CAMBRIDGE LATIN COURSE

BOOK III

CAMBRIDGE SCHOOL CLASSICS PROJECT

Shaftesbury Road, Cambridge CB2 8EA, United Kingdom

One Liberty Plaza, 20th Floor, New York, NY 10006, USA

477 Williamstown Road, Port Melbourne, VIC 3207, Australia

314–321, 3rd Floor, Plot 3, Splendor Forum, Jasola District Centre, New Delhi – 110025, India

103 Penang Road, #05–06/07, Visioncrest Commercial, Singapore 238467

Cambridge University Press & Assessment is a department of the University of Cambridge.

We share the University's mission to contribute to society through the pursuit of education, learning and research at the highest international levels of excellence.

www.cambridge.org
Information on this title: www.cambridge.org/9781009162739

© University of Cambridge School Classics Project 2025

First published 1972

Second edition 1983

Third edition 1990

Fourth edition 2001

Fifth edition 2025

20 19 18 17 16 15 14 13 12 11 10 9 8 7 6 5 4 3 2 1

Printed in Poland by Opolgraf

A catalogue record for this publication is available from the British Library

ISBN 978-1-009-16273-9 Paperback with Digital Access (5 Years)

ISBN 978-1-009-16271-5 Digital Access (5 Years)

Cambridge University Press & Assessment has no responsibility for the persistence or accuracy of URLs for external or third-party internet websites referred to in this publication and does not guarantee that any content on such websites is, or will remain, accurate or appropriate.

For EU product safety concerns, contact us at Calle de José Abascal, 56, 1°, 28003 Madrid, Spain, or email eugpsr@cambridge.org.

Contents

Introduction

The Cambridge School Classics Project and the Cambridge Latin Course

The Cambridge School Classics Project (CSCP) is part of the Faculty of Education at the University of Cambridge and has been supporting Classics education for over fifty years. CSCP comprises a small team of Classics education and technology specialists supported by a wide community of educators and academics. All CSCP materials are based on the latest research not only in Classics but also in language acquisition and educational theory.

While CSCP have numerous projects and initiatives supporting Classics education around the world, their first ever undertaking – the Cambridge Latin Course – remains their most successful and influential, leading the way in evidence-based teaching of Classical languages. The underlying course structure and inductive methods of the CLC have proven effective and adaptive, responding well to the ever-changing educational environment. Most of the funding which enables CSCP's work comes from sales of the Cambridge Latin Course and associated products; therefore every CLC purchase directly funds Classics educational research and development; grātiās!

Why study Latin with the CLC?

Languages are all about communication, and learning a language enables you to access the culture of the people who use it.

With this in mind, the Cambridge Latin Course has two main aims:

1   To teach you to understand Latin so that you can read Latin texts confidently

2   To develop your knowledge and understanding of Roman culture, especially in the first century AD.

The CLC uses a specific approach to language learning called the 'Reading Method'. As you study with the course you will read lots of Latin stories; this is so you get used to seeing Latin in action and focusing on its meaning rather than just learning rules in isolation. The stories are set in a Roman context, and as you study you will meet real historical characters – as well as fictional ones – and learn about the social, political and historical aspects of Roman culture. The many illustrations have also been created or chosen to give you extra information about the Roman world and are meant to be looked at alongside the text.

Time chart

Throughout this book BC and AD are used when referring to dates as this is the system you are most likely to encounter in your wider studies of Ancient History and Latin. This system was created in the sixth century AD and it uses the 'birth of Jesus Christ' as its point of reference. Many other dating systems exist and have existed over the course of human history.

An easy alternative should you not wish to use BC and AD is that which uses BCE (Before Common Era) and CE (Common Era). This system uses the same point of reference as BC and AD, so you can simply swap BC for BCE and AD for CE.

Date	Britain	The Roman World	The Wider World
BC			
2500–1000	c.2500: Stonehenge built c.1800: First large-scale copper mines c.1500–800: Burial in barrows replaced by cremation in cemeteries c.1500: First hill forts constructed c.1200–800: Smaller groups begin to combine into the tribal kingdoms of the Iron Age		c.2000: Invention of scissors, Mesopotamia; extinction of last population of woolly mammoth, Wrangle Island, Arctic Sea c.1750–1050: Mycenaean civilisation in Greece; earliest cultivation of the tea plant, China c.1650: Domestication of chickens, Thailand c.1600–400: Olmec civilisation in Mexico c.1500: Earliest settlements in Oceania (Mariana archipelago) c.1300: Earliest notated music: Hurrian Hymn to Nikkal, Ugarit, Syria
1000–500	c.700–500: Ironworking becomes widespread c.500: The first 'brochs' (stone towers) built in Scotland	753: Traditional date of the foundation of Rome 509: Traditional start of the Roman Republic 508: Roman-Etruscan Wars	814: Traditional date of the foundation of Carthage 630: Earliest known use of coinage (Ionia or Lydia, Anatolia) 600–500: Creation of the medical/surgical text the Sushruta-samhita, India
500–300	c.450: Maiden Castle in Dorset is the largest hillfort in Britain (possibly Europe) c.350: Many hillforts abandoned 330–320: Earliest known written record of the British Isles written by Pytheas of Massilia	451–450: The Law of the 12 Tables 390: Gauls sack Rome 343–304: First and Second Samnite and Latin Wars	c.500: Probable life of Lao-Tzu, founder of Taoism, China; beginning of the earlier phase of creation of the Nasca line drawings, southern Peru 431–404: Peloponnesian War between Athens and Sparta 399: Death of Socrates 336: Alexander the Great becomes king of Macedon
300–100	c.250 Earliest settlement at the Glastonbury lake village, Somerset c.150–50 'Waterloo helmet' probably created c.100: Settlement with monumental timber structures at Stanwick, North Yorkshire	298–290: Third Samnite War: Romans control the Italian peninsula 264–241: First Punic War 218–201: Second Punic War 192–188: War with the Seleucid Empire 146: Third Punic War; destruction of Carthage	c.300: Earliest farming of chickens outside of East Asia c.250: Earliest watermills as reported by Strabo, Egypt and Anatolia c.200: Compass invented in China; start of the final phase of creation of the Nazca line drawings, southern Peru (lasts until c.AD 500) c.100: The Antikythera Mechanism created by the Greeks, described as the first analogue computer; acupuncture described in Nei Qing, a Chinese medical text
100–50	c.80–60: First coins produced and used in Britain 55–54: Caesar's first and second invasions of Britain	91–89: Social War 88–79: Sulla's first civil war and dictatorship 89–85: First Mithridatic War 73–71: Spartacus revolt 60: Political alliance of Pompey, Julius Caesar and Crassus 58–50: Caesar's Gallic Wars	90–70: Probable date of the oldest extant Buddhist paintings found in the Ajanta Caves, India 76: Death of Salome Alexandra, the last sovereign to die ruling an independent Judaea 57: Base year of the Vikrama era Indian calendar 53: Birth of Chinese poet Yang Xiong

Date	Britain	The Roman World	The Wider World
50–1	c.50: Burial of the 'Snettisham hoard' c.25: Settlement at Colchester develops c.20: Trade between Britain and the Roman Empire increases	49–45: Civil War between Caesar and Pompey 44: Julius Caesar assassinated 43: Triumvirate of Octavian, Mark Antony and Lepidus 43: Death of orator and politician, Cicero 27: Octavian given the title 'Augustus' and becomes the first emperor	48: Ptolemy XIII deposes his co-ruler, wife and sister Cleopatra VII; she is restored in 47 with help from Julius Caesar 43: According to legend the Emerald Buddha is created 37: With the support of Rome, Herod I becomes king of Judaea 31–30 Cleopatra and her Roman partner Mark Antony are defeated at the Battle of Actium by Octavian; Cleopatra takes her own life; Egypt becomes a Roman province 27: Kushite Queen Amanirenas leads armies against the Romans
		AD	
1–50	39–40: After death of Cunobelinus, king of the Catuvellauni, one of his sons flees to Caligula; the other two, Caratacus and Togodumnus, become rulers 42: Verica, king of the Atrebates driven out by Caratacus and Togodumnus; appeals to Claudius 43: Romans land in Kent; death of Togodumnus; retreat of Caratacus; Noviomagus (Chichester) founded 44: Second phase of conquest led by general Vespasian 47–50: Foundation of Londinium (London) and Viroconium (Wroxeter)	8: The poet Ovid is exiled 14: Death of Augustus; Tiberius becomes emperor 37: Death of Tiberius; Caligula becomes emperor 41: Caligula assassinated; Claudius becomes emperor	9: Emperor Wang Mang usurps the Han Dynasty in China 18: Rebel group – 'The Red Eyebrows'– forms against Wang Mang 23: The Red Eyebrows help to overthrow Wang Mang; Han Dynasty restored c.30: Chinese prefect Tu Shih invents a water-powered engine for pumping air into furnaces used in metal-smelting 45: Birth of China's first female historian Ban Zhao
50–70	50: Verulamium (St Albans) granted municipium status 51: Caratacus captured 55: Isca Dumnoniorum (Exeter) founded 58–62: Agricola serves as military tribune 60–61: Boudica's revolt 60–70: Construction of Aquae Sulis (Bath)	54: Death of Claudius; Nero become emperor 68: Death of Nero 69: Year of the Four Emperors: Galba, Otho, Vitellius, Vespasian	53–54: First Letter of Paul to the Corinthians 68: China's first Buddhist temple, White Horse Temple, is built
70–100	71: Eboracum (York) founded Mid-70s: Foundation of Deva (Chester) and Corinium (Cirencester) 77: Agricola appointed governor 78: Destruction of last major druidic centre c.80: Salvius probably arrives in Britain as iuridicus c.83/84: Battle of Mons Graupius 100: Trajan orders withdrawal of troops from modern Scotland	73: Siege of Masada 79: Death of Vespasian; Titus becomes emperor; eruption of Vesuvius 81: Death of Titus; Domitian becomes emperor 86: Salvius made consul by Domitian sometime after 86 96: Death of Domitian; Nerva becomes emperor 98: Death of Nerva; Trajan becomes emperor	75: Date of latest known cuneiform text c.75: Hero, a Greek scientist in Alexandria, invents an early form of steam engine 78: The beginning of the Indian calendar Saka Era 100: Death (in Rome) of Jewish military commander, priest, scholar, and historian Josephus c.100 Theravada Buddhism, strong in southern India and Sri Lanka, travels through SE Asia; Teotihuacan, main city in the highlands of central America, introduces the god Quetzalcoatl
100–122	101–105: Death of Salvius 122: Emperor Hadrian orders the construction of a wall across northern Britain	117: Death of Trajan; Roman Empire at its greatest extent; Hadrian becomes emperor c.120: Rebuilding of Pantheon by Hadrian 120: Death of Tacitus 121: Hadrian begins tour of Roman Empire, first to Gaul and Germany and then Britain	c.105: Paper-making developed in China by Cai Lon c.118: First known depiction of a wheelbarrow in a tomb wall painting near Chengdu, China c.119: Death of Greek author Plutarch

Using quotations

This book includes more references to written evidence than Books I and II. When historians use quotations or references to primary or secondary sources, they are careful to do so clearly and in the correct format. Here are a few notes to help you to understand these references and use them in your own work.

Where something is quoted exactly as it was said or written, it is placed in quotation marks. Longer quotations are usually set apart from the main text, while shorter snippets can be blended into it. Ideas and information from primary or secondary sources can also be put into different words to make them work better in context. Such references do not use quotation marks.

It is important to make it clear where an idea or information is from, even if you are not using the exact words of the original source. This information is often placed in brackets after the content you are reusing.

Sometimes it is not necessary to write long passages out in full. Where words have been missed out of a direct quotation this is indicated by three dots … or, if a large section of the text has been omitted, three dots in square brackets […].

When a quotation is pulled out of a longer text, it can be helpful to add words or phrases so that it makes sense to the reader. These words or phrases are placed in brackets.

If a source has text missing or unreadable (this often happens with inscriptions, for example) historians may be able to work out what it originally said. If this has happened, the suggestion of what the missing words or letters might have been is also placed in brackets.

Thinking point: The following passage contains some of the features described above (written in green). Explain the purpose of each of them.

Roman and Greek authors often give the impression that they consider the Britons to be strange, unsophisticated and sometimes even savage.

'(The Britons) have an old-fashioned and primitive way of life … their houses are humble … their habits are simple' (Diodorus Siculus, *Historical Library* 5.21). Julius Caesar in the *Gallic Wars* gives very little information about ancient British society and politics beyond mentioning a series of tribes and some aristocratic names (*Gallic Wars* 5.12), although he does mention Britain in the context of religious leaders in Gaul, known as druids:

'It is believed that (the druids' way of life) originated in Britain and then spread to Gaul [...] people suffering from serious illnesses or who are heading into battle either sacrifice human victims or promise to do so, employing the druids to perform such sacrifices …' (*Gallic Wars* 6.13–16)

Inscriptional evidence

A lot of important evidence about the Roman occupation of Britain comes from inscriptions, particularly on the tombstones of soldiers. The study of inscriptions is called **epigraphy**. You saw some examples in Books I and II, but in Book III they are more common and the historical claims that can be made by reading them are considered in more detail.

Here is an example from the tombstone of a soldier who was buried at Deva (Chester):

This may look difficult to understand, but such inscriptions usually follow a standard pattern. The items are typically arranged in the following order:

1 The dedication at the top of the stone – D M – is short for **Dīs Mānibus** (to the spirits of the departed).

2 The praenomen. This is the first of a citizen's three names and is usually abbreviated to a single letter. Here L stands for **Lūcius**.

3 The nomen. Given in full here: **Licinius**.

4 The father's name, usually just the praenomen represented by a single letter. This usually comes before an F meaning **fīlius** (son). In this inscription the F has been left out, so when it is written out for interpretation an F will be added in brackets. As is the case here, the son often had the same praenomen as his father; here L F stands for **Lūciī fīlius** (son of Lucius).

5 Tribe. Roman citizens were organised into thirty-five tribes, used for voting purposes. The name of the tribe was given in a shortened form; here TER for **Teretīna**.

6 The cognomen. This is the last of the three names, usually placed after the father's name and the individual's voting tribe. Having three names was a mark of Roman citizenship and therefore an important indication of status. This soldier's cognomen is given in full: **Valēns**.

7 Birthplace. Usually written as an abbreviation which can be identified as a town in the Roman Empire. Here we see ARE for **Arelātē** (modern Arles in the south of France).

8 Rank and legion. Usually both written in a shortened fashion. In this inscription, VETERAN for **veterānus** (a retired soldier or one coming up to retirement); LEG XX VV for **legiōnis XX Valeriae Victrīcis** (Twentieth Legion Valeria Victrix).

9 Age. This is represented by AN or ANN for **annōrum**, followed by a number. This number is often rounded to a multiple of 5. Sometimes VIX for **vīxit** (lived) is placed before AN.

10 Length of service (not included in the inscription above) represented by STIP followed by a number. **Stipendium** was the annual pay of a soldier, so STIP X for **stipendia X** means ten years of paid service.

11 The final statement. This is abbreviated, and usually takes the form of H S E for **hīc situs est** (is buried here) or H F C for **hērēs faciendum cūrāvit** (his heir had this stone set up). In this inscription the scribe has written HFFC in error, so when it is written out this extra F is placed in curly brackets.

The inscription can therefore be interpreted as follows:

D M	D(IS) M(ANIBUS)	This stone is dedicated to the spirits of the departed.
L LICINIUS L (F) TER VALENS	L(UCIUS) LICINIUS L(UCII) F(ILIUS) TER(ETINA) VALENS)	Lucius Licinius Valens, son of Lucius of the Teretine tribe
ARE VETERAN LEG XX VV	ARE(LATE) VETERAN(US) LEG(IONIS) XX V(ALERIAE) V(ICTRICIS)	from Arelate, veteran of the Twentieth Legion Valeria Victrix
AN VL	AN(NORUM) VL	aged forty-five
H F {F} C	H(ERES) F(ACIENDUM) C(URAVIT)	His heir set this up.
H S E	H(IC) S(ITUS) EST	He (Lucius) is buried here.

Reproductions of two other soldiers' tombstones found at Chester.

> **Thinking point:** Study these tombstones. Try to find out the following information:
>
> **1** the soldier's name
>
> **2** his rank
>
> **3** his legion
>
> **4** his age at death
>
> **5** the length of his service.

Britain in the later first century AD

Britain in the later first century AD.

AQUAE SULIS

Stage 21

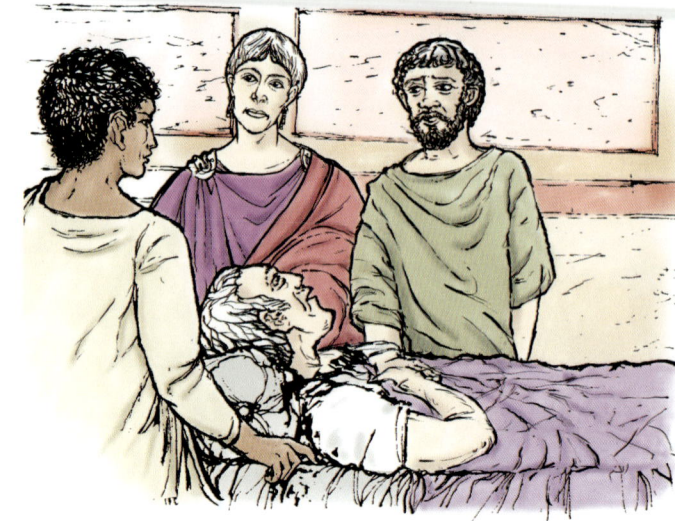

1 Quīntus apud Salvium manēbat per tōtam hiemem.
rēx Togidubnus Quīntum ad aulam saepe invītāvit.
Quīntus, ā Togidubnō invītātus, dē urbe Alexandrīā
nārrābat.

2 ubi vēr appropinquābat, Togidubnus in morbum
gravem incidit.
rēgīna Catia multōs medicōs ad aulam arcessīvit.
medicī, ā Catiā arcessītī, remedium morbī frūstrā
quaesīvērunt.

3 Quīntus Dumnorigem dē remediō anxius cōnsuluit.
Dumnorix, ā Quīntō cōnsultus, cōnsilium libenter dedit:
'rēx ad oppidum Aquās Sūlis īre dēbet, ubi fōns sacer est.
ibi dea Sūlis precēs hominum audīre solet.'

4 Vitelliānus Quīntō dē oppidō Aquīs Sūlis nārrāvit:
'Rōmānī fabrōs perītissimōs ad illud oppidum
mīsērunt.
fabrī, ā Rōmānīs missī, templum deae Sūlis et
thermās maximās ibi aedificāvērunt.'

5 Quīntus Salvium et Rūfillam dē deā quaesīvit.
'Togidubnus deam Sūlem saepe honorāvit,'
respondit illa.
'nunc fortasse dea, ā Togidubnō honorāta,
eum sānāre potest.'

6 'Togidubnus est vir sapiēns,' inquit Salvius.
'melius est eī testāmentum facere.'

Lūcius Marcius Memor

When you have read this story, answer the questions at the end.

oppidum Aquae Sūlis parvum erat, turba maxima. ex omne parte imperiī Rōmānī ad fontem sacrum conveniēbant hominēs. prōcūrātor thermārum erat Lūcius Marcius Memor, nōtissimus haruspex, vir magnae dignitātis.

quamquam prīma hōra erat, Memor iam in tablīnō dīligēns labōrābat. nam librum longissimum dē vītā suā scrībēbat. post duās hōrās Cephalus, haruspicis lībertus, tablīnum intrāvit.   5

'domine! domine!' clāmābat.

haruspex, ā lībertō vexātus, nihil respondit.

'dominus homō occupātus est,' sibi dīxit lībertus. tum

'domine!' clāmāvit. 'venī! hōra tertia est.'   10

tandem Memor lībertum spectāvit; vultus eius erat sevērus.

'fer mihi plūs vīnī!' inquit. 'tum abī!'

'domine! domine! necesse est tibi venīre,' inquit Cephalus.

'cūr mē vexās, Cephale?' inquit Memor. 'cūr tū rem administrāre ipse nōn potes?'   15

'rem huius modī administrāre nōn possum,' respondit lībertus. 'sunt multī servī, multī fabrī, quī mandāta prōcūrātōris exspectant. tē exspectat architectus ipse. tē cōnsulere volunt sacerdōtēs. adsunt mīlitēs, ab hostibus vulnerātī. adsunt nōnnūllī mercātōrēs, quōs arcessīvistī. tū rem ipse administrāre dēbēs.'   20

oppidum *town*
Aquae Sūlis *Bath*
fontem: fōns *spring*
prōcūrātor *manager*
haruspex *soothsayer*
vir magnae dignitātis
    a man of great importance
dīligēns *hardworking, careful*

sevērus *severe, stern*

fer! *bring!*
plūs vīnī *more wine*

huius modī *of this kind*
mandāta *instructions, orders*
cōnsulere *consult*
hostibus: hostis *enemy*

'nimium labōris habeō,' clāmāvit Memor. 'quam fessus sum! cūr ad hunc populum barbarum umquam vēnī? vīta mea est dūra. nam in Britanniā ad summōs honōrēs ascendere nōn possum. necesse est mihi virōs potentēs colere. ēheu! in hāc īnsulā sunt paucī virī potentēs, paucī clārī.'

'quid vīs mē facere, domine?' inquit lībertus.   25

'iubeō tē omnēs dīmittere,' clāmāvit Memor. 'nōlī mē iterum vexāre!'

Memor, postquam haec dīxit, statim scrībere coepit.

Cephalus, ā dominō īrātō territus, invītus exiit. in thermīs plūrimōs hominēs invēnit, vehementer clāmantēs et Memorem absentem vituperantēs. eōs omnēs Cephalus dīmīsit.   30

nimium labōris *too much work*
populum: populus *people*
umquam *ever*
honōrēs: honor *honour, public office*
potentēs: potēns *powerful*
colere *cultivate, make friends with*

absentem: absēns *absent*

Questions

1 **oppidum Aquae Sūlis parvum erat, turba maxima** (line 1): why might a visitor to Aquae Sulis have been surprised on seeing the town?

2 **prōcūrātor thermārum erat Lūcius Marcius Memor, nōtissimus haruspex, vir magnae dignitātis** (lines 2–3): what three things do we learn about Lucius Marcius Memor?

3 Look at lines 4–5: **quamquam prīma hōra erat … scrībēbat.**
   a **prīma hōra** (line 4). Was this early or late in the morning? Give a reason for your answer.
   b Memor is described as **dīligēns**. What was he doing?

4 Look at lines 5–8: **post duās … nihil respondit.**
   a Who entered the study?
   b How did Memor react to their entrance?

5 **'fer mihi plūs vīnī!' inquit. 'tum abī!'** (line 12): what two orders did Memor give?

6 **'cūr mē vexās, Cephale?' inquit Memor. 'cūr tū rem administrāre ipse nōn potes?'** (lines 14–15): what two questions did Memor ask?

7 Why do you think that Cephalus used the words **mandāta prōcūrātōris** (line 17) rather than **mandāta tua**?

8 **vīta mea … paucī clārī** (lines 22–24): what explanation does Memor give for his claim that his life is hard?

9 **'iubeō tē omnēs dīmittere,' clāmāvit Memor. 'nōlī mē iterum vexāre!'** (line 26): how did Memor react to Cephalus' question? Make two points.

10 **Cephalus, ā dominō īrātō territus, invītus exiit** (line 28): which two Latin words show how Cephalus was feeling when he left Memor's study?

11 **in thermīs plūrimōs hominēs invēnit, vehementer clāmantēs et Memorem absentem vituperantēs** (lines 28–29): what did Cephalus find when he arrived at the baths?

12 Read Cephalus' speech in lines 16–20 again. Pick out one example of the different words or phrases which he repeats and suggest why he used them to try to get Memor to act.

A statuette of a haruspex, the religious office held by Memor.

About the language 1: perfect passive participles

1 In Stage 20, you met sentences like these, containing present participles:

amīcī ad vīllam contendērunt, dōna **portantēs**.
*The friends hurried towards the house, **carrying** gifts.*

Lūcia amīcōs in cubiculō **lacrimantēs** audīvit.
*Lucia heard the friends **crying** in the bedroom.*

2 In Stage 21, you have met sentences like these:

haruspex, ā lībertō **vexātus**, nihil respondit.
*The soothsayer, **having been annoyed** by the freedman, said nothing in reply.*

thermae, ā Rōmānīs **aedificātae**, maximae erant.
*The baths, **having been built** by the Romans, were very big.*

The words in bold are **perfect passive participles**.

3 A participle is used to describe a noun. For instance, in the second example in paragraph 2, **aedificātae** describes the baths. Participles change their endings to agree with the nouns they describe. In this way they behave like adjectives.

Compare the following pair of sentences:

singular   faber, ā Rōmānīs **missus**, perītissimus erat.
         *The craftsperson, **having been sent** by the Romans, was very skilful.*

plural   fabrī, ā Rōmānīs **missī**, perītissimī erant.
         *The craftspeople, **having been sent** by the Romans, were very skilful.*

4 Translate the following examples:

   a   amīcus, ā Quīntō salūtātus, vīllam intrāvit.

   b   nūntiī, ā rēge arcessītī, rem terribilem nārrāvērunt.

   c   puella, ā patre laudāta, laetissima erat.

   d   templum, ā fabrīs perītīs aedificātum, erat splendidum.

   e   mīlitēs, ab hostibus vulnerātī, thermās vīsitāre voluērunt.

   f   epistulae, ā Catiā missae, longissimae erant.

In each sentence, identify the perfect passive participle and the noun which it describes. State whether each pair is singular or plural, and masculine, feminine or neuter.

5 Notice that the perfect passive participle can be translated in a number of ways:

nūntius, ā Togidubnō ipsō missus, cēnam magnificam nūntiāvit.

The messenger, having been sent by Togidubnus himself, announced a magnificent dinner.

Or, in more natural English:

The messenger, sent by Togidubnus himself, announced a magnificent dinner.

Vitelliānus, ā Rūfillā arcessītus, statim ad ātrium festīnāvit.

Vitellianus, having been summoned by Rufilla, hurried at once to the atrium.

Or, in more natural English:

Vitellianus, summoned by Rufilla, hurried at once to the atrium.

Vitellianus, who had been summoned by Rufilla, hurried at once to the atrium.

When Vitellianus had been summoned by Rufilla, he hurried at once to the atrium.

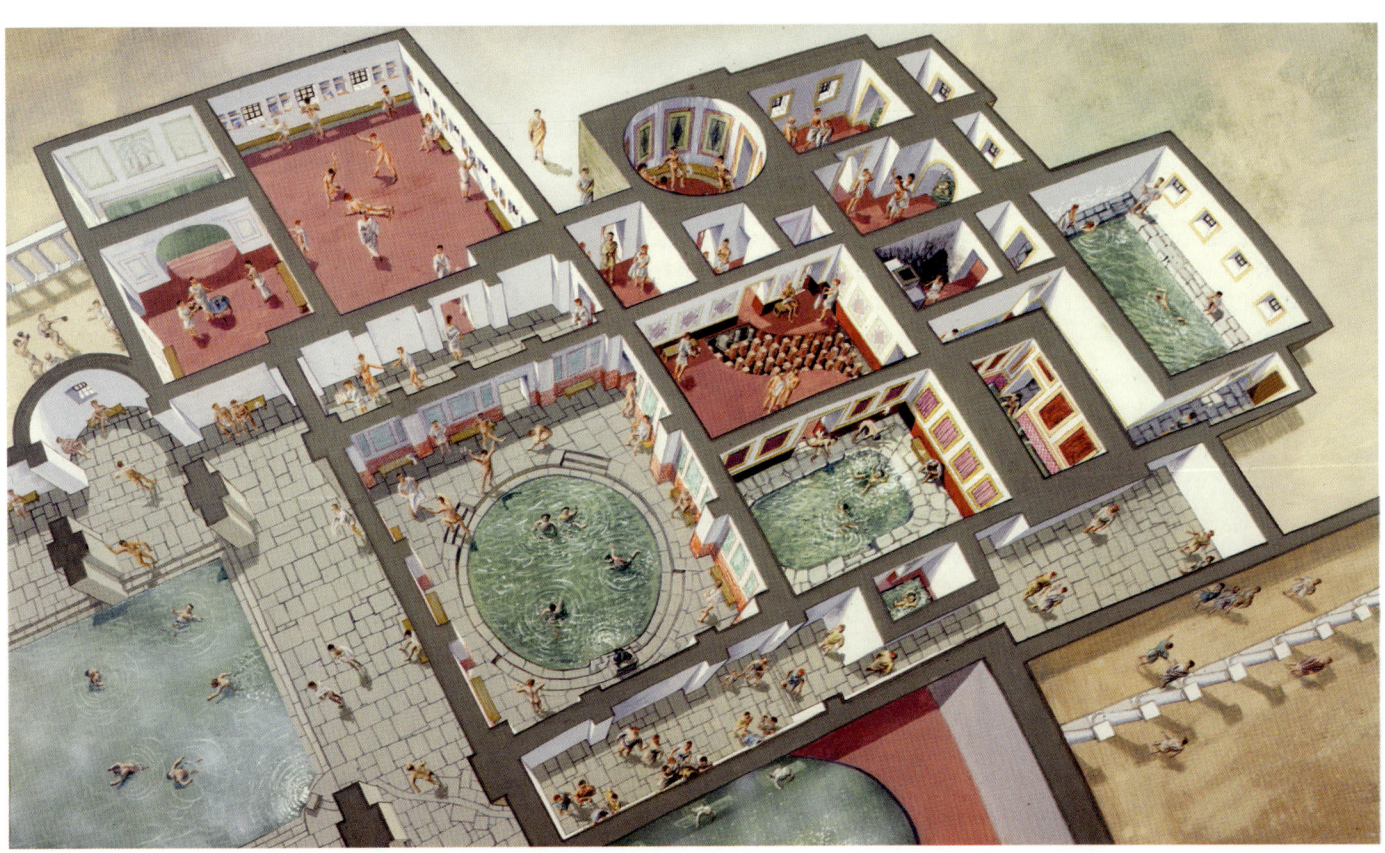

What the bathing complex at Aquae Sulis may have looked like.

senātor advenit

Cephalus ā thermīs rediit. tablīnum rūrsus intrāvit Memoremque labōrantem salūtāvit. Memor, simulac Cephalum vīdit, īrātus clāmāvit,

'cūr prohibēs mē labōrāre? cūr mihi nōn pārēs? stultior es quam asinus!'

'sed domine,' inquit Cephalus, 'aliquid novī nūntiāre volō. postquam hinc discessī, mandāta, quae mihi dedistī, effēcī. ubi tamen sacerdōtēs fabrōsque dīmittēbam, senātōrem thermīs appropinquantem cōnspexī.'   5

Memor, ā Cephalō permōtus,

'quis est ille senātor?' inquit. 'unde vēnit?'

'necesse est tibi hunc senātōrem quam celerrimē vidēre,' inquit Cephalus. 'nam hic senātor, ab omnibus laudātus, Gāius Salvius est.'   10

'num Gāius Salvius Līberālis?' exclāmāvit Memor. 'nōn crēdō tibi.'

Cephalus tamen facile eī persuāsit, quod Salvius iam in āream thermārum equitābat.

Memor laetissimus statim clāmāvit,

'fer mihi togam! fer calceōs! ōrnāmenta mea ubi sunt? vocā servōs!   15 quam fēlīx sum! Salvius hūc venit, vir summae auctōritātis, quem colere maximē volō.'

Cephalus, ā dominō incitātus, celerrimē togam calceōsque quaesīvit. tum Memorī ōrnāmenta trādidit, ex armāriō raptim extracta. haruspex lībertum innocentem vituperābat, lībertus Salvium.   20

rūrsus *again*

prohibēs: prohibēre *prevent*

aliquid novī *something new*
hinc *from here*
effēcī: efficere *carry out, accomplish*
permōtus *alarmed, disturbed*

equitābat: equitāre
    ride (on horseback)

calceōs: calceus *shoe*
ōrnāmenta *badges of office, insignia*
auctōritātis: auctōritās
    authority
raptim *hastily, quickly*

Memor set up a statue near the altar of the goddess Sulis. The statue had disappeared, but this is the statue base with Memor's name on it.

The people of Aquae Sulis

In the late first century AD, Aquae Sulis was a small but growing community based around the famous bath complex and temple. While plenty of people made their home there, the site's reputation also drew visitors from far and wide. The wide variety of people living in and passing through Aquae Sulis is evidenced by the inscriptions they left behind, such as those made as offerings to the goddess or on tombstones. Below are two inscriptions which inspired some of the characters in our stories. We cannot know the real stories of these people, however; how long they stayed, exactly why they came, and what they thought about Aquae Sulis, are all lost to us.

This stone statue base was found near the altar of the goddess Sulis. The statue has disappeared, but the base records that it was dedicated to the goddess by Lucius Marcius Memor, a Roman **haruspex** (official who interpreted omens by inspecting the entrails of sacrificial animals).

Thinking point: As with most inscriptions, the ones on this page are written using abbreviations. Using the guidance on reading inscriptions at the front of the book (pages viii–ix), see if you can work out which parts of the inscriptions correspond to different parts of the translations.

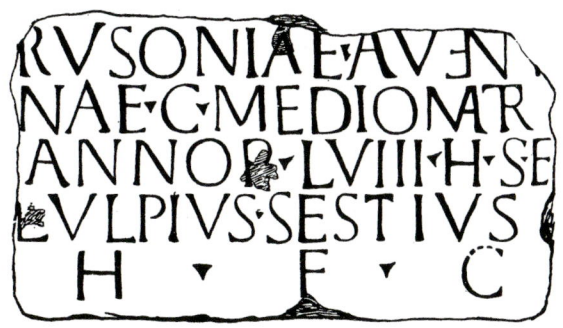

'To the goddess Sulis, Lucius Marcius Memor, Haruspex, gave this as a gift.'

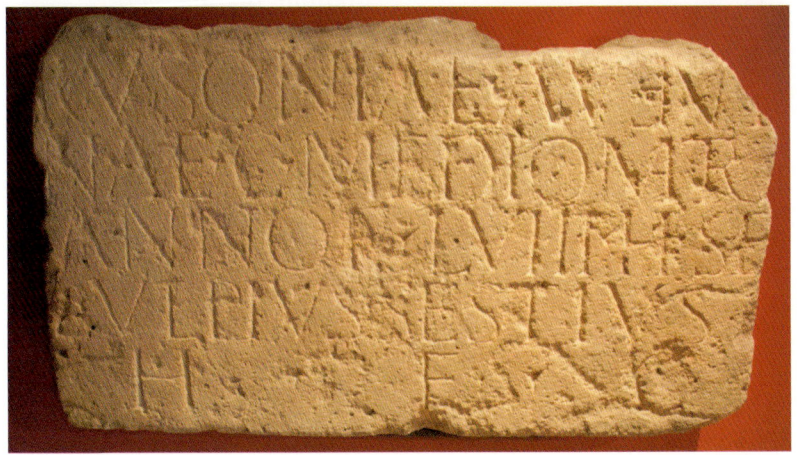

'To Rusonia Aventina, a tribeswoman of the Mediomatrici, aged 58; she lies here; Lucius Ulpius Sestius, her heir, had this erected.'

This tombstone is for Rusonia Aventina, a woman who travelled all the way from Divodurum in eastern Gaul (modern Metz in France). We will meet Aventina later in our stories.

Memor rem suscipit

I

Salvius et Memor, in hortō sōlī ambulantēs, sermōnem gravem habent.

Salvius: Lūcī Marcī Memor, vir summae prūdentiae es. volō tē rem magnam suscipere.

Memor: tālem rem suscipere velim, sed occupātissimus sum. exspectant mē sacerdōtēs. vexant mē architectus et magnus numerus fabrōrum. sed quid vīs mē facere? 5

Salvius: Tiberius Claudius Togidubnus, rēx Rēgnēnsium, hūc nūper advēnit. Togidubnus, quī in morbum gravem incidit, remedium petit.

Memor: difficile est mihi tē adiuvāre, mī senātor. Togidubnus est vir octōgintā annōrum. difficile est deae Sūlī Togidubnum sānāre. 10

Salvius: nōlō tē reddere Togidubnum sānum. volō tē rem contrāriam efficere.

Memor: quid dīcis? num mortem Togidubnī cupis?

Salvius: ita vērō! porrō, quamquam tam occupātus es, volō tē ipsum hanc rem efficere. 15

Memor: vīsne mē rēgem occīdere? rem huius modī facere nōlō. Togidubnus enim est vir clārissimus, ā populō Rōmānō honōrātus.

Salvius: es vir summae calliditātis. hanc rem efficere potes. nōn sōlum ego, sed etiam imperātor Domitiānus hoc cupit. Togidubnus enim Rōmānōs saepe vexāvit. imperātor mihi, nōn Togidubnō, cōnfīdit. imperātor tibi praemium dignum prōmittit. num praemium, ab imperātōre prōmissum, recūsāre vīs? 20

Memor: quō modō rem facere possum? 25

Salvius: nescio. hoc tantum tibi dīcō: imperātor mortem Togidubnī exspectat.

Memor: ō mē miserum! rem difficiliōrem numquam fēcī.

Salvius: vīta, mī Memor, est plēna rērum difficilium.

(exit Salvius.) 30

---

gravem: gravis *serious*

prūdentiae: prūdentia *good sense, intelligence*

tālem: tālis *such*
velim *I would like*

morbum: morbus *illness*

octōgintā *eighty*

reddere *make (again)*
sānum: sānus *well, healthy*
rem contrāriam: rēs contrāria *the opposite*

occīdere *kill*

calliditātis: calliditās *shrewdness, cleverness*
nōn sōlum ... sed etiam *not only ... but also*
dignum: dignus *worthy, appropriate*

nescio: nescīre *not know*
tantum *only*

II

Memor: Cephale! Cephale! (*lībertus, ā Memore vocātus, celeriter intrat.
pōculum vīnī fert.*) cūr mihi vīnum offers? nōn vīnum, sed
cōnsilium quaerō. iubeō tē mihi cōnsilium quam celerrimē dare.
rēx Togidubnus hūc vēnit, remedium morbī petēns. imperātor
Domitiānus, ā Togidubnō saepe vexātus, iam mortem eius cupit. 5
imperātor ipse iubet mē hoc efficere. quam difficile est!

cōnsilium *advice*

Cephalus: minimē, facile est! pōculum venēnātum habeō, mihi ā latrōne
Aegyptiō ōlim datum. venēnum, in pōculō cēlātum, vītam
celerrimē exstinguere potest.

venēnātum: venēnātus
poisoned
venēnum *poison*
exstinguere *extinguish, destroy*

Memor: cōnsilium, quod mihi prōpōnis, perīculōsum est. Togidubnō 10
venēnum dare timeō.

prōpōnis: prōpōnere *propose,
put forward*
nihil perīculī *no danger*
quotiēns *whenever*
balneō: balneum *bath*
praebēre *present, provide*
sapiēns *wise*

Cephalus: nihil perīculī est. rēx, quotiēns ē balneō exiit, pōculum vīnī
postulat. deinde ad fontem sacrum prōcēdere solet. necesse
est servō prope balneum stāre et pōculum rēgī praebēre.

Memor: (*dēlectātus*) quam sapiēns es! cōnsilium optimum est. nūllīs 15
tamen servīs cōnfīdō. sed tibi cōnfīdō, Cephale. iubeō tē ipsum
Togidubnō pōculum praebēre.

Cephalus: ēheu! mihi rem difficillimam impōnis.

impōnis: impōnere *impose*

Memor: vīta, mī Cephale, est plēna rērum difficilium.

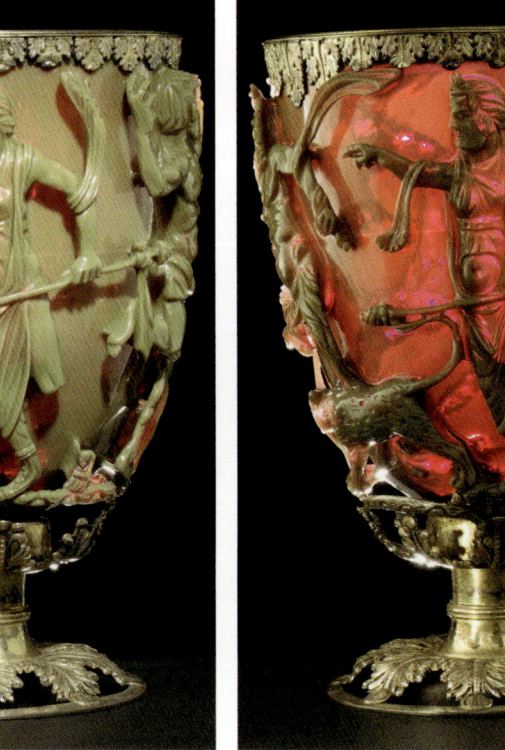

Some cups which have survived from the ancient world have hidden surprises. This fourth-century AD cup demonstrates how clever Roman artisans could be. Due to tiny particles of colloidal gold and silver contained within the special type of glass with which it is made, this green cup turns red when light is shone through it.

About the language 2: more about infinitives

1 In Book II, you met sentences with the infinitive like these:

num tū familiārēs ad vīllam **invītāre** vīs?
*Surely you don't want **to invite** your relatives to our house?*

Catia multās epistulās **mittere** solet.
*Catia is accustomed **to send** many letters.*

In each example, notice the nouns **tū** and **Catia**.

They are in the nominative case because they are the subject of the sentence.

2 In Stage 21, you have now met sentences with the infinitive like these:

nōlō tē familiārēs ad vīllam **invītāre**.
*I don't want you **to invite** your relatives to our house.*

volō Catiam multās epistulās **mittere**.
*I want Catia **to send** many letters.*

Notice that the nouns **tē** and **Catiam** are now in the accusative case.

3 Further examples:

a nōlō tē rēgem adiuvāre.

b iubeō vōs in vīllā manēre.

c volō omnēs prīncipēs ad aulam appropinquāre.

d rēgīna vult medicōs rēgī remedium dare.

e Cephalus Memorem librum scrībere nōn vult.

f Memor lībertum cōnsilium capere voluit.

This dolphin is part of a mosaic uncovered in Bath (Aquae Sulis).

Building words: adjectives and adverbs

1   Study the form and meaning of the following words:

laet**us**, laet**a**	*happy*	laet**ē**	*happily*
perīt**us**, perīt**a**	*skilful*	perit**ē**	*skilfully*
splendidissim**us**, splendidissim**a**	*very splendid*	splendidissim**ē**	*very splendidly*

2   As you already know, the words in the left-hand columns are adjectives; the Latin adjectives are given in their nominative singular masculine and feminine forms. The words in the right-hand columns are known as **adverbs**. The form of a Latin adverb always stays the same.

3   Using the pattern in paragraph 1 as a guide, work out the words that are missing from this table:

adjectives		*adverbs*	
cautus	*cautious*	cautē	. . . .
superba	*proud*	. . . .	*proudly*
suāvissimus	*very sweet*	. . . .	. . . .

4   Divide the following words into two lists, one of adjectives and one of adverbs. Then give the meaning of each word.

   intentē; gravissimus; callida; tacitē; avida; dīligentissimus; firmē; saevissimē.

5   Choose the correct Latin words to translate the words in **bold** in the following sentences:

   a   The palace of Togidubnus was **very tasteful**. (ēlegāntissima, ēlegāntissimē)

   b   The merchant always treated his customers **honestly**. (probus, probē)

   c   The queen **very generously** promised a large gift. (līberālissima, līberālissimē)

   d   A **cautious** (cautus, cautē) man proceeds **slowly**. (lentus, lentē)

A seahorse from the same mosaic.

Practising the language

fōns sacer

On the journey to Aquae Sulis, Togidubnus tells Quintus a version of the history of the town and its baths.

Togidubnus et Quīntus oppidō Aquīs Sūlis lentē appropinquābant.
rēx, in raedā recumbēns, īnfirmus

    'mī Quīnte,' inquit, 'vīsne mē tibi dē fonte sacrō nārrāre?'

    'ita vērō,' avidē respondit Quīntus.

    'iamprīdem,' inquit Togidubnus, 'fōns, ē quō aquae calidae effluunt,   5
in valle dēsertā situs erat. ibi Britannī, deam Sūlem adōrantēs et eī
dōna cōnsecrantēs, gemmās et aliās rēs pretiōsās in fontem inicere
solēbant. aliī deae grātiās agēbant, aliī ā deā auxilium petēbant.

    'Rōmānī, postquam ad Britanniam advēnērunt, dē fonte mox
cognōvērunt. deinde architectus magnae perītiae, ā Rōmānīs missus,   10
splendidissimum templum deae Sūlī Minervae aedificāvit et thermās
magnificās. simul fabrī, ab architectō incitātī, mūrum circum fontem
posuērunt. nunc inter templum et thermās fōns situs est, unde aquae
per fistulam plumbeam ad balneōs rēctā perveniunt.'

    'euge!' inquit Quīntus.'tālem locum adhūc nōn vīsitāvī.'   15

raedā: raeda *carriage*

calidae: calidus *hot, warm*
valle: vallis *valley*
situs *located, situated*

Minervae: Minerva
    Minerva (goddess of wisdom)
fistulam: fistula *pipe*
plumbeam: plumbeus *(made of) lead*
adhūc *until now, so far*

---

1   **Explore the story**

    a   **Togidubnus et Quīntus oppidō Aquīs Sūlis lentē appropinquābant** (line 1):
       in what way were Togidubnus and Quintus approaching Aquae Sulis?

    b   Look at lines 2–3: **rēx, in raedā ... sacrō nārrāre?'**

       i   How is Togidubnus described?

       ii   What question did Togidubnus ask Quintus?

    c   **'ita vērō,' avidē respondit Quīntus** (line 4): how can we tell that Quintus' response
       to Togidubnus' question was enthusiastic? Give a reason for your answer.

    d   **'iamprīdem,' inquit Togidubnus, 'fōns, ē quō aquae calidae effluunt, in valle
       dēsertā situs erat** (lines 5–6): what information did Togidubnus give Quintus about
       the spring?

    e   Look at lines 6–8: **ibi Britannī, ... auxilium petēbant**.

       i   According to Togidubnus, what were the Britons doing at the spring?

       ii   What two possible reasons are given for the Britons' actions?

    f   **'Rōmānī, postquam ad Britanniam advēnērunt, dē fonte mox cognōvērunt**
       (lines 9–10): what happened soon after the Romans arrived in Britain?

g Look at lines 10–12: **deinde architectus … thermās magnificās**.

    i How is the architect described?

    ii How did the architect come to be at Aquae Sulis?

    iii What buildings did the architect build?

h **simul fabrī, ab architectō incitātī, mūrum circum fontem posuērunt** (lines 12–13): what did the craftspeople do and why?

i Look at lines 13–14: **nunc inter … rēctā perveniunt.'**

    i According to Togidubnus, what was the current location of the spring?

    ii Where did the waters from the spring now go?

j **'euge!' inquit Quīntus. 'tālem locum adhūc nōn vīsitāvī.'** (line 15): do you think that Quintus was eager to visit Aquae Sulis after hearing Togidubnus' description? Give a reason for your answer.

2 Explore the language

When Togidubnus briefly tells Quintus about the site of Aquae Sulis, his language reveals what he thinks of certain facts. How does his choice of words show us

a what he thinks the sacred fountain was like as a place of worship before the Romans came?

b what he thinks of the changes the Romans made to the site?

3 Explore further

When we are dealing with the history of sites such as Aquae Sulis, we are often working with incomplete evidence. For example, there is little evidence left now to show us what Britons thought of the site, both before and after the Romans came to Britain. It can be useful to think about what we would like to know about places and events, even if we can never find out the answers to all our questions.

What questions would you like to ask a Briton about Aquae Sulis?

Are there any questions which you would like to ask a Roman?

Natural hot springs.

Reviewing the language Stage 21: page 212

Aquae Sulis and its baths

The Roman town of Aquae Sulis lies beneath the streets of the modern city of Bath in the valley of the River Avon. In a small area enclosed by a bend in the river, over a quarter of a million litres of hot (between 40 and 49 degrees Celsius) water emerge each day from underground springs. This water fell as rain 10 000 years ago and filtered just over 3 kilometres (2 miles) down into the earth before rising to the surface as hot springs containing minerals such as calcium, magnesium and sodium. These waters, considered sacred by both the Britons and Romans, gave Aquae Sulis its Latin name: the Waters of (the goddess) Sulis.

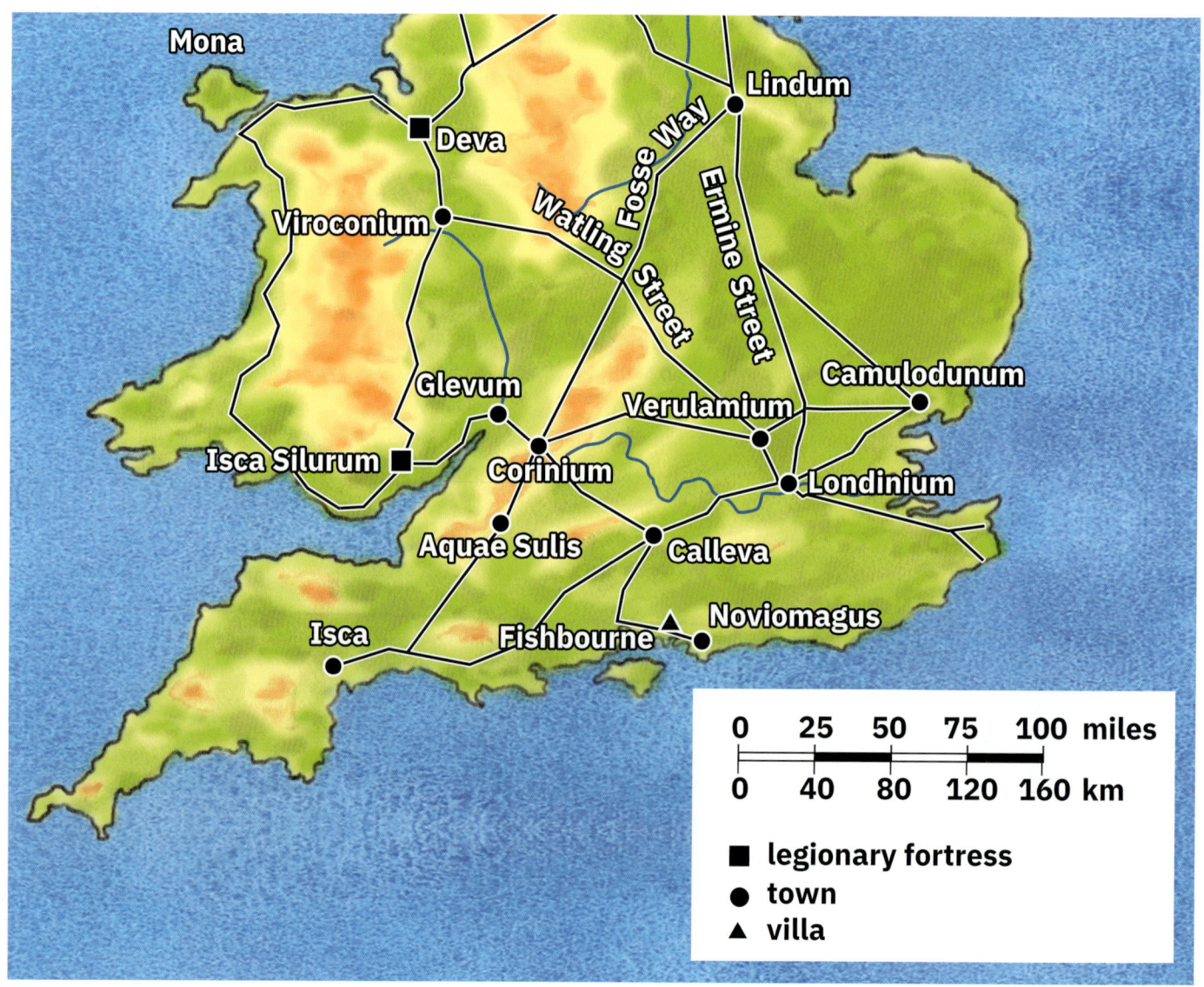

Aquae Sulis and other major Roman settlements.

The sacred spring as it is today. The buildings there now are later constructions. The Romans enclosed it using a wall of stone blocks, lined with lead sheets nearly one centimetre (half an inch) thick.

Bubbles form as the naturally hot water rises to the top of the pool.

Before the Romans enclosed the hot spring, it was a place of great mystery to the tribes of Britain. We remember a time when the approach to the divine spring was through marshy woodland. Steam hung between the trees and the ground was muddy and red with the bubbling waters.

Then the Romans came. They drove wooden stakes into the ground and dug for weeks to remove the mud and create a stone pool. Then they built their temple and channelled the waters into their drains and bath house. Roman engineering is a force of nature all its own.

Although archaeologists suspect that the spring was sacred to the Britons before the Romans built Aquae Sulis, the work of the Roman engineers in the first century AD destroyed all evidence for British worship at the site. Pre-Roman coins found at Bath indicate that the people of Iron Age Britain threw them into the spring, but very little else can be said about whom the Britons worshipped here and what they believed. It is possible that they had a goddess of their own called Sulis, whom the Romans came to associate with Minerva, but since the only evidence we have for Sulis is Roman, we cannot say for sure.

This bronze head was probably made in Gaul. It was most likely part of a standing cult statue of Sulis-Minerva.

A visitor to Aquae Sulis in AD 83, the time of our story, would have arrived at a Roman temple complex built only a decade or two before. Visitors entering the precinct would have seen an altar and an imposing temple ahead of them. To their left was a traditional Roman bathing complex and the lead-lined reservoir of the sacred spring which fed it.

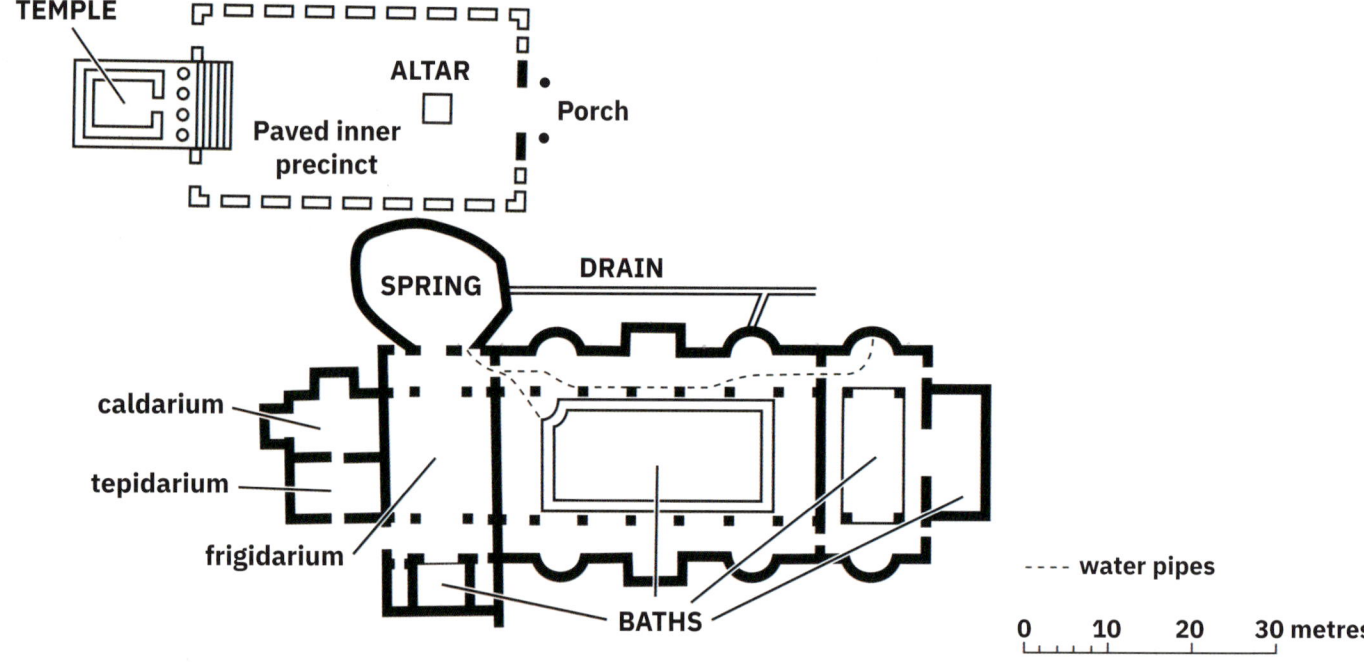

Plan of the temple complex around the time of our stories.

Water flowed from the spring into the baths through lead pipes that are still in place today.

This is the largest of the three plunge baths, now called the Great Bath. Its naturally warm waters still give off a haze of rolling steam, just as they would have in Roman times.

How the Great Bath probably looked around the time of our stories.

In addition to the pools of naturally hot water, there was a set of baths heated by a hypocaust, with a caldarium, tepidarium and frigidarium.

Thinking point 1: What can you remember about Roman bath complexes? Explain what is meant by each of the following terms: hypocaust, caldarium, tepidarium, frigidarium.

In addition to the impressive temple and bath house, there were probably a few other public buildings, such as a basilica for the administration of law and local government, and possibly a theatre. Most other buildings would have been houses for those who lived there and inns for the town's visitors.

Thinking point 2: What changes did the Romans make to the spring and its surroundings? Why do their actions make it difficult to learn about how the Britons used the site before the Romans arrived?

The Romans continued to build at Aquae Sulis. This is what the precinct would have been like by the early fourth century AD.

One of the most striking features of Aquae Sulis is the temple pediment, high above the steps leading into the temple building. At its centre is a male face, with a beard and hair floating around it as if submerged in water. This face is surrounded on both sides by winged victories, female figures that symbolise military conquest, each standing on a globe. If you look closely, you can even see Minerva's owl, perched on her helmet.

Archaeologists have long debated the identity of the male figure in the centre of the pediment. Scholars think he is a male gorgon, a (usually female) mythical monster, made to resemble a water god or spirit sacred to the people of Britain and Gaul.

Thinking point 3: Look at the picture of the pediment and identify each of the elements described by Cephalus. Why might the Romans have chosen these specific images for use at Aquae Sulis?

The remains of the temple pediment and a reconstruction of what it may have looked like.

The bathing complex was built using local stone, but specialised craftspeople were brought from Gaul to work on the temple. It is likely that the local Roman government was responsible for these grand building projects; few others would have had access to the necessary wealth, connections and engineering skill.

The Roman baths at Aquae Sulis were fed by the sacred spring. Some Roman authors, such as Pliny the Elder, thought that mineral springs like these had healing properties, but there is little evidence to suggest that visitors to Aquae Sulis bathed in the water for healing. It was not until the late sixteenth century that Bath became a famous spa town, to which wealthy visitors flocked to 'take the waters' for their health. Ancient visitors, like Togidubnus, made the journey for the sacred spring and its goddess. Countless offerings were left for Sulis-Minerva at Aquae Sulis, including the **dēfīxiōnēs** (curse tablets) we will meet in Stage 22.

When they arrived at the site, visitors could approach the sacred spring from the temple precinct and lean over the railing to look down into the water. This was the moment they had come for. If they had brought something to offer the goddess, they dropped it into the pool and watched it disappear into the bubbling silt at the bottom. Offerings thrown into the spring included precious objects such as coins, jewellery and cups made of silver and pewter. It is hard to know exactly what such offerings meant to the people who made them, but perhaps they were given in exchange for the goddess's intervention in people's everyday lives and struggles.

Thinking point 4: The initial building programme at Aquae Sulis was undertaken not long after the Boudican revolt (AD 60–61). It has been suggested that this was an attempt by the local Roman authorities to mark their victory and express their authority. Suggest how the building programme might be seen as a demonstration of Roman power in Britannia.

Some of the objects thrown into the spring as offerings.

Thinking point 5: Look at the picture of objects found in the spring. What sort of things have survived? What factors do you think affect the type of objects found in the spring?

Enquiry: What might the site of Aquae Sulis reveal about Roman attitudes towards the culture of the Britons?

You may wish to consider the following:

- the sacred spring before Aquae Sulis
- how the Romans changed the site of the sacred spring
- how the Romans financed and built the site
- who visited it and why
- how the material evidence reflects cultural interactions between the Romans and Britons.

Vocabulary checklist 21

From now on, most verbs in the checklists are listed as in the Book III Language information section (i.e. perfect passive participles are usually included).

ā, ab	*from; by*
aliī … aliī	*some … others*
annus, annī	*year*
circum	*around*
clārus, clāra, clārum	*famous*
cōnfīdō, cōnfīdere	*trust*
dīligēns, *gen.* **dīligentis**	*hardworking, careful*
dūrus, dūra, dūrum	*harsh, hard*
fōns, fontis	*fountain, spring*
gravis, grave	*heavy, serious*
hōra, hōrae	*hour*
iubeō, iubēre, iussī, iussus	*order*
maximē	*very greatly, very much*
morbus, morbī	*illness*
nūper	*recently*
oppidum, oppidī	*town*
plēnus, plēna, plēnum	*full*
praemium, praemiī	*reward, prize*
sapiēns, *gen.* **sapientis**	*wise*
unde	*from where*

An earring found in the spring.

1 Belimicus, quī ad oppidum Aquās Sūlis vēnerat, thermās intrāvit.
Belimicus, thermās ingressus, ad fontem sacrum festīnāvit.

2 Belimicus, prope fontem stāns, Dumnorigem cōnspexit.
Belimicus, Dumnorigem cōnspicātus, post columnam sē cēlāvit.

3 Dumnorix, parvam tabulam tenēns, ad fontem prōcessit.
Dumnorix, ad fontem prōgressus, manūs ad caelum sustulit et deae Sūlī tabulam obtulit.

4 Belimicus, quī parvam tabulam vīderat, ad fontem
cautē revēnit.
Belimicus, ad fontem regressus, precēs Dumnorigis
plānē audīvit.

5 Dumnorix, deam precātus, tabulam in fontem
iniēcit et dīxit:
'mortem inimīcīs Togidubnī!'

6 Dumnorix, haec verba locūtus, ē thermīs exiit.
Belimicus ā fonte contendit, attonitus.

in vīllā Aventīnae

erat vīlla nova prope thermās. in ātriō huius vīllae garriēbant Quīntus et Dumnorix. illī exspectābant Aventīnam, quae vīllam nūper ēmerat et Dumnorigem bene nōverat. Aventīna erat fēmina magnae dīligentiae et summae benignitātis.

mox ancilla iānuam aperuit, quod domina revēnerat. Dumnorix, Aventīnam cōnspicātus, statim surrēxit.   *5*

'exspectātissima es, Aventīna nostra!' inquit. 'quid agit rēx?'

'morbus nōn peior est,' respondit Aventīna. 'omnia mandāta, quae rēgīna Catia tibi dederat, cum summā cūrā effēcī.'

'bene,' inquit prīnceps. 'tibi gratiās maximās agimus, Aventīna.   *10* dē Togidubnō sollicitī sumus.'

dīligentiae: dīligentia
  carefulness, attentiveness
benignitātis: benignitās
  kindness
cōnspicātus
  having caught sight of

peior *worse*

	Dumnorix, haec verba locūtus, prope Aventīnam cōnsēdit.	**locūtus** *having spoken*
Aventīna:	Vilbia autem, fīlia meī frātris, mihi aliquid novī rettulit.	**autem** *but*
Dumnorix:	hanc rem audīre velim. Vilbia est puella maximae prūdentiae.	
Aventīna:	tabernam possideō in extrēmā parte oppidī. hanc tabernam, *15* ubi aliquandō Vilbia labōrat, prīnceps quīdam vīsitāre solet. vīsne mē illum prīncipem hūc invītāre? nōmen eius est Belimicus.	**extrēmā parte: extrēma pars** *edge*
Quīntus:	ēheu! ille prīnceps est vir ingeniī prāvī.	**prāvī: prāvus** *evil*
Aventīna:	quid? vērum dīcis? *20*	
Quīntus:	prīncipem Cantiacōrum bene nōvimus.	
Dumnorix:	nōlī timēre, Aventīna mea! paulum perīculī est. Dumnorix, fortissimus prīncipum, adest!	**paulum perīculī** *little danger*
Quīntus:	sine dubiō Belimicus ad oppidum Aquās Sūlis vēnit, quod ultiōnem petit. *25*	**ultiōnem: ultiō** *revenge*
Dumnorix:	mī Quīnte, nōlī illam pestem commemorāre! iste Belimicus, saepe dē ultiōne locūtus, nihil umquam effēcit. (*rīdēns*) praetereā ego sum leō, iste rīdiculus mūs. semper eum superāre possum.	**praetereā** *besides* **mūs** *mouse*
Aventīna:	fortasse tū fortior es quam Mārs ipse, mī amīce. ego tamen *30* Belimicō vix crēdere possum. volō tē in tabernā eī obviam īre.	**Mārs** *Mars (god of war)* **obviam īre** *(go to) meet*

fībula

Two silver brooches joined by a chain.

fībula *brooch, decorative pin*

prīdiē prōcēdit Aventīna ad tabernam, in quā labōrat Vilbia. tabernam ingressa, Aventīna Vilbiam petit, cui ōsculum dat.

ingressa *having entered*
ōsculum *kiss*
mea lūx! *light of my life!*
amita *aunt*

Aventīna: mea lūx! quid hodiē agis?

Vilbia: (*misera*) tam occupāta sum, amita! ecce, pōcula sordida ubīque iacent. mihi necesse est omnia lavāre. nimium labōris habeō. pōcula lavāre diūtius nōlō.   5

Aventīna: mea Vilbia, tibi favet fortūna. pater tuus nūntium ad mē mīsit: 'domum nūper rediī. Vilbiam exspectō.' placetne?

Vilbia: (*Aventīnam amplexa*) mihi placet, amita cārissima!

amplexa *having hugged*

*Vilbia autem, haec locūta, pōculum lavāre nōn incipit. amitae fībulam   10
ostendit. Aventīna fībulam, quam fīlia frātris tenet, intentē spectat.*

incipit: incipere *begin, start*

Aventīna: quam pulchra, quam pretiōsa est haec fībula, mea Vilbia. eam īnspicere velim. num argentea est?

Vilbia: sānē argentea est. herī prīnceps Britannicus, cui pōculum vīnī praebēbam, eam mihi grātīs dedit.   15

sānē *obviously*
grātīs *free*

Aventīna: (*sollicita*) quālis est hic prīnceps? estne homō probus aut mendāx?

quālis *what sort of person?*

Vilbia: nescio. eum in hōc oppidō numquam anteā vīdī. fortasse rēgem Togidubnum colere vult. (*anxia*) quid prōpōnis, amita? vīsne mē fībulam prīncipī reddere? adeō cupiō eam retinēre. tam pulchra   20
est. quid facere dēbeō?

Aventīna: (*rem breviter cōgitāns*) nōs hunc prīncipem cavēre dēbēmus. nēmō tālia dōna grātīs dat.

breviter *briefly*

Vilbia, amitam iterum amplexa, pōculum lavāre incipit, cantāns.

Explore further

In the story **in vīllā Aventīnae**, Aventina was described as **fēmina magnae dīligentiae et summae benignitātis**, and Vilbia was described as **puella maximae prūdentiae**.

To what extent do you think that these are good or bad descriptions of these characters? Support your answers with examples from the stories you have read so far.

About the language 1: perfect active participles

1   In Stage 21, you met sentences containing perfect passive participles:

perfect passive participles: page 6

rēx, ā Rōmānīs **honōrātus**, semper fidēlis manēbat.
*The king, **having been honoured** by the Romans, always remained loyal.*

puellae, ā patre **laudātae**, rīdēbant.
*The girls, **having been praised** by their father, were smiling.*

2   In Stage 22, you have met another kind of perfect participle.
Study the way it is translated in the following examples:

Vilbia, tabernam **ingressa**, Aventīnae fībulam ostendit.
*Vilbia, **having entered** the inn, showed the brooch to Aventina.*

senex, deam **precātus**, abiit.
*The old man, **having prayed** to the goddess, went away.*

The words in **bold** are **perfect active participles**.
Like other participles they change their endings to agree with the nouns they describe.
Compare the following pair of sentences:

singular   puer, mīlitēs **cōnspicātus**, valdē timēbat.
plural   puerī, mīlitēs **cōnspicātī**, valdē timēbant.

3   Translate the following examples:

    a   Dumnorix, vīllam ingressus, Aventīnam cōnspexit.

    b   rēgīna, multa verba locūta, tandem tacuit.

    c   mercātōrēs, ad forum prōgressī, negōtium agere coepērunt.

    d   fēmina, deam Sūlem precāta, dōnum in aquam iniēcit.

    e   puellae, equum cōnspicātae, eum īnspicere volēbant.

In each sentence, pick out the perfect active participle and the noun which it describes.
State whether each pair is singular or plural.

4   Only a small group of verbs have a perfect active participle; they do not have a perfect passive participle.

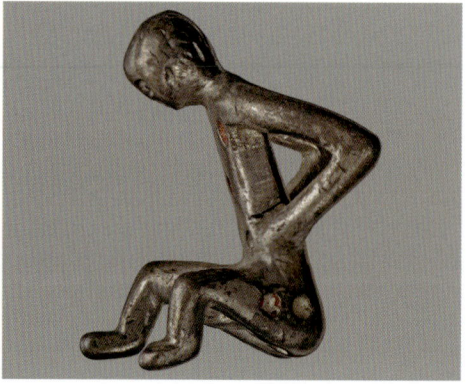

The Romans were very fond of games involving types of dice, both the kind we are used to (left), and more novel varieties such as the little man (right), who can fall six ways up; here he scores 2. The larger of the cubic dice has a hollow in it, possibly for loading the dice.

prīnceps īnfēlīx

scaena prīma

diēs vesperāscit. Vilbia in tabernā hūc illūc ruit, quod tam occupāta est. Dumnorix, ab Aventīnā missus, cum Belimicō āleam lūdit. Dumnorix Belimicō multam pecūniam dēbet.

Belimicus: quid agit Togidubnus? valēscitne? heus! Venerem iēcī! caupō! iubeō tē plūs cibī ferre.   5

Dumnorix: cotīdiē valēscit rēx. nunc tacē, amīce! ego āleās iaciō.

Belimicus: hercle! quam īnfēlīx es, Dumnorix! canem iterum iēcistī. alium dēnārium mihi dēbēs.

Dumnorix: satis pecūniae iam āmīsī. accipe dēnāriōs quōs tibi dēbeō, Belimice. ad vīllam Aventīnae redeō.   10

    (Dumnorix, haec locūtus, ē tabernā exit. simul Vilbia, plūs cibī portāns, Belimicō appropinquat.)

Belimicus: *(cachinnāns)* tanta est stultitia hōrum Rēgnēnsium! Dumnorix, ā mē dēceptus, multam pecūniam āmīsit. sed Togidubnus, nūllam fraudem suspicātus, etiam īnfēlīcior est. melius est   15 eī cavēre. rēgī nōn tūtum est thermās huius oppidī vīsitāre.

    (Vilbia, ubi verba Belimicī audīvit, est attonita.)

Vilbia: *(sēcum cōgitāns)* nōnne prīnceps, quī Dumnorigem dēcēpit, est homō magnae arrogantiae? porrō, rēx Togidubnus, vir summae auctōritātis, in magnō perīculō est. ēheu! necesse est mihi   20 quam celerrimē Dumnorigem monēre.

    (exit currēns.)

hūc illūc *here and there, up and down*
āleam lūdit *is playing dice*
Venerem: Venus *Venus (highest dice throw)*

canem: canis *dog (lowest dice throw)*

stultitia *foolishness*

fraudem: fraus *trick*
suspicātus *having suspected*

arrogantiae: arrogantia *arrogance, conceit*

scaena secunda

Vilbia, ē tabernā ēgressa, per silentium noctis currit. Dumnorix, quī prope fontem deae Sūlis stat, Vilbiam currentem videt.

Dumnorix:	Vilbia? quid quaeris? puellīs nōn tūtum est per viās noctū īre. domī manēre dēbēs.	
Vilbia:	(*commōta*) ā tabernā, in quā sedet Belimicus, cucurrī.	5
Dumnorix:	(*attonitus*) Diāna altera es! celerius quam cerva cucurristī.	
Vilbia:	rēx Togidubnus in maximō perīculō est.	
Dumnorix:	quid dīcis? volō tē mihi tōtam rem explicāre, Vilbia.	
Vilbia:	thermās vīsitāre nōn dēbet rēx. nam aliquis in hōc oppidō Togidubnum laedere cupit.	10
Dumnorix:	quō modō hoc cognōvistī?	
Vilbia:	prīnceps Cantiacōrum, postquam ē tabernā exiistī, id apertē dīxit.	
Dumnorix:	hercle! Togidubnum saepe monuī, 'nōlī Cantiacīs crēdere, praesertim Belimicō.'	
Vilbia:	sine dubiō Belimicus vir perfidus est.	15
Dumnorix:	ita vērō, Vilbia. nunc abī! fortasse dea Sūlis mihi cōnsilium dare potest.	

(exit Vilbia. Dumnorix prope fontem sacrum manet manūsque ad caelum tollit.)

Dumnorix:	ō dea Sūlis! auxilium ā tē iam petīvī. tē precātus, tabulam plumbeam in fontem sacrum iniēcī. dīra imprecātiō, in tabulā scrīpta, iam in fonte tuā iacet. volō tē precēs meās audīre.	20

paulīsper silentium est. tum 'ehem!' audit Dumnorix. sē vertēns, Belimicum videt. ad Dumnorigem prōgressus, Belimicus īrātus eum vituperāre incipit.

Belimicus:	quid dicēbās, furcifer? auxilium ā deā Sūle petis? asine! tē ipsum in fontem sacrum inicere velim.	25
Dumnorix:	mī amīce, verba tua cum summā cūrā ēligere dēbēs. tibi perīculōsum est aquae appropinquāre.	

(Vilbia, ad fontem regressa, ubi clāmōrēs audīvit, post columnam sē cēlat.)

		30
Belimicus:	homuncule! Vilbiam auferre audēs? porrō, ista puella est fūr. ubi est fībula argentea mea, quam Vilbia abstulit?	
Dumnorix:	īnsānus es, Belimice. melius est tibi domum redīre.	
Belimicus:	audēsne mihi ita dīcere, Dumnorix? (*gladium dēstringēns*) nēmō mē impūne vexat.	35

ēgressa *having gone out*

noctū *at night*

Diāna *Diana (goddess of hunting)*
altera *another, a second*

aliquis *someone*

apertē *openly*

praesertim *especially*
perfidus *treacherous, untrustworthy*

precātus *having prayed to*
tabulam: tabula *(writing) tablet*
dīra *dreadful*
imprecātiō *curse*
prōgressus *having advanced*

regressa *having returned*

(Vilbia invīsa Belimicō appropinquat. puella prīncipem, simulac tergum vertit, in aquam dēicit.)

Dumnorix: *(susurrāns)* optimē fēcistī! sed nōlō tē ad illam tabernam redīre, Vilbia. tibi perīculōsum est in hōc oppidō manēre.

Vilbia: consentiō. tūtius est mihi Dēvam redīre, ubi mē exspectat pater.   *40*

exeunt Dumnorix et Vilbia. Belimicus ē fonte cum magnā difficultāte madidus sē extrahit et abit saeviēns.

invīsa *unseen*
tergum *back*

Dēvam *to Chester*

difficultāte: difficultās
   difficulty
madidus *soaking wet*

The reservoir of the spring as it is today.

About the language 2: more about the genitive

1 In Book II, you met examples of the genitive case like these:

marītus **Galatēae** erat Aristō.
*The husband **of Galatea** was Aristo.*

prō templō **Caesaris** stat āra.
*In front of the Temple **of Caesar** stands an altar.*

2 In Stage 21, you met another use of the genitive. Study the following examples:

satis pecūniae	*enough money*, literally, *enough of money*
nimium vīnī	*too much wine*
plūs sanguinis	*more blood*
multum cibī	*much food*

Each phrase is made up of two words:

a A word like **plūs** or **nimium** indicating an amount or quantity.

b A noun in the genitive case.

3 Further examples:

a nimium pecūniae   **c** plūs labōris

b nihil perīculī   **d** multum aquae

4 In Stage 22, you have met examples like these:

fēmina ingeniī prāvī   vir minimae auctōritātis
a woman of evil character   *a man of very little authority*

In both examples, a noun (**fēmina, vir**) is described by another noun and an adjective both in the genitive case. Such phrases can be translated in different ways. For example:

puella magnae virtūtis   homō summae benignitātis
a girl of great courage   *a man of the utmost kindness*
Or, in more natural English: Or, in more natural English:
a very courageous girl   *a very kind man*

5 Further examples:

a homō magnae prūdentiae   **d** fābula huius modī

b iuvenis vīgintī annōrum   **e** puella maximae calliditātis

c fēmina magnae dignitātis   **f** vir ingeniī optimī

Building words: adjectives and adverbs

1   In Stage 21 you met the following pattern:

adjectives		adverbs	
laetus, laeta	*happy*	laet**ē**	*happily*
perītus, perīta	*skilful*	perit**ē**	*skilfully*

2   Study another common pattern of adjectives and adverbs:

adjectives		adverbs	
brevis	*short*	brevi**ter**	*shortly*
ferōx	*fierce*	ferōci**ter**	*fiercely*

3   Using this pattern as a guide, work out the words that are missing from this table:

suāvis	*sweet*	suāviter	. . . .
neglegēns	. . . .	neglegenter	*carelessly*
audāx	. . . .	audācter	. . . .

4   Divide the following words into two lists, one of adjectives and one of adverbs.
    Then give the meaning of each word.

fortis; fidēliter; īnsolēns; fortiter; sapienter; īnsolenter; fidēlis; sapiēns.

5   Choose the correct Latin word to translate the words in **bold** in the following sentences:

a   Vilbia was a **sensible** young person. (prūdēns, prūdenter)

b   Salvius rode **quickly** into the courtyard. (celer, celeriter)

c   Belimicus was **happy** because he had eaten well. (laetus, laetē)

d   The soldier always worked **diligently**. (dīligēns, dīligenter)

e   Aventina listened **very sadly** to Dumnorix. (trīstissima, trīstissimē)

6   Notice the different pattern for these two adjectives and their related adverbs:

adjectives		adverbs	
facilis	*easy*	facil**e**	*easily*
difficilis	*difficult*	difficil**ē**	*with difficulty*

Practising the language

pallium et pugiō

In the town of Aquae Sulis, two Roman soldiers attempt to capture a thief.

duo mīlitēs Rōmānī ad tabernam quondam ambulābant. alter Crīspus,
alter Frontō erat. Crīspus vītam dēplōrābat, quod pallium novum
āmīserat. Frontō, quamquam amīcus Crīspī erat, eum dērīdēbat.

'umquam fuit mīles neglegentior quam tū, Crīspe?' inquit.
'quō modō pallium āmīsistī?' 5

'thermās ingressus, servō pallium trādidī.' respondit Crīspus miser.
'tum vestīmenta in apodytēriō dēposuī et balneum intrāvī. ēheu!
ē balneō ēgressus, neque servum neque pallium invēnī.'

'mīles minimae prūdentiae es,' inquit Frontō. 'sānē fūr persōnam
servī agēbat.' 10

subitō Crīspus hominem pallium gerentem cōnspicātus, 'heus!'
clāmāvit. 'pallium meum geris! venī hūc!'

ille tamen, ā Crīspō vocātus, statim fūgit. amīcī eum agitāre
coepērunt. per multās viās oppidī fūrem persecūtī, eum tandem in viā
dēsertā invēnērunt. 15

'effugere nōn potes!' clāmāvit Frontō. 'mīlitēs Rōmānī sunt
callidiōrēs quam vōs Brittunculī!'

fūr, ā Frontōne vituperātus, pallium Crīspō reddidit. tum Frontō
attonitus

'hercle!' exclāmāvit. 'pugiō meus abest!' 20

fūr, quī pugiōnem Frontōnis cēperat, 'valēte, amīcī!' clāmāvit,
et fūgit rīdēns.

pallium *cloak*

dēplōrābat: dēplōrāre
complain about

minimae: minimus
very little
persōnam ... agēbat:
persōnam agere
play the part (of)

persecūtī: persecūtus
having pursued

Brittunculī: Brittunculus
poor little Briton

---

1 Explore the story

a **duo mīlitēs Rōmānī ad tabernam quondam ambulābant. alter Crīspus,
alter Frontō erat** (lines 1–2): what are we told about Crispus and Fronto here?

b Look at lines 2–3: **Crīspus vītam ... eum dērīdēbat**.

   i Why was Crispus complaining about his life?

   ii How was Fronto reacting to Crispus' complaints?

c **'umquam fuit mīles neglegentior quam tū, Crīspe?' inquit. 'quō modō pallium
āmīsistī?'** (lines 4–5): what two questions did Fronto ask Crispus?

d Look at lines 6–8: **'thermās ingressus ... pallium invēnī.'**

   i What had Crispus done immediately after going into the baths?

   ii What had Crispus done before he entered the bath itself?

   iii What problem had Crispus faced after getting out of the bath?

e 'sānē fūr persōnam servī agēbat' (lines 9–10): what explanation did Fronto offer for what had happened at the baths?

f Look at lines 11–12: **subitō Crīspus … 'venī hūc!'**

    i Why did Crispus shout at the man?

    ii What did Crispus want the man to do?

g Look at lines 13–15: **ille tamen … dēsertā invēnērunt**.

    i What did the man do after being called by Crispus?

    ii What did Crispus and Fronto do in response to this?

h 'mīlitēs Rōmānī sunt callidiōrēs quam vōs Brittunculī!' (lines 16–17): what claim did Fronto make?

i fūr, ā Frontōne vituperātus, pallium Crīspō reddidit (line 18): what are we told here about the **fūr**?

j Look at lines 18–22: **tum Frontō … fūgit rīdēns**.

    i What did Fronto notice?

    ii What had the **fūr** done?

    iii What two things did the **fūr** do at the end of the story?

2 Explore the language

Romans enjoyed different types of humour, including wordplay, satire and farce. Traditional elements of a farce include deception, slapstick, disguises, coincidences and sudden twists.

What elements of Roman farce can you find in this story?

3 Explore further

This story is inspired not only by Roman comedy but also by one of the **dēfīxiōnēs** found at Aquae Sulis. These tablets are one way in which we can see what ordinary people were thinking about: in this case, theft!

You have met other types of written Latin which give us glimpses into the lives of ordinary people. What kinds of things can we learn from

a tombstones?

b graffiti and wall paintings?

c letters such as the Vindolanda tablets?

d business documents such as Caecilius' accounts?

Reviewing the language Stage 22: page 214

Enquiry: The UNESCO Memory of the World programme records remarkable and important pieces of cultural heritage from all over the world. In 2014 the curse tablets found at Bath (Aquae Sulis) became the only items from Roman Britain to be added to the UK Memory of the World Register. Why might the Bath curse tablets have been recognised in this way?

Curses and curse tablets

When excavating Roman religious sites, such as the spring at Aquae Sulis, archaeologists sometimes find small sheets of lead or pewter inscribed with curses which call for the punishment of an enemy. These are called **dēfīxiōnēs** (curse tablets) and over 300 have been found in Britain alone. These tablets give historians a rare glimpse into the lives of ordinary people, directly and in their own words.

The method of putting a curse on someone followed a general formula. The name of the offender, if known, was written on a tablet along with details of the crime. A god was then called upon to punish them, often in a very unpleasant way. If the exact offender was unknown, the tablet might contain a list of suspects or, if there were not even any suspects, a vague statement about the possible culprit such as 'whether enslaved or free, whether man or woman'. The completed tablet was rolled or folded up and 'delivered' to the gods. In Britain, almost all curses were placed in temples, household shrines or somewhere with water, such as a well or spring. Elsewhere in the empire, they were often buried in tombs so that the dead could either carry out the curse or deliver it to the gods of the underworld.

Around 130 curse tablets have been found in the sacred spring at Aquae Sulis (around 117 of which have writing that can be read). Some curses were very simple: just 'I dedicate' followed by the intended victim's name; however, they could also be brutal and vivid in their requests for punishment.

This curse tablet asks the Roman god Neptune and Niskus (possibly a local river god) to punish a thief of gold and silver coins. It was found in a small river near Southampton. Other curse tablets appealing to Neptune have been found in the River Thames in London, the Little Ouse in Norfolk and the Tas in Suffolk.

> BASILIA GIVES TO THE TEMPLE OF MARS HER SILVER RING, THAT SO LONG AS SOMEONE, SLAVE OR FREE, KEEPS SILENT OR KNOWS ANYTHING ABOUT IT, HE MAY BE ACCURSED IN HIS BLOOD AND EYES AND EVERY LIMB, OR EVEN HAVE ALL HIS INTESTINES ENTIRELY EATEN AWAY, IF HE HAS STOLEN THE RING OR BEEN AN ACCOMPLICE.

> DOCILIANUS, SON OF BRUCERUS, TO THE MOST HOLY GODDESS SULIS. I CURSE HIM WHO HAS STOLEN MY HOODED CLOAK, WHETHER MAN OR WOMAN, WHETHER SLAVE OR FREE, THAT ... THE GODDESS SULIS INFLICT DEATH UPON ... AND NOT ALLOW HIM SLEEP OR CHILDREN NOW OR IN THE FUTURE, UNTIL HE HAS BROUGHT MY HOODED CLOAK TO THE TEMPLE OF HER DIVINITY.

Thinking point 1: For each of these curse tablets identify who is doing the cursing and why. Neither of these people knew who had stolen their property. How do they get around this when writing their curse?

One of the most famous tablets of Aquae Sulis is this one, which inspired the character of Vilbia in this Stage:

> MAY HE WHO HAS STOLEN VILBIA FROM ME DISSOLVE LIKE WATER. MAY SHE WHO HAS DEVOURED HER BE STRUCK DUMB, WHETHER IT BE VELVINNA, EXSUPEREUS, VERIANUS SEVERINUS, AUGUSTALIS, COMITIANUS, CATUS, MINIANUS, GERMANILLA OR JOVINA.

This example illustrates how difficult curse tablets can be to read and interpret. The author of this curse tablet was once assumed to be a jealous lover, but this is no longer a popular view among historians. Most curse tablets found in Britain deal with the theft of items such as jewellery and clothing. This would suggest that, rather than a girlfriend, Vilbia was an enslaved woman who was considered someone's property. It is also possible that the curse refers to an actual object; the word **vilbia** may be a corruption of **fibula** (brooch). Some historians have suggested that it may be a lost British word for a pointed tool.

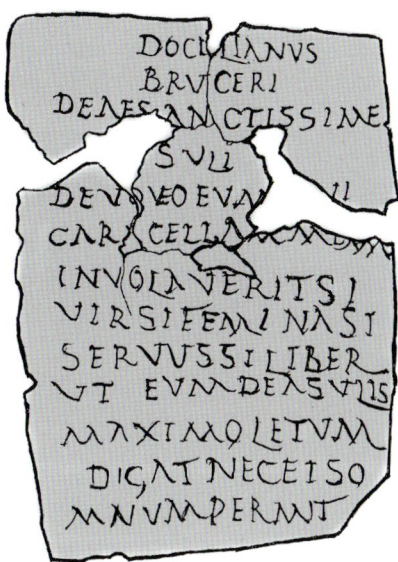

A reconstruction of the first side of Docilianus' curse.

> **Thinking point 2:** Explain how historians' understanding of the Vilbia tablet has changed and the possible interpretations that have been suggested.

The Vilbia curse, like many others, was written backwards to increase the mystery of the process and perhaps the strength of the curse. Curse tablets found elsewhere in the empire, especially in big cities such as Rome and Carthage, sometimes add magical words with no apparent meaning in human language such as bescu, berebescu, bazagra (rather like 'abracadabra', a word which actually appears in the ancient Greek Magical Papyri).

The Vilbia curse.

> **Thinking point 3:** In what ways are British curse tablets different from those found elsewhere in the empire?

It has been suggested that the following tablet found at the Temple of Mercury at Uley – about 35 kilometres (22 miles) north of Aquae Sulis – was written by the same Docilianus who asked Sulis to punish the thief who stole his cloak:

> TO THE GOD MERCURY FROM DOCILINUS ... VARIANUS AND PEREGRINA AND SABINIANUS, WHO HAVE BROUGHT EVIL HARM ON MY BEAST AND ARE ... I ASK YOU TO DRIVE THEM TO THE GREATEST DEATH, AND DO NOT ALLOW THEM HEALTH OR SLEEP UNLESS THEY PAY BACK TO YOU WHAT THEY HAVE DONE TO ME.

This is the only example in Britain of two different tablets thought to be by the same person. The names Docilinus and Docilianus may be different Romanised spellings of the British name Docca. The handwriting on the tablets also seems to match, and the punishments requested are very similar in nature.

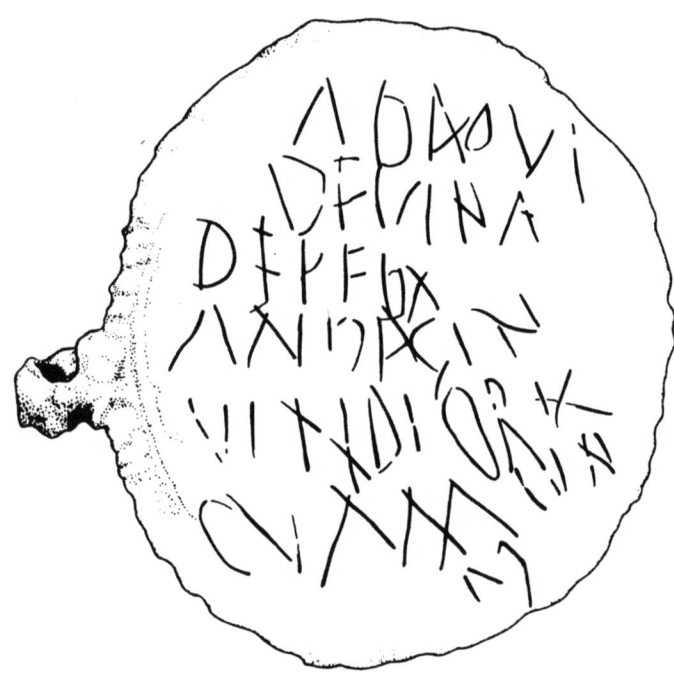

This defixio has a small ring at one end, suggesting it may have been a pendant that was re-purposed as a curse tablet. The inscription lists a mix of Roman and 'Celtic' names which have been Latinised, perhaps the intended victims of the curse.

Some curse tablets from elsewhere in the Roman world include a roughly drawn figure, such as this example from the region of modern Tunisia. A bearded spirit stands in a boat carrying an urn and a torch, symbols of death. None of the curse tablets found in Britain contain pictures.

This curse tablet is unique. You may not be able to see them, but the letters are from the Latin alphabet, while the words they spell seem to be in an indigenous British language.

Although not everyone in the ancient world approved of or believed in such practices, it is important to remember that rituals like curses were part of everyday life. Individuals such as Docilianus would not have called repeatedly on the gods if they did not think their curses worked. Spells, charms and recipes have also survived which claim to offer protection against magic and curses.

> 'There is indeed no one who does not fear being spell-bound by means of evil curses.'
> (Pliny the Elder, *Natural History* 28.4)

Due to their widespread use and very personal nature, curse tablets provide historians with valuable evidence about the everyday lives of a huge range of people.

No community ever lives in complete harmony, and practices such as curse tablets gave people a way to feel more in control of their problems. When there was no human way of righting a wrong, perhaps because there was no way of knowing who was to blame, a person could appeal to the supernatural for help. This might have helped them to feel less powerless or give them hope for future justice. Cursing the person who stole his cloak might have brought Docilianus some peace; at least the unknown thief would not get away with it. The possibility of being cursed may also have affected those with a guilty conscience: perhaps the threat of divine justice would weigh heavily. A thief might initially dismiss the power of curses, but the next time a business deal went wrong or they suffered an injury they might have felt a little anxious: *what if ...?*

Enquiry: The UNESCO Memory of the World programme records remarkable and important pieces of cultural heritage from all over the world. In 2014 the curse tablets found at Bath (Aquae Sulis) became the only items from Roman Britain to be added to the UK Memory of the World Register. Why might the Bath curse tablets have been recognised in this way?

Entries on the UK Memory of the World Register must meet at least one of the following criteria. You may wish to consider which of these, if any, you think the Bath tablets meet.

- Time – is it representative of its time?
- Place – does it highlight certain features of the place where it was created?
- People – does it illustrate a significant aspect of human social, industrial or artistic development?
- Subject and theme – does it relate to something historically or intellectually important?
- Form and style – is it an outstanding example of a certain type of thing?
- Social/spiritual/community significance – is the community emotionally attached to it or does it contribute to that community's sense of identity?

Vocabulary checklist 22

caelum, caelī	*sky*
cēlō, cēlāre, cēlāvī, cēlātus	*hide*
ēgressus, ēgressa, ēgressum	*having gone out*
iaciō, iacere, iēcī, iactus	*throw*
incipiō, incipere, incēpī, inceptus	*begin, start*
īnfēlīx, *gen.* īnfēlīcis	*unlucky*
ingressus, ingressa, ingressum	*having entered*
locūtus, locūta, locūtum	*having spoken*
moneō, monēre, monuī, monitus	*warn, advise*
-ne	(turns a statement into a question)
plūs, *gen.* plūris	*more*
praebeō, praebēre, praebuī, praebitus	*offer, provide*
precātus, precāta, precātum	*having prayed (to)*
prōgressus, prōgressa, prōgressum	*having advanced*
quīdam, quaedam, quoddam	*one, a certain*
quō modō?	*how? in what way?*
regressus, regressa, regressum	*having returned*
simul	*at the same time*
tālis, tāle	*such*
verbum, verbī	*word*

One of the Bath curse tablets, folded as it was when it was found.

1

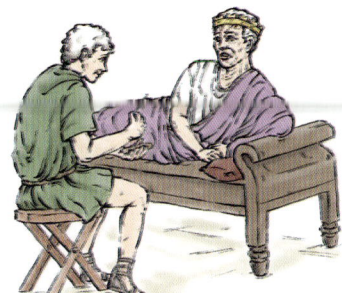

Togidubnus epistulam nūntiō dictat.
in hāc epistulā Togidubnus Catiae
dē oppidō Aquīs Sūlis nārrat.
'haruspex Rōmānus valdē occupātus est.'

Catia amīcae dē epistulā Togidubnī nārrat.
'Togidubnus dīcit haruspicem Rōmānum
valdē occupātum esse.'

2

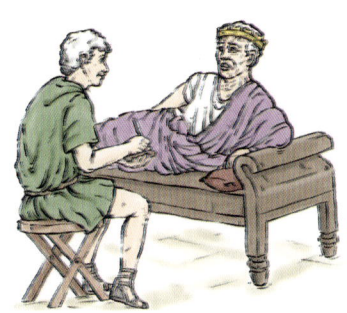

'nōn sōlum Britannī sed etiam cīvēs Rōmānī
deam Sūlem adōrant.'

'Togidubnus dīcit nōn sōlum Britannōs
sed etiam cīvēs Rōmānōs deam Sūlem adōrāre.'

3

Vitelliānus epistulam Philō dictat.
in hāc epistulā Vitelliānus patrī dē Catiā nārrat.
'rēgīna Catia saepe molestissima est.'

'Vitelliānus dīcit rēgīnam Catiam
saepe molestissimam esse.'

4

'nōn sōlum amīcae
sed etiam prīncipēs Britannicī
aulam vīsitant.'

'Vitelliānus dīcit nōn sōlum amīcās
sed etiam prīncipēs Britannicōs
aulam vīsitāre.'

in thermīs

I

prope thermās erat templum, ā fabrīs Rōmānīs aedificātum.
rēx Togidubnus cum multīs prīncipibus servīsque prō templō sedēbat.
Quīntus prope sellam rēgis stābat. rēgem prīncipēsque manus mīlitum
custōdiēbat. prō templō erat ingēns āra, quam omnēs aspiciēbant.
Memor, togam splendidam gerēns, prope āram stābat immōtus.   5

    Dumnorix ūnum ē servīs arcessīvit.

    'dīc haruspicī: rēx parātus est,' servō dīxit.

    servus ad Memorem festīnāvit.

    'domine,' inquit, 'prīnceps Rēgnēnsis dīcit rēgem parātum esse.'

    duo sacerdōtēs, agnum dūcentēs, ad āram statim prōcessērunt.   10
postquam rēx signum dedit, ūnus sacerdōs agnum sacrificāvit. deinde
Memor, quī iam tremēbat, alterī sacerdōtī,

    'iubeō tē,' inquit, 'ōmina īnspicere. dīc mihi: quid vides?'

    sacerdōs, postquam iecur agnī īnspexit, anxius,

    'iecur est līvidum,' inquit. 'nōnne hoc mortem significat? nōnne mortem   15
virī clārī significat?'

    Memor, quī perterritus pallēscēbat, sacerdōtī respondit,

    'minimē! dea Sūlis, quae precēs aegrōrum audīre solet, nōbīs ōmina
optima mīsit.'

    haec locūtus, ad Togidubnum sē vertit.   20

    'ōmina sunt optima!' inquit. 'ōmina tibi remedium mīrābile significant,
quod dea Sūlis Minerva tibi favet.'

    tum rēgem ac prīncipēs Memor in apodytērium dūxit.

aspiciēbant: aspicere
  look towards

ōmina: ōmen *omen, sign*
  (from the gods)
iecur *liver*
līvidum: līvidus *dull,*
  greyish blue
significat: significāre
  mean, indicate
pallēscēbat: pallēscere
  grow pale

ac *and*

II

deinde omnēs in eam partem thermārum intrāvērunt, ubi balneum
maximum erat. Quīntus, prīncipēs secūtus, circumspectāvit et attonitus,

'hae thermae,' inquit, 'maiōrēs sunt quam thermae Pompēiānae!'

Dumnorix eī respondit, 'Togidubnus putat hās thermās meliōrēs esse
quam omnēs thermās Rōmānās.'   5

servī cum magnā difficultāte Togidubnum in balneum dēmittere
coepērunt. maximus clāmor erat. rēx prīncipibus mandāta dabat, prīncipēs
libertīs. tandem rēx, ē balneō ēgressus, vestīmenta, quae servī tulerant,
induit. tum omnēs fontī sacrō appropinquāvērunt.

Cephalus, quī anxius tremēbat, prope fontem stābat, pōculum   10
ōrnātissimum tenēns.

'domine,' inquit, 'pōculum vīnī Britannicī tibi offerō. vīnum est dulce.'

haec locūtus, rēgī pōculum obtulit. Togidubnus ad Quīntum sē convertit.

'ecce pōculum vīnī Britannicī, mī Quīnte! lībertus dīcit vīnum esse dulce.'

Quīntus autem, pōculum cōnspicātus, id rapuit et clāmāvit,   15

'nōlī bibere! hoc est pōculum venēnātum. pōculum huius modī in urbe
Alexandrīā vīdī.'

Cephalus tamen pōculum ē manibus Quīntī rapere temptābat. maxima
pars spectātōrum stābat immōta. sed Dumnorix saeviēns pōculum rapuit
et Cephalō obtulit.   20

'facile est nōbīs vērum cognōscere,' clāmāvit. 'iubeō tē pōculum haurīre.
num vīnum dulce bibere timēs?'

Cephalus pōculum haurīre nōluit, et ad genua rēgis prōcubuit.
rēx immōtus stābat. cēterī prīncipēs lībertum frūstrā resistentem
comprehendērunt. Cephalus, ā prīncipibus coāctus, venēnum hausit.   25
deinde, vehementer tremēns, ingentem gemitum dedit et mortuus
prōcubuit.

secūtus *having followed*

difficultāte: difficultās
difficulty

dulce: dulcis *sweet*

genua: genū *knee*

coāctus: cōgere *force, compel*

The altar at Bath. The base and
the sculptured corner blocks are
original; the rest of the Roman
stone must have been re-used
elsewhere during the Middle
Ages. Compare the drawing
on page 44. At the top left of
the photograph can be seen
the stone statue base which is
inscribed with Memor's name.

About the language 1: indirect statement

1 In Book I, you met sentences like these:

'mercātor multam pecūniam habet.' *'The merchant has a lot of money.'*

'amīcī ad forum ambulant.' *'The friends are walking to the forum.'*

'thermae splendidae sunt.' *'The baths are splendid.'*

In each example, a statement is being made. These examples are known as **direct statements**. Notice the nouns **mercator**, **amīcī** and **thermae**, and the verbs **habet**, **ambulat** and **sunt**.

2 In Stage 23, you have met sentences like these:

Aventīna crēdit **mercātōrem multam pecūniam habēre**.
*Aventina believes **the merchant to have a lot of money**.*

Or, in more natural English: *Aventina believes that **the merchant has a lot of money**.*

Vilbia scit **amīcōs ad forum ambulāre**.
*Vilbia knows **the friends to be walking to the forum**.*

Or, in more natural English: *Vilbia knows that **the friends are walking to the forum**.*

Quīntus crēdit **thermās splendidās esse**.
*Quintus believes **the baths to be splendid**.*

Or, in more natural English: *Quintus believes that **the baths are splendid**.*

In each of these examples, the statement is not being made, but is being reported or mentioned. These examples are known as **indirect statements**. Notice that the nouns **mercatorem**, **amīcōs** and **thermās** are now in the accusative case, and the verbs **habēre**, **ambulāre** and **esse** are now in the infinitive form.

nouns: page 184
infinitives: page 199

3 Compare the following examples:

direct statements	indirect statements
'līberī dormiunt.'	pater dīcit līberōs dormīre.
'The children are asleep.'	*Father says that the children are asleep.*
'Lūcia in vīllā Barbillī habitat.'	audiō Lūciam in vīllā Barbillī habitāre.
'Lucia is living in Barbillus' villa.'	*I hear that Lucia is living in Barbillus' villa.*

4 Further examples of direct and indirect statements:

a 'senātor appropinquat.'

b nūntius dīcit senātōrem appropinquāre.

c 'Memor in tablīnō semper labōrat.'

d audiō Memorem in tablīnō semper labōrāre.

e 'mea soror longam fābulam nārrat.'

f scīmus meam sorōrem longam fābulam nārrāre.

g Vitelliānus putat Catiam multās epistulās scrībere.

h Salvius dīcit imperātōrem īrātum esse.

i Cephalus nūntiat haruspicem abesse.

epistula Cephalī

postquam Cephalus periit, servus eius rēgī epistulam trādidit, ā Cephalō ipsō scrīptam:

'rēx Togidubne, in maximō perīculō es. Memor īnsānit. mortem tuam cupit. iussit mē rem efficere. invītus Memorī pāruī. fortasse nōn crēdis mē vērum dīcere. sed tōtam rem tibi nārrāre velim.   5

ubi tū ad hās thermās advēnistī, remedium quaerēns, Memor mē ad vīllam suam arcessīvit. vīllam ingressus, eum perterritum invēnī. Memor mihi nūntiāvit imperātōrem Domitiānum mortem rēgis cupere.

"iubeō tē hanc rem administrāre," inquit. "iubeō tē venēnum parāre. Togidubnus enim est homō ingeniī prāvī."   10

Memorī respondī,

"longē errās. Togidubnus est vir ingeniī optimī summaeque fideī."

ego eī quoque dīxī mē nōlle tālem rem facere. Memor tamen īrātus,

"sceleste!" inquit. "lībertus meus es. mandāta mea facere dēbēs. cūr mihi obstās?"   15

rēx Togidubne, diū recūsāvī obstinātus. diū beneficia tua commemorāvī. tandem Memor custōdem arcessīvit, quī mē verberāvit. ā custōde paene occīsus, Memorī tandem cessī.

ad casam meam regressus, venēnum invītus parāvī. scrīpsī tamen hanc epistulam et servō fidēlī trādidī. iussī servum tibi epistulam trādere.   20 veniam petō, quamquam facinus scelestum parāvī. Memor coēgit mē hanc rem efficere. Memorem, nōn mē, pūnīre dēbēs.'

īnsānit: īnsānīre *be mad, be insane*

longē errās: longē errāre *make a big mistake*
fideī: fidēs *loyalty, trustworthiness*

beneficia: beneficium *act of kindness, favour*

facinus *crime*
coēgit: cōgere *force, compel*

Britannia perdomita

perdomita *conquered*

When you have read this story, answer the questions at the end.

Salvius cum Memore anxius sermōnem habet. servus ingressus Memorī nūntiat Togidubnum ipsum advenīre, togam splendidam ōrnāmentaque pretiōsa gerentem. servus addit rēgem magnam manum mīlitum dūcere.

Memor:	rēx mīlitēs sēcum hūc dūcit?
Salvius:	Togidubnus, nōs suspicātus, ultiōnem petit. Memor, tibi necesse est mē adiuvāre. nōs ambō enim Rōmānī sumus, Togidubnus barbarus.

(intrat Togidubnus. in manibus epistulam tenet, ā Cephalō scrīptam.)

Togidubnus:	Memor, tū illās īnsidiās parāvistī. tū iussistī Cephalum venēnum comparāre et mē necāre. sed Cephalus, lībertus tuus, mihi omnia patefēcit.
Memor:	Togidubne, id quod dīcis absurdum est. nōs omnēs scīmus Cephalum esse mortuum.
Togidubnus:	Cephalus homō magnae prūdentiae erat. tibi nōn crēdidit. invītus tibi pāruit. simulac mandāta ista dedistī, scrīpsit Cephalus epistulam in quā omnia patefēcit. servus, ā Cephalō missus, epistulam mihi tulit.
Memor:	epistula falsa est, Cephalus mendācissimus. innocēns sum.
Togidubnus:	tū, nōn Cephalus, es mendāx. lībertus enim, magnam iniūriam passus, vērum patefacere volēbat.
Salvius:	Togidubne, cūr mīlitēs hūc dūxistī?
Togidubnus:	Memorem ē cūrā thermārum iam dēmōvī.
Memor:	quid dīcis? tū mē dēmōvistī? iam tibi dīxī mē innocentem esse.
Salvius:	rēx Togidubne, quid fēcistī? tū, quī barbarus es, haruspicem Rōmānum dēmovēre audēs? tū, summōs honōrēs ā nōbīs adeptus, numquam contentus fuistī. nunc perfidiam apertē ostendis. imperātor Domitiānus, arrogantiam tuam diū passus, ad mē epistulam nūper mīsit. in hāc epistulā iussit mē rēgnum tuum occupāre. iubeō tē igitur ad aulam statim redīre.
Togidubnus:	ēn iūstitia Rōmāna! ēn fidēs! nūllī perfidiōrēs sunt quam Rōmānī. stultissimus fuī, quod Rōmānīs adhūc crēdidī. nunc, ā Rōmānīs dēceptus, ista ōrnāmenta, mihi ā Rōmānīs data, humī iaciō. Salvī, mitte nūntium ad Domitiānum: 'nōs tandem Togidubnum vīcimus. Britannia perdomita est.'

(senex, haec locūtus, lentē per iānuam exit.)

5

10   **īnsidiās: īnsidiae** *trap, ambush*
patefēcit: patefacere *reveal*

absurdum: absurdus *absurd*

15

falsa *false, untrue*

20   **passus** *having suffered*

dēmōvī: dēmovēre *dismiss, remove*

25

adeptus *having received, having obtained*
perfidiam: perfidia *treachery*
rēgnum *kingdom*
occupāre *seize, take over*

ēn iūstitia! *so this is justice!*

35   **humī** *on the ground*
nūntium: nūntius *message, news*
vīcimus: vincere *conquer*

Questions

1   **Salvius cum Memore anxius sermōnem habet** (line 1): who is described as **anxius**?

2   **servus ingressus … mīlitum dūcere** (lines 2–3): from what the enslaved man says, why might Salvius and Memor think that Togidubnus' visit to them is not an ordinary one? Make two points.

3   Look at lines 5–7: **Togidubnus, nōs … Togidubnus barbarus**.

   a   What is Salvius' explanation for Togidubnus' visit?

   b   Why does Salvius think that Memor should help him?

4   **Memor, tū illās īnsidiās parāvistī. tū iussistī Cephalum venēnum comparāre et mē necāre** (lines 10–11): what accusations does Togidubnus make against Memor?

5   **Togidubne, id quod dīcis absurdum est. nōs omnēs scīmus Cephalum esse mortuum** (lines 13–14): why is Memor certain that Togidubnus is unable to prove his accusation?

6   Look at lines 16–18: **simulac mandāta … mihi tulit**.

   a   What proof does Togidubnus in fact have?

   b   How did that proof come into Togidubnus' possession?

7   **tū, nōn Cephalus, es mendāx. lībertus enim, magnam iniūriam passus, vērum patefacere volēbat** (lines 20–21): what reason does Togidubnus give for Cephalus wanting to reveal the truth?

8   Look at line 22: **Togidubne, cūr mīlitēs hūc dūxistī?**.

   a   What question does Salvius ask Togidubnus?

   b   Why do you think that Salvius has been silent from Togidubnus' arrival until now?

9   **quid dīcis? tū mē dēmōvistī? iam tibi dīxī mē innocentem esse** (line 24): why is Memor upset?

10   Look at lines 26–28: **tū, summōs … apertē ostendis**. What three points does Salvius make here as he accuses Togidubnus of being ungrateful?

11   Look at lines 28–30: **imperātor Domitiānus … tuum occupāre**.

   a   What order does Salvius say that he has received?

   b   Who sent that order to Salvius?

12   Look at lines 34–35: **ista ōrnāmenta, mihi ā Rōmānīs data, humī iaciō**.

   a   What is Togidubnus doing as he says these words?

   b   Why do you think he is doing this?

13   How are the attitudes or situations of Memor, Salvius and Togidubnus different at the end of this story from what they were at the beginning? Make one point about each character.

Britannia perdomita, on a Roman coin.

About the language 2: more about the indirect statement

1   Look at the following pairs of statements:

direct statements   *indirect statements*

'Togidubnus advenit!'   Cephalus dīcit Togidubnum advenīre.
'Togidubnus is arriving!'   *Cephalus says that Togidubnus is arriving.*

'Aventīna in magnā villa habitat.'   audiō Aventīnam in magnā vīllā habitāre.
'Aventina lives in a big house.'   *I hear that Aventina lives in a big house.*

'Rōmānī molestissimī sunt.'   prīncipēs putant Rōmānōs molestissimōs esse.
'The Romans are very disruptive.'   *The chieftains think that the Romans are very disruptive.*

In these sentences indirect statements are introduced by a verb in the present tense, such as **dīcit**, **audiō**, **putant**, etc.

> **indirect statement**: page 46

2   Indirect statements can also be introduced by a verb in the perfect or imperfect tense, such as **dīxit**, **audīvī**, **putābant**, etc.

direct statements   *indirect statements*

'Togidubnus advenit!'   Cephalus dīxit Togidubnum advenīre.
'Togidubnus is arriving!'   *Cephalus said that Togidubnus was arriving.*

'Aventīna in magnā villa habitat.'   audīvī Aventīnam in magnā vīllā habitāre.
'Aventina lives in a big house.'   *I heard that Aventina was living in a big house.*

'Rōmānī molestissimī sunt.'   prīncipēs putābant Rōmānōs molestissimōs esse.
'The Romans are very disruptive.'   *The chieftains thought that the Romans were very disruptive.*

Compare the indirect statements in paragraph 1 with the indirect statements in paragraph 2. How do they differ?

3   Further examples:

  a   'Salvius ad tablīnum Memoris ambulat.'

  b   Vitelliānus dīcit Salvium ad tablīnum Memoris ambulāre.

  c   Vitelliānus dīxit Salvium ad tablīnum Memoris ambulāre.

  d   'Catia cum multīs amīcīs sermōnem habet.'

  e   Rūfilla audit Catiam cum multīs amīcīs sermōnem habēre.

  f   Rūfilla audīvit Catiam cum multīs amīcīs sermōnem habēre.

  g   sacerdōs putābat haruspicem sacrificium facere.

  h   imperātor crēdēbat Togidubnum Rōmānōs vexāre.

  i   scīvimus Belimicum mendācem esse.

Building words: verbs and nouns

1   Study the form and meaning of the following verbs and nouns.

infinitive	*perfect passive participle*	*noun*
scrībere *to write*	scrīptus, -a, -um	scrīptor *writer*
vincere *to win*	victus, -a, -um	victor *winner, victor*
imperāre *to command*	imperātus, -a, -um	imperātor *commander, emperor*

2   Using the pattern in paragraph 1 as a guide, work out the words that are missing from this table:

emere *to buy*	ēmptus, -a, -um	ēmptor . . . .
legere	lēctus, -a, -um	. . . . *reader*
spectāre	spectātus, -a, -um	. . . .

3   Sometimes masculine nouns that end in -or have a feminine equivalent that ends -rīx.

infinitive	*perfect passive participle*	*noun*	
		masculine	feminine
līberāre *to set free*	līberātus, -a, -um	līberātor	līberātrīx *liberator*
vincere *to win*	victus, -a, -um	victor	victrīx *winner, victor*

4   Using what you know about how nouns can be formed from verbs, give the meanings of the following nouns:

dēfēnsor; vēnditor; prōditor; amātor.

5   Many English nouns ending in -**or** are derived from Latin verbs. Which verbs do the following English nouns come from? Use the Vocabulary to help you if necessary.

demonstrator, curator, navigator, narrator, tractor, doctor.

6   Can you suggest what the ending -**or** / -**trix** might indicate in Latin and English?

The Romans did not sentence people to prison. They used prisons to hold people captive until they could be put on trial or their punishments carried out. People of higher status could expect to be put under house arrest rather than in a prison. This scene from Trajan's Column shows high-ranking prisoners crowded together in a Roman fort being guarded by an auxiliary soldier.

Practising the language

Minerva victrīx

victrīx *victor, winner*

Aventina uses a famous Greek myth to illustrate the power of Rome.

Aventīna, quae per oppidum cum Vilbiā ambulābat, eī fābulam
nārrāre coepit.

'fuit ōlim puella īnfēlīx, nōmine Arachnē.'

'cūr īnfēlīx erat puella?' rogāvit Vilbia.

Aventīna Vilbiae respondit, 'Arachnē erat puella summae perītiae, 5
ab omnibus magnopere laudāta, quod pulcherrimam tēlam texere
poterat. etiam crēdidit artem suam esse mīrābiliōrem quam artem
deae Minervae. amīcīs assiduē dīcēbat, "cūr Minerva hūc nōn venit?"
puella īnfēlīx adeō cupiēbat cum deā certāre.

'dea autem, postquam haec audīvit, fōrmam anīlem induit. casam 10
puellae ingressa, "stultissima fuistī," inquit. "tibi melius est ā Minervā
veniam petere." Arachnē tamen cōnsilium eius recūsāvit. Minerva igitur,
ā puellā valdē vexāta, fōrmam dēposuit. ecce! appāruit dea ipsa.

'longum erat certāmen, in quō ambae tēlās splendidās texuērunt.
Minerva tamen, tēlam pulcherrimam puellae cōnspicāta, saeviēbat. 15
ēheu! Arachnē poenās dedit. puellam in arāneam mūtāvit Minerva.
tāle est imperium Rōmānum, Vilbia. nēmō eī resistere potest.'

magnopere *greatly*
tēlam: tēla *cloth, tapestry*
texere *weave*
artem: ars *skill*

anīlem: anīlis
  of an old woman

arāneam: arānea *spider*
mūtāvit: mūtāre *change*

---

1 **Explore the story**

a **Aventīna, quae per oppidum cum Vilbiā ambulābat, eī fābulam nārrāre coepit**
(lines 1–2): what did Aventina do as she was walking through the town?

b **fuit ōlim puella īnfēlīx, nōmine Arachnē** (line 3): how did Aventina describe Arachne?

c Look at lines 5–8: **Arachnē erat ... deae Minervae**.

  i Why did everybody praise Arachne?

  ii What was Arachne's opinion of her own skill?

d Look at lines 8–9: **amīcīs assiduē ... cum deā certāre**.

  i What was Arachne challenging Minerva to do?

  ii To what extent did Arachne want to compete against Minerva?

e **dea autem, postquam haec audīvit, fōrmam anīlem induit** (line 10):
what are we told about Minerva here?

f Look at lines 10–12: **casam puellae ... eius recūsāvit**.

  i How did Minerva describe Arachne when she entered her house?

  ii What advice did Minerva offer Arachne?

  iii What was Arachne's reaction to Minerva's advice?

g Look at lines 12–13: **Minerva igitur ... dea ipsa**.

    i How did Minerva react to the attitude shown by Arachne?

    ii What was the surprise for Arachne?

h **longum erat certāmen, in quō ambae tēlās splendidās texuērunt** (line 14):
what was the outcome of the weaving contest?

i Look at lines 15–16: **Minerva tamen ... arāneam mūtāvit**.

    i Why was Minerva so furious with Arachne?

    ii What was the outcome for Arachne of Minerva's fury?

j **tāle est imperium Rōmānum, Vilbia. nēmō eī resistere potest** (line 17):
what comparison was Aventina making between Minerva and the Roman Empire?

2 Explore the language

This famous myth has been told many times throughout the ancient and modern worlds, and in many different ways. Some versions show Arachne as an arrogant character, others as a sympathetic one.

How does Aventina create sympathy for Arachne in the way she tells this story?

How does Aventina make Minerva appear terrifying in the way she tells this story?

3 Explore further

Myths were often used by storytellers to convey a message. The same myth could be used by different people to convey slightly different messages.

Think carefully about the message Aventina is trying to convey here and how she has presented Arachne and Minerva.

If one of the Roman characters in our stories was telling this myth, how different do you think it would be? What do you think they would present differently?

Reviewing the language Stage 23: page 215

A Greek vase of the sixth century BC showing women weaving.

Roman religion

For the Romans, a pool might be the home of a nymph and every crossroad might be a meeting place of spirits. People interacted with the divine and the supernatural on a regular basis, in a wide variety of ways. These included the curse tablets you looked at in Stage 22 and the offerings made at Aquae Sulis mentioned in Stage 21.

There was no Roman holy book full of teachings, or a religious focus on personal salvation and morality. Instead, the Romans performed rituals in the hope of pleasing the gods and gaining their favour, therefore ensuring their personal success and prosperity, as well as that of Rome and the empire.

> **Thinking point 1:** What do you already know about Roman religion and belief?

> Rituals and ceremonies are often held in public, but the majority of people cannot enter most temples or take an active role in what is going on. We attend and watch respectfully. There are also regular festivals throughout the year, in which the whole community takes part. A person might also choose to develop a more personal connection with a specific power; like Clemens when he became an initiate of Isis in Alexandria.

Following tradition and worshipping in the proper manner was very important to make sure the gods were kept happy. The Roman state took a leading role, and worship of the main gods involved approved rituals and ceremonies organised by religious officials on its behalf. Being a religious official was not necessarily a full-time or lifelong role; many of the men who served as priests also had political careers as senators. One of the most important officials was the chief priest of Jupiter, the **flāmen Diālis**. He shared his sacred duties with his wife, the **flāminica Diālis**. These two shared responsibility for the proper worship of Jupiter, leading rituals both together and separately to ensure his continued support for Rome and its people.

A flamen was a priest who led worship of one of the main Roman gods on behalf of the state. Chosen from politically powerful upper-class Roman families, they followed strict rules and wore the distinctive cap you can see in this picture.

'It is generally believed that it is useless to perform a sacrifice without a specific form of prayer; without it the gods are not thought to be properly consulted. Furthermore, there is one form of words for getting good omens, another to ward off evil, and yet another to offer praise. We can also see how our chief magistrates follow a strict routine when performing their prayers: to prevent a single word being missed out or said in the wrong place, one person reads a script of the prayer beforehand, another is appointed as a guard to keep watch, and a third is put in charge of maintaining strict silence other than a musician who plays the flute, so that the only words that can be heard are those of the prayer.'

(Pliny the Elder, *Natural History* 28.3)

> **Thinking point 2:** What can we learn from this passage about the importance of prayer to the Romans?

From Augustus onwards, the emperor always held the position of **Pontifex Maximus** or Chief Priest. There were also priests, festivals and rituals dedicated to the emperor's – and by extension the empire's – well-being. The historical Salvius, for example, was a member of the Arval Brotherhood, whose religious duties included praying for the emperor and his family. His wife Rufilla was also a priestess for the welfare of the emperors.

Early emperors were not generally worshipped as gods during their lifetime; Rome had no tradition of worshipping its rulers and the idea was discouraged. People in the eastern provinces of the Roman Empire, however, were used to regarding their rulers as divine and so honouring the Roman emperors in this way did not seem inappropriate. By the mid-second century AD, Romans in the west had become more comfortable with the idea as well. The Britons and other peoples in the west of the empire were encouraged to worship the **genius** (protecting spirit) of the emperor, linked with the goddess Roma.

This scene depicts the emperor Antoninus Pius and his wife Faustina transforming into gods after death. They are being carried to heaven by a winged figure watched by the goddess Roma. This relief is from the base of a monument built in c.AD 161 by Antoninus' successors.

This temple in the Pompeian forum is thought to be dedicated to the Roman emperors as its altar is decorated with imperial symbols such as an oak wreath and laurels, and the relief depicts a sacrifice of a bull to the emperor. Such temples can be found all over the Roman Empire.

Altars were erected in honour of 'Rome and the emperor'. When an emperor died, it was common for him to be declared a god, and temples were often built to honour the deified emperor. One such temple, that of Claudius in Camulodunum (Colchester), became a symbol of oppression in the eyes of angry local Britons:

> 'They could not avoid seeing the temple erected to Divine Claudius and it seemed to them like the fortress of a never-ending tyranny. Local men chosen as priests were forced to pour out their fortunes like water under the pretence of religious duty.'
>
> (Tacitus, *Annals* 14.31)

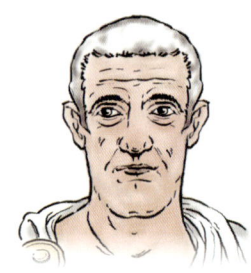

The temple was destroyed before it was even finished during Boudica's revolt in AD 60–61.

This bronze head may depict Emperor Claudius. It has been suggested that it was wrenched from one of the statues in Camulodunum and thrown into a river.

Thinking point 3:
What was the role of the Roman emperor and state in Roman religion?

Gods and goddesses

Roman religion included a huge variety of gods, demigods and spirits. The Roman state respected this variety – as long as nothing interfered with official religious rites – but particularly promoted the worship of Jupiter and his family of gods and goddesses, especially Juno, Minerva, Ceres, Apollo, Diana, Mars and Venus. They were closely linked with their equivalent Greek deities and their mythology but were not exactly the same. For example, Mars was a war god and in Latin versions of Greek myths his name is used instead of the Greek god Ares, but for the Romans he also had agricultural associations. The Romans also gave far more importance to their goddess of the home and family, Vesta, than the Greeks did to their equivalent, Hestia. In the temple to Vesta in the Roman forum, priestesses called the Vestal Virgins were responsible for keeping alight the sacred flame, which was linked to the well-being of Rome.

The Vestal Virgins were not the only high-profile Roman priestesses; those who served Ceres, Venus and Liber (the god associated with wine, fertility and the harvest) were also very important. Women were involved at every level of Roman religion, participating in and leading rituals relating to political, military and commercial matters as well as those focused on family and the home.

Thinking point 4:
Which gods and goddesses do you know of that were worshipped by the Romans? What connections do some of them have to other ancient cultures?

The Romans generally tolerate our traditional religious beliefs and practices, as long as they don't think we're threatening their power. In turn, many people adapt Roman culture, including religion, to suit their own needs. My husband likes to show his commitment to the Romans and their culture. He dedicated his new temple to Neptune and Minerva, rather than to British gods, and included the welfare of the emperor in the dedicatory inscription.

As well as worshipping the Roman gods, some people depict British gods with Roman clothing and symbols and combine them with the Roman pantheon. At Aquae Sulis, a Roman temple to Sulis-Minerva has been built in a place that we Britons already considered sacred and powerful. Their bath house and fancy temple may not be in keeping with our traditions, but we can still visit the spring and feel connected to our sacred place, no matter the changes the Romans make to it.

A drawing of the dedicatory inscription mentioned by Catia. It reads:

'To Neptune and Minerva, for the welfare of the Divine House, by the authority of Tiberius Claudius Togidubnus, great king of the Britons, the Guild of Smiths and those in it gave this temple at their own expense … ens, son of Pudentinus, presented the forecourt.'

Thinking point 5: What does this source suggest about Togidubnus' attitude toward Roman religion? Look back at the passage from Tacitus about the Temple of Claudius at Camulodunum. How does Togidubnus' view compare to that of the British people described by Tacitus?

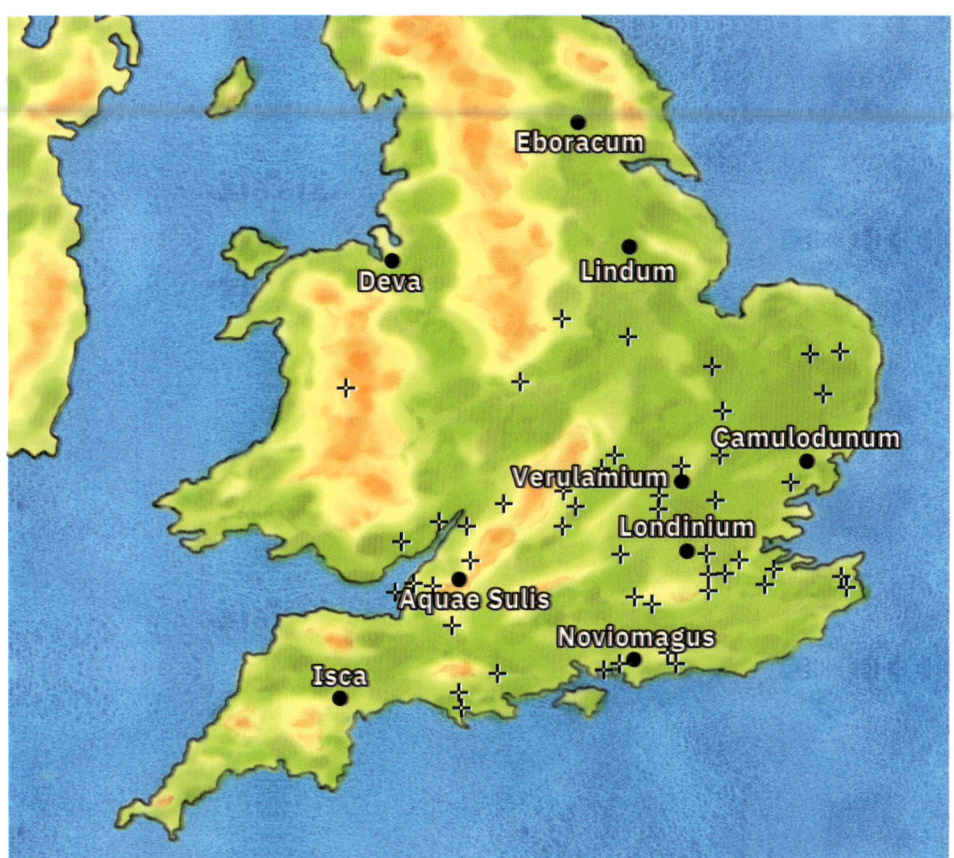

A map showing all known locations of temples to Romano-British gods.

This priest's headdress, probably originally attached to a cap, was found at Wanborough Roman Temple in Surrey. The headdress probably dates to the first century AD, and the wheel symbol at the top is linked with the British version of Jupiter.

Three sculptures from Aquae Sulis: Left: a gilded bronze head of Sulis-Minerva, presumably from her statue in the temple, showing the goddess as the Romans pictured her. Middle: three Celtic mother-goddesses. Right: the originally Gallic goddess Nemetona and the horned Gallo-Roman god Loucetius-Mars.

> **Thinking point 6:** What can you infer from these three sculptures about the combination of religious traditions at Aquae Sulis?

Sacrifices and offerings

From earliest times the Romans believed that all things were controlled by spirits or divinities (**nūmina**). The power of these beings was seen, for example, in fire or in the changing of the seasons. To ensure that these beings used their power for good rather than harm, the early Romans presented them with offerings of food and wine. This created a sort of contract in which both parties got something they wanted: the spirits got good offerings, while the humans received their help and good will. Sometime after the third century BC these spirits and deities became the system of Roman gods, and the idea of a contract between mortals and the gods continued.

Public festivals often included animal sacrifices. This was a lengthy process. Sacrificial victims were paraded to the altar, the plinth on which the sacrifice would be performed. This was often in the open air rather than inside a temple. The priest would then say a prayer and make an offering such as incense or wine before pouring wine and ground grain over the animal's head. The victim was then killed and its entrails examined for omens. Finally, parts of the sacrificial victim were burned on the altar. Any parts left over were eaten by the participants as part of a celebratory meal. Many Romans also offered animal sacrifices or gave gifts to the gods in a personal capacity, sometimes setting up their own altars to honour their chosen deity.

An emperor in his role as Chief Priest leads a solemn procession. He covers his head with a fold of his toga. A bull, a sheep and a pig are to be sacrificed.

Giving or promising offerings to the gods makes it more likely that your prayers will be answered. At Aquae Sulis I sacrificed a lamb to Sulis-Minerva in the hope that she would be pleased and restore me to health. People at all levels of society do this. If a general is going off to war, there will be a solemn public ceremony at which prayers and expensive sacrifices are offered to the gods. Ordinary people might make offerings or sacrifices while praying for things such as a successful business deal, a safe journey or the birth of a child.

In many Roman homes offerings of food were made to Vesta, the goddess of the hearth, and to the **larēs** and **penatēs**, the spirits of the household and food cupboard. Each household shrine was different, depending on the preferences and priorities of the family. The statuettes representing the gods would pass down the family, with each generation adding or removing from the collection as they saw fit.

Reconstruction of a lararium dedicated to Ceres standing in the atrium of a Roman villa. The paintings of snakes represent spirits who protect the house.

Reconstruction of a domestic shrine of Venus. The statuette is original and would have been imported to Britain from Gaul.

Statuette of a Lar found in Norfolk.

People accompanied their prayers with promises of offerings if the favours were granted. These promises were known as **vōta** (votives in English). If the prayer was considered granted, then the individual would make the promised offering. This might be a small altar, presumably accompanied by a sacrifice, or some other object such as a plaque. People left inscriptions dedicating their offering to the god or gods, sometimes with details of what prayer they felt the god had answered.

> **Thinking point 7:** What different types of offerings did the Romans give to their gods? Give some of the reasons they did this.

Examples of vota from Roman Britain

'C. Tetius Veturius Micianus, captain of the Sebosian cavalry squadron, set this up as he promised to Silvanus the unconquered, in thanks for capturing a beautiful boar, which many people before him tried to do but failed.'

'To Jupiter, Best and Greatest, and to the Genius of this place Gaius Verecundius Severus, willingly and deservedly fulfilled his vow.'

DEAE
DIANAE ṢA
ÇRV · AEL·
TIMO · P ·
V · Ṣ · T · L · M ·

This inscription was found on an altar in 1601, although the altar itself has since been lost:

'To the goddess Diana, Aelia Timo set up this holy offering, gladly, willingly and deservedly fulfilling her vow.'

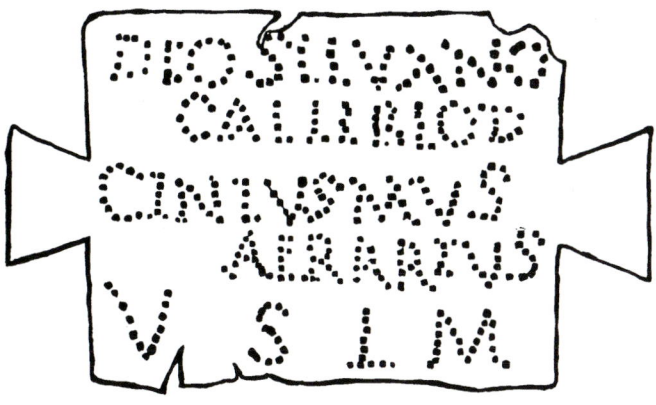

'To the god Silvanus Callirius, Cintusmus, the coppersmith, willingly and deservedly fulfilled as a gift his vow.'

Thinking point 8: For each inscription, identify who is giving thanks and to which god they are making their dedication.

Divination

A haruspex, like Memor, might be present at important sacrifices. He and his assistants would watch the way in which the victim fell; observe the smoke and flames when parts of the victim were placed on the altar fire; and, most importantly, cut the victim open and examine its entrails, especially the liver. They would look for anything unusual about the liver's size or shape, observe its colour and texture, and note whether it had spots on its surface. They would then interpret what they saw and announce to the priest overseeing the sacrifice whether the signs from the gods were favourable or not.

A model liver with labels to help haruspices interpret any markings. This model is from Etruria, a region in central Italy, where the Romans thought the practices of haruspices originated.

A haruspex examining a sacrificed bull.

Such attempts to discover the future are known as divination and the Romans took them very seriously. The Roman politician and author Cicero offers Julius Caesar – famously assassinated during a meeting of the Roman Senate – as an example of the dangers involved in ignoring the interpretations of the haruspices:

'… no heart was found in the entrails of the sacrificial ox. … Caesar was not worried by this discovery, even though (the haruspex) warned him to beware in case he lost both his wits and his life, as both of these things, he said, come from the heart. The next day part of the liver of the sacrifice was missing. These omens were sent by the immortal gods to Caesar so that he might foresee his death …'

(Cicero, *On Divination* 1.119)

Another type of divination was performed by priests known as **augurēs** (augurs), who based their predictions on observations of birds. They would note the direction of flight, whether the birds flew together or separately, what kind of birds they were and what noises they made.

Before committing to any significant course of action, particularly battles, a Roman leader might want to consult the sacred chickens, which were raised by priests for use in auguries. The chickens would be offered food and their behaviour interpreted by an augur. Publius Claudius Pulcher, a Roman naval commander during the First Punic War (264–241 BC), became a famous example of the importance of respecting the auspices. Before an attack on the enemy fleet, the chickens were consulted:

'The chickens were released from their cage. When they refused to eat, he ordered them to be thrown overboard into the water, stating "since they will not eat, maybe they will drink". But the joke brought the jester many tears and the Roman people a great disaster, for the fleet was brutally defeated. Similarly, his colleague Junius lost his fleet in a storm after failing to obey the auspices. Due to these disasters Claudius was tried and condemned for high treason and Junius took his own life.'

(Cicero, *Natura Deorum* 2.7)

Thinking point 9: What Roman beliefs about divination can you infer from these extracts from Cicero's works?

Enquiry: The Classicist Jörg Rüpke wrote that Roman religion 'was not confined to temples and festivals; it permeated all areas of society.' Explain how the evidence supports this claim.

You may wish to consider the following:

- the role and nature of the gods and their relationship with mortals
- the different levels of Roman religious practice: state, local community, family and personal
- the relationship between politics and religion, including the role of the emperor
- different religious practices including prayer, sacrifice and offerings, and divination.

You may find information from previous Stages, especially Stages 21 and 22, to be useful in exploring this question.

Vocabulary checklist 23

adiuvō, adiuvāre, adiūvī	*help*
āra, ārae	*altar*
autem	*but*
cēdō, cēdere, cessī	*give in, give way*
cōnspicātus, cōnspicāta, cōnspicātum	*having caught sight of*
cūra, cūrae	*care*
efficiō, efficere, effēcī, effectus	*carry out, accomplish*
faber, fabrī	*craftsman, craftsperson*
ingenium, ingeniī	*character*
lentē	*slowly*
maior, *gen.* maiōris	*bigger, larger, greater*
mandātum, mandātī	*instruction, order*
modus, modī	*manner, way, kind*
nūntius, nūntiī	*message, news*
pāreō, pārēre, pāruī	*obey*
putō, putāre, putāvī	*think*
rapiō, rapere, rapuī, raptus	*seize, grab*
scelestus, scelesta, scelestum	*wicked*
scio, scīre, scīvī	*know*
vestīmenta, vestīmentōrum	*clothes*

This bronze statuette represents a Romano-British worshipper bringing offerings to a god.

FUGA

Stage 24

in itinere

Aventīna et Vilbia, ex oppidō Aquīs Sūlis ēgressae, Dēvam in plaustrō iter faciēbant. in itinere ad flūmen altum et lātum vēnērunt, ubi erat pōns. cum ad pontem vēnissent, Aventīna exclāmāvit

'ēheu! pōns sēmirutus est.'

subitō nūntius Rōmānus appāruit equitāns.   5

'cēdite!' clāmāvit. 'epistulam magnī momentī ferō.'

Aventīna nūntium monuit pontem sēmirutum esse. nūntius igitur ex equō dēscendit. cum dēscendisset, equus statim trānsiit.

'nimis cauta es!' Aventīnae dīxit nūntius. 'ecce! nihil perīculī est.'

nūntius, cum haec dīxisset, trānsīre coepit. cum ad medium pontem   10
vēnisset, dēcidit pōns, dēcidit nūntius.

Vilbia rīsit.

'mālim cauta esse potius quam caudex!'

altum: altus *deep*
lātum: lātus *wide*
cum *when*
sēmirutus *rickety*

magnī momentī
    of great importance
trānsiit: trānsīre *cross*

mālim *I would prefer*
potius *rather*

Roman roads

The movement of people and goods throughout the provinces of the Roman Empire was made possible by its network of roads, which at its peak is estimated to have stretched 92 000 kilometres (57 000 miles). Each section of road took the shortest possible route across plains, forests, mountains, rivers, valleys, marshes and deserts, with tunnels and bridges where necessary. They had to divert around river valleys and impassable mountains, but once past the obstructions, the roads usually continued along their original line. A fully paved Roman road usually lasted eighty to a hundred years. Some are even still in use today and many modern European roads still follow the Roman routes.

After the line was chosen, a cut the width of the planned road (between 2 and 6 metres, or between 6 and 20 feet) was made. This needed to be deep enough to hold the four layers that would make up the road (up to 1.5 metres, or 5 feet). If the earth was soft at that depth, piles (wooden posts) were driven in to strengthen it. A footing of large stones was then laid at the bottom of the trench. This was covered with a layer of smaller stones, concrete or rubble, and then a layer of rolled sand concrete. The road surface (**pavīmentum**) was made of local materials, usually large, flat paving stones. This final surface was curved to provide effective drainage. The Romans liked to raise their roadways on an embankment of earth about 1 metre (just over 3 feet) high, called an **agger**, to aid drainage and give marching troops a good view of the territory. Ditches on either side of the agger also provided drainage.

Military surveyors used an instrument called a groma (pictured) to make sure the roads were straight. Where trees or hills were in the way, they took sightings from high points using smoke from fires.

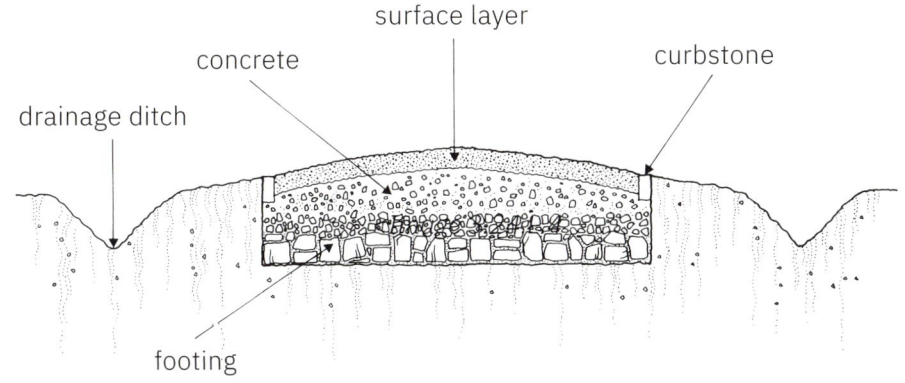

surface layer

concrete

curbstone

drainage ditch

footing

> **Thinking point:** Roads were a vital part of Rome's imperial infrastructure. How do you think good roads helped the Romans to maintain their empire?

Roman flagstones.

A stretch of Roman road in Britain known as Wade's Causeway. In local legend, Wade was a giant who was said to have built the road by throwing stones at his wife. Only the lower layers of road remain; the road surface has disappeared over the centuries.

Quīntus cōnsilium capit

When you have read this story, answer the questions at the end.

cum Togidubnus trīstis īrātusque ē vīllā Memoris exiisset, Salvius
quīnquāgintā mīlitēs arcessīvit. eōs iussit rēgem prīncipēsque Rēgnēnsium
comprehendere et in carcere retinēre. hī mīlitēs, tōtum per oppidum missī,
mox eōs invēnērunt. Dumnorix tamen, ē manibus mīlitum noctū ēlāpsus,
Quīntum quaesīvit, quod eī crēdēbat.   5

    cubiculum Quīntī ingressus, haec dīxit:

    'amīce, tibi crēdere possum. adiuvā mē, adiuvā Togidubnum. paucīs
Rōmānīs crēdō; plūrimī sunt perfidī. nēmō quidem perfidior est quam iste
Salvius quī Togidubnum interficere nūper temptāvit. nunc Togidubnus,
ā mīlitibus Salviī comprehēnsus, in carcere iacet. etiam audīvī rēgem   10
omnīnō dē vītā suā dēspērāre.

    'ego tamen crēdō tē esse virum summae virtūtis magnaeque prūdentiae.
quamquam Salvius potentissimus est, nōlī rēgem, amīcum tuum, dēserere.
nōlī eum in carcere inclūsum relinquere. tū anteā eum servāvistī. nōnne
iterum servāre potes?'   15

    cum Dumnorix haec dīxisset, Quīntus rem sēcum anxius cōgitābat.
auxilium Togidubnō ferre volēbat, quod eum valdē dīligēbat; sed rēs
difficillima erat. subitō cōnsilium cēpit.

    'nōlī dēspērāre!' inquit. 'rēgī auxilium ferre possumus. hanc rem lēgātō
Gnaeō Iūliō Agricolae clam referre dēbēmus. itaque nōbīs necesse est   20
festīnāre ad ultimās partēs īnsulae ubi Agricola bellum gerit. Agricola
sōlus Salviō obstāre potest, quod summam potestātem in Britanniā habet.
nunc nōbīs necesse est hinc effugere.'

    Dumnorix, cum haec audīvisset, cōnsilium audāx magnopere laudāvit.
tum pistōrem vīcīnum arcessīvit, cui mandāta dedit. pistor exiit. mox   25
regressus, cibum quīnque diērum Quīntō et Dumnorigī trādidit. illī,
ē vīllā ēlāpsī, equōs cōnscendērunt et ad Agricolam abiērunt.

carcere: carcer *prison*
ēlāpsus *having escaped*

quidem *indeed*

omnīnō *completely*
virtūtis: virtūs *courage, virtue*

inclūsum: inclūsus *imprisoned*

dīligēbat: dīligere *be fond of*

lēgātō: lēgātus *governor*

ultimās: ultimus *furthest*
potestātem: potestās *power*

cōnscendērunt: cōnscendere
    mount, climb onto

Questions

1   cum Togidubnus trīstis īrātusque ē vīllā Memoris exiisset (line 1): what two emotions did Togidubnus feel as he left Memor's house?

2   eōs iussit rēgem prīncipēsque Rēgnēnsium comprehendere et in carcere retinēre (lines 2–3): what orders did Salvius give the fifty soldiers?

3   Look at lines 4–5: **Dumnorix tamen ... eī crēdēbat**.

   a   Which Latin word shows why Dumnorix was not seen by the soldiers?

   b   Why did Dumnorix seek out Quintus?

4   Look at lines 7–9: **amīce, tibi ... nūper temptāvit**.

   a   What did Dumnorix want Quintus to do?

   b   What was Dumnorix's opinion of the Romans?

   c   What did Dumnorix tell Quintus that Salvius had tried to do?

5   nunc Togidubnus, ā mīlitibus Salviī comprehēnsus, in carcere iacet. etiam audīvī rēgem omnīnō dē vītā suā dēspērāre (lines 9–11): what three things did Dumnorix tell Quintus about Togidubnus?

6   'ego tamen ... servāre potes?' (lines 12–15): how did Dumnorix try to persuade Quintus in these lines? Make three points.

7   Look at lines 17–18: **auxilium Togidubnō ... difficillima erat**.

   a   Why was Quintus willing to help Togidubnus?

   b   Which Latin word indicates that Quintus knew that it would be challenging to help the king?

8   hanc rem lēgātō Gnaeō Iūliō Agricolae clam referre dēbēmus (lines 19–20): what did Quintus suggest to Dumnorix that they should do to help the king?

9   Look at lines 20–21: **itaque nōbīs ... bellum gerit**.

   a   Where did Quintus suggest that he and Dumnorix needed to go?

   b   Why did Quintus believe that they needed to go there?

10 Agricola sōlus Salviō obstāre potest, quod summam potestātem in Britanniā habet (lines 21–22): why did Quintus think that Agricola could block Salvius' plans?

11 mox regressus, cibum quīnque diērum Quīntō et Dumnorigī trādidit (lines 25–26): what indication is given by the baker's actions that Quintus' and Dumnorix's journey was likely to be a long one?

12 Do you think that this story supports the opinion of Quintus that Dumnorix expresses in line 12 (**ego tamen crēdō tē esse virum summae virtūtis magnaeque prūdentiae**)? Support your answer with three examples taken from the story.

About the language 1:
cum and the pluperfect subjunctive

1   Study the following sentences:

cum Dumnorix haec verba **dīxisset**, Quīntus anxius erat.
*When Dumnorix **had said** these words, Quintus was worried.*

cum amīcae ad pontem **advēnissent**, Aventīna trānsīre nōluit.
*When the friends **had arrived** at the bridge, Aventina did not want to cross.*

The form of the verb in **bold** is known as the **subjunctive**.

2   The subjunctive is often used with the word **cum** meaning *when*, as in the examples above.

3   Further examples:

    a   cum rēx exiisset, Salvius mīlitēs ad sē vocāvit.

    b   cum fēminae cōnsilium cēpissent, ex oppidō discessērunt.

    c   cum architectus haec mandāta dedisset, fabrī ad aulam rediērunt.

    d   artificēs, cum vīllam intrāvissent, pictūrās pingere coepērunt.

4   The examples of the subjunctive in paragraphs 1 and 3 are all in the same tense,
the **pluperfect subjunctive**. Compare the 3rd person of the pluperfect subjunctive
with the ordinary, or **indicative**, form of the pluperfect:

	pluperfect indicative		pluperfect subjunctive	
	singular	*plural*	*singular*	*plural*
first conjugation	portāverat	portāverant	portāvisset	portāvissent
second conjugation	docuerat	docuerant	docuisset	docuissent
third conjugation	trāxerat	trāxerant	trāxisset	trāxissent
fourth conjugation	dormīverat	dormīverant	dormīvisset	dormīvissent
irregular verbs				
esse (*to be*)	fuerat	fuerant	fuisset	fuissent
velle (*to want*)	voluerat	voluerant	voluisset	voluissent

Travelling by road

Travellers on Roman roads walked, used carriages or carts, or rode, generally on mules or ponies. Horses were ridden mainly by cavalrymen or government officials. In good conditions a traveller might cover 32 kilometres (20 miles) on foot, 40–48 kilometres (25–30 miles) by carriage or perhaps a little more by mule.

On long journeys, where possible, people stayed with family, friends, acquaintances or business associates. Those unable to do this could stay at roadside inns, which may not always have been pleasant. One unhappy guest in Pompeii wrote his complaint on the wall:

> 'Innkeeper, I confess I urinated in the bed. If you want to know why, there was no chamber pot.'

Inns in Roman literature are often portrayed as dirty, uncomfortable and full of thieves, prostitutes and drunks; the Roman poet Horace wrote of the 'wicked **caupōnēs** (innkeepers)' and Pliny the Younger complained about bedbugs. In reality there were different types of lodging available along major routes, some of which no doubt had excellent reputations.

Thinking point:
What factors would have affected the journey time of a Roman traveller?

A light carriage with two horses, passing a milestone (a stone used to mark distance along Roman roads).

A copy of a carving found on a tombstone. A traveller in a hooded cloak pays for a meal for himself and his mule.

The Roman postal system

Letters came and went in all directions across the Roman Empire. Letters written by government officials or containing matters of state could be sent using the Imperial Post (**cursus pūblicus**). Someone carrying such letters would have a government permit (**diplōma**) which indicated that they were on official business and therefore entitled to fresh horses at the **mānsiōnēs**. These were official stopping places with stables, food and accommodation, found along all main roads.

It has been estimated that an official courier could average 80 kilometres (50 miles) a day. In an emergency, he could triple this distance by travelling night and day. Private letters took much longer. These were either carried by an enslaved person or sent with a trusted traveller, such as a friend or a merchant with a good reputation.

Many letters have been found during the excavations of the Roman fort at Vindolanda on Hadrian's Wall, including this one sent by Severus to his friend Candidus:

> **'Severus to his Candidus, greetings. Regarding the ... for the Saturnalia, I ask you, brother, to see to them at a price of 4 or 6 asses, and radishes costing no less than ½ denarius. Farewell, brother.'**

On the back:

> **'To Candidus, slave of Genialis the prefect, from Severus, slave of ...'**

An enclosed coach of the Imperial Post drawn by two mules. There is seating inside and on top.

Salvius cōnsilium cognōscit

postrīdiē, cum Quīntus et Dumnorix ad ultimās partēs īnsulae
contenderent, mīlitēs Dumnorigem per oppidum frūstrā quaerēbant. rem
dēnique Salviō nūntiāvērunt. ille, cum dē fugā Dumnorigis cognōvisset,
vehementer saeviēbat. tum Quīntum quaesīvit; cum eum quoque nusquam
invenīre potuisset, Belimicum, prīncipem Cantiacōrum, arcessīvit. 5

'Belimice,' inquit, 'iste Dumnorix ē manibus meīs effūgit; abest quoque
Quīntus Caecilius. neque Dumnorigī neque Quīntō crēdō. putō eōs ambōs
auxilium Togidubnō quaerere. ī nunc; dūc mīlitēs tēcum; illōs quaere
in omnibus partibus oppidī. quaere comitēs quoque eōrum.'

Belimicus, multīs cum mīlitibus ēgressus, per oppidum dīligenter 10
quaerēbat. intereā Salvius anxius reditum eius exspectābat. cum
Salvius rem sēcum cōgitāret, Belimicus subitō rediit exsultāns.
pistōrem dēplōrantem in medium ātrium trāxit.

'pistōrem, quī prope vīllam Aventīnae habitat, comprehendī.'

Salvius ad pistōrem conversus, 15

'ubi est Quīntus Caecilius?' inquit. 'quō fūgit Dumnorix?'

'nescio,' inquit pistor quī, tantam iniūriam passus, quicquam dīcere
nōlēbat. 'nihil scio,' iterum inquit.

Belimicus, cum haec audīvisset, gladium dēstrictum ad iugulum
pistōris tenuit. 20

'melius est tibi,' inquit, 'vērum Salviō dīcere. num perīre māvīs?'

fugā: fuga *escape*
nusquam *nowhere*

ī: īre *go*

reditum: reditus *return*
exsultāns: exsultāre *exult,
be triumphant*

conversus *having turned*

quicquam *anything*

dēstrictum: dēstringere
draw out
iugulum: iugulus *throat*
māvīs: mālle *prefer*

pistor, quī iam dē vītā suā dēspērābat,

'cibum quīnque diērum tantum parāvī,' inquit susurrāns.'nihil aliud fēcī. crēdō Quīntum Caecilium cum Dumnorige ad ultimās partēs Britanniae festīnāre.'

'Salvius 'hercle!' inquit. 'ad Agricolam iērunt. Quīntus, ā Dumnorige incitātus, mihi obstāre temptat; homō tamen magnae stultitiae est; mihi resistere nōn potest, quod auctōritās senātōris nōn minor est quam illius.'

Salvius, cum haec dīxisset, Belimicō mandāta dedit. eum iussit cum trīgintā equitibus exīre et fugitīvōs comprehendere. pistōrem custōdibus trādidit. deinde ūnum ē servīs suīs arcessīvit cui epistulam dictāvit. nūntium iussit hanc epistulam quam celerrimē lēgātō Agricolae ferre.

intereā Belimicus, Quīntum et Dumnorigem per trēs diēs persecūtus, eōs tandem in fundō dēsertō invēnit. equitēs statim impetum in eōs fēcērunt. amīcī, ab equitibus circumventī, fortiter sē dēfendēbant. dēnique Dumnorix humī cecidit mortuus. cum equitēs corpus Dumnorigis in puteum altum inicerent, Quīntus, graviter vulnerātus, magnā cum difficultāte per agrōs effūgit.

25

minor *smaller, less*

30

impetum: impetus *attack*

35

corpus *body*

Aerial view of the Shropshire section of the Roman road followed by Quintus and Dumnorix to Chester.

About the language 2: cum and the imperfect subjunctive

1   In this Stage, you have met sentences with **cum** and the pluperfect subjunctive:

cum and the pluperfect subjunctive: page 70

cum rem **cōnfēcissent**, abiērunt.
*When they **had finished** the job, they went away.*

senex, cum pecūniam **invēnisset**, ad vīllam laetus rediit.
*The old man, when he **had found** the money, returned happily to the villa.*

2   Now study the following examples:

cum custōdēs **dormīrent**, fūrēs ē carcere effūgērunt.
*When the guards **were sleeping**, the thieves escaped from the prison.*

Aventīna, cum in viā **stāret**, Belimicum cōnspexit.
*Aventina, when she **was standing** in the street, caught sight of Belimicus.*

In these sentences, **cum** is being used with a different tense of the subjunctive, the **imperfect subjunctive**.

3   Further examples:

a   cum hospitēs cēnam cōnsūmerent, fūr cubiculum intrāvit.

b   cum prīnceps rem cōgitāret, nūntiī subitō revēnērunt.

c   iuvenēs, cum bēstiās agitārent, mīlitem vulnerātum cōnspexērunt.

d   puella, cum epistulam scrīberet, sonitum mīrābilem audīvit.

4   Compare the 3rd person of the imperfect subjunctive with the infinitive:

	infinitive	imperfect subjunctive	
		singular	*plural*
first conjugation	portāre	portāret	portārent
second conjugation	docēre	docēret	docērent
third conjugation	trahere	traheret	traherent
fourth conjugation	audīre	audīret	audīrent
irregular verbs			
	esse	esset	essent
	velle	vellet	vellent

Vilbia fugitīvum invenit

Stonehenge and other Neolithic sites in Britain predate the Roman occupation by thousands of years.

cum plaustrum Aventīnam Vilbiamque per silvam dēnsam lentē veheret, Vilbia amitam dē monumentīs antīquīs, quae fabrī Britannicī iamprīdem posuerant, rogāvit.

'ūnum ex hīs monumentīs nōn procul ab oppidō Aquīs Sūlis situm est,' eī respondit Aventīna. 'templum aut aedificium magnificius quam illud nusquam vīdī. aliī dīcunt neque templa urbis Athēnārum neque pȳramidēs Aegyptiās huic monumentō sacrō praestāre.'   5

cum Aventīna haec dīxisset, Vilbia sonōs subitō audīvit. ē plaustrō dēscendēns, vestīgia humī cōnspexit. deinde inter arborēs contendit, vestīgia secūta.   10

'Vilbia! cavē!' clāmāvit Aventīna. 'fortasse animal saevum, ā vēnātōribus vulnerātum, sub arboribus latet.'

Vilbia, brevī regressa, amitam vocāvit.

'festīnā hūc!' inquit. 'Rōmānum vulnerātum invēnī! putō eum esse moribundum!'   15

Aventīna, cum ad Vilbiam accurrisset, attonita,

'agnōscō eum!' inquit. 'est amīcus Togidubnī, Quīntus Caecilius. ēheu! multum sanguinis ē vulneribus iam efflūxit. Vilbia, eum movēre nōn audeō. fer aquam! eī necesse est bibere.'

cum Vilbia revēnisset, Quīntus aquam bibit oculōsque paulātim aperuit.   20
suspīrāvit Vilbia commōta.

Aventīna tamen 'fer mihi mel!' eī dīxit. 'volō tē mihi duo ligāmenta quoque ferre!'

Vilbia amitae statim pāruit. cum Aventīna ligāmenta parāret, Vilbia mel in vulnera Quīntī collocāvit. Quīntus īnfirmus,   25

'soror mea ōlim dīxit nihil melius esse quam mel,' inquit.

tandem Quīntus, ab Aventīnā Vilbiāque optimē cūrātus, ad plaustrum claudicāre potuit. tum Aventīna ad eum conversus,

'Dēvam iter facimus,' inquit. 'frāter meus ferrārius est Dēvae. apud nōs quiēscere potes.'   30

Quīntus 'Dēvam?' susurrāvit. 'ergō spēs manet …'

praestāre *be superior to, surpass*

vestīgia: vestīgium *footprint, track*
arborēs: arbor *tree*

brevī *in a short time*

suspīrāvit: suspīrāre *sigh, draw breath*
ligāmenta: ligāmentum *bandage*

ferrārius *blacksmith*
Dēvae *at Chester*

ergō *therefore*
spēs *hope*

Building words: opposites

1 You have already met the following opposites:

volō	*I want*	nōlō	*I do not want*
scio	*I know*	nescio	*I do not know*

2 Study these opposites and work out the meanings that are missing:

homō	*person*	nēmō	....
ōtium	*leisure*	negōtium	....
umquam	*ever*	numquam	....
usquam	*anywhere*	nusquam	....

3 Study these further ways of forming opposites and work out the meanings that are missing:

patiēns	*patient*	impatiēns	....
mortālis	*mortal*	immortālis	....
ūtilis	*useful*	inūtilis	....
nocēns	*guilty*	innocēns	....
nōtus, -a	*well-known*	ignōtus	....
cōnsentīre	*to agree*	dissentīre	....
persuādēre	*to persuade*	dissuādēre	....
facilis	*easy*	difficilis	....

4 From the box choose the correct Latin words to translate the words in **bold** in the following sentences:

certa	fēlīx	similis	inimīcus
dissimilis	incerta	amīcus	īnfēlīx

a A black cat was thought to be **lucky**, but a stumble was **unlucky**.

b Catia was **uncertain** whether she was in danger.

c Dumnorix is the **friend** of Quintus, but Belimicus is his **enemy**.

d Vilbia is **like** Aventina in character, but **different** in age.

A case (capsa) could be used to carry multiple scrolls.

Practising the language

Catia captīva

Vitellianus arrives unexpectedly at the palace, and he has not come alone.

cum sōl lūcēret, Catia et Rūfilla in hortō Togidubnī garriēbant,
inter flōrēs variōs ambulantēs.

    'aliquid novī dē marītō tuō audīvistī?' Catiam rogāvit Rūfilla.
'valēscetne?'

    Catia eī respondit, 'in epistulā rēx nūper dīxit morbum paulō   5
minus gravem esse.'

    'quam fēlīx es!' inquit Rūfilla. 'nihil dē meō marītō audīvī.
Vitelliānus dīcit Salvium esse nimis occupātum.'

    cum Rūfilla haec dīxisset, Vitelliānus ipse, hortum ingressus,
ad duās fēminās adiit. manum quattuor mīlitum dūcēbat.   10

    'quid facis, mī fīlī?' rogāvit mātrōna attonita. 'cūr adsunt mīlitēs?
nōn decōrum est tibi …'

    'nōn decōrum est mihi iussa patris neglegere,' eī dīxit Vitelliānus.
'ille iussit mē rēgīnam in hāc aulā retinēre. Togidubnus perfidus,
in oppidō Aquīs Sūlis comprehēnsus, iam in carcere iacet.'   15

    'num vērum dīcis?' inquit Rūfilla. 'quanta est īnsānia marītī meī?'

    Catia tamen, quae adhūc tacuerat, ad Rūfillam sē vertit atque
'valē, amīca' placidē dīxit. vultus eius erat serēnus. tum mīlitēs,
ad rēgīnam prōgressī, eam intrā aulam dūxērunt.

minus *less*

nimis *too*

iussa: iussum *order, instruction*
neglegere *ignore, disregard*

quanta? *how great?*
īnsānia *madness, insanity*

placidē *calmly*
intrā *inside, within*

---

1 **Explore the story**

    a Look at lines 1–2: **cum sōl … variōs ambulantēs**.

        i What were Catia and Rufilla doing in Togidubnus' garden?

        ii What was the weather like while they were there?

    b **'aliquid novī dē marītō tuō audīvistī?' Catiam rogāvit Rūfilla. 'valēscetne?'**
        (lines 3–4): what two questions did Rufilla ask Catia?

    c **Catia eī respondit, 'in epistulā rēx nūper dīxit morbum paulō minus
        gravem esse.'** (lines 5–6): what has Togidubnus told Catia in a letter?

    d Look at lines 7–8: **'quam fēlīx … nimis occupātum.'**

        i What has Rufilla heard from Salvius?

        ii What has Vitellianus told Rufilla about Salvius?

    e **cum Rūfilla haec dīxisset, Vitelliānus ipse, hortum ingressus,
        ad duās fēminās adiit** (lines 9–10): what happened after Rufilla had spoken?

f Look at lines 10–11: **manum quattuor ... adsunt mīlitēs?**

    i What had Vitellianus done to make his mother **attonita**?

    ii What two questions did Rufilla ask her son?

g 'nōn decōrum est mihi iussa patris neglegere,' eī dīxit Vitelliānus (line 13):
what did Vitellianus say about his father's instructions?

h Look at lines 14–15: 'ille iussit ... carcere iacet.'

    i What has Salvius ordered Vitellianus to do?

    ii What has happened to Togidubnus?

    iii How is Togidubnus described by Vitellianus?

i 'num vērum dīcis?' inquit Rūfilla. 'quanta est īnsānia marītī meī?' (line 16):
what did Rufilla say in response to what Vitellianus had said?

j Look at lines 17–19: **Catia tamen ... aulam dūxērunt**.

    i What had Catia been doing until this point?

    ii How did Catia seem when she spoke to Rufilla?

    iii How is Catia's appearance described?

    iv What happened to Catia at the end of the story?

2 Explore the language

Speech can tell us about a character's personality and feelings. Catia, Rufilla and Vitellianus all have very different ways of speaking. This includes how often they ask questions, whether they use long or short sentences, and the types of words they use.

Look closely at what each of these characters says and how they say it.
What can you learn about them from this?

3 Explore further

A single event might be interpreted very differently by various people observing it. Think about Catia's actions at the end of the story and the possible reasons why she behaved in this way.

How do you think that Vitellianus interpreted these actions? What about Rufilla? What factors might affect their interpretations?

How do you interpret Catia's actions?

Reviewing the language Stage 24: page 216

Governing the empire

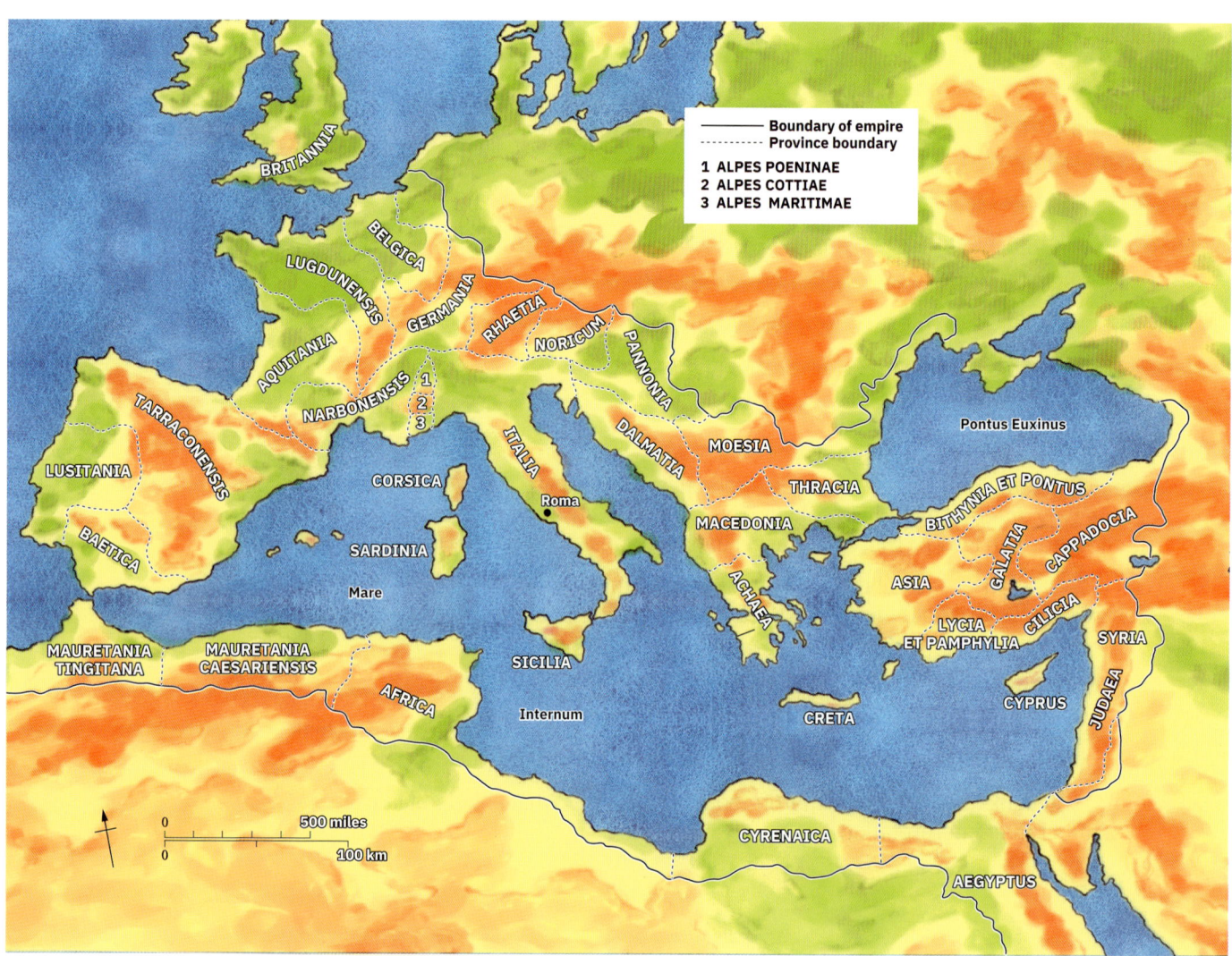

The provinces of the Roman Empire at its greatest extent, during the reign of Emperor Trajan.

> **Thinking point 1:** Look at the map of the Roman Empire. What might be the challenges of governing this territory?

The Romans conquered their empire gradually over several centuries, starting with the island of Sicily in the third century BC and ending in the late first and early second centuries AD with Trajan's conquests in Dacia (modern Romania) and the east. Some provinces, such as Britannia, became part of the empire as a result of military invasion. Others were acquired by other means: Bithynia, for example, was left to Rome in the will of King Nicomedes IV in return for support from the Romans in his struggle for the throne.

However they were obtained, once provinces were part of the empire the Romans aimed to govern them for the benefit of Rome and the emperor. Provinces were run by governors appointed by the emperor and Senate (the main governing and advisory body in Rome). Governors were the ultimate authorities in their province. In our story, Quintus and Dumnorix decide to consult Britannia's governor, Agricola, about Salvius' actions. Governing a province was a difficult task and Roman politics was full of intrigue. Agricola may have outranked him, but men like Salvius could amass a great deal of power and influence; they were useful allies and dangerous enemies.

Most provinces are 'senatorial provinces' and their governors are appointed by the Senate for one year. Some, such as Egypt and Britannia, are 'imperial provinces', with governors chosen personally by the emperor. In the case of Egypt, no senator can even visit without the emperor's permission. Imperial provinces are often more dangerous, and their governors usually serve three years. I work with Gnaeus Julius Agricola, who was made governor of Britannia by Emperor Vespasian. Britannia is a relatively new, not very peaceful province on the edge of the empire; so it requires a permanent military presence and strong military leadership.

Men who are appointed as governors have always had distinguished careers in which they held important offices. The Senate and the emperor take care to select suitable people for such important jobs, keeping a lookout for men who show special skill or talent during the earlier part of their career.

Thinking point 2: Most governors were appointed for one year. Why do you think governors were appointed for three years in imperial provinces?

In this letter from Vindolanda, a man (probably a trader) appeals to the provincial governor to stop his violent and unjust punishment at the hands of the military. He says that he has tried complaining to the officers with no success, and that the local commander cannot hear his case due to ill health. The governor is, therefore, his last hope for justice.

Aspirational Roman politicians like Agricola had to work their way up a set sequence of military and administrative offices. In AD 64 Agricola was appointed quaestor in Asia; he served as tribune of the people in AD 66 and was made praetor in AD 68.

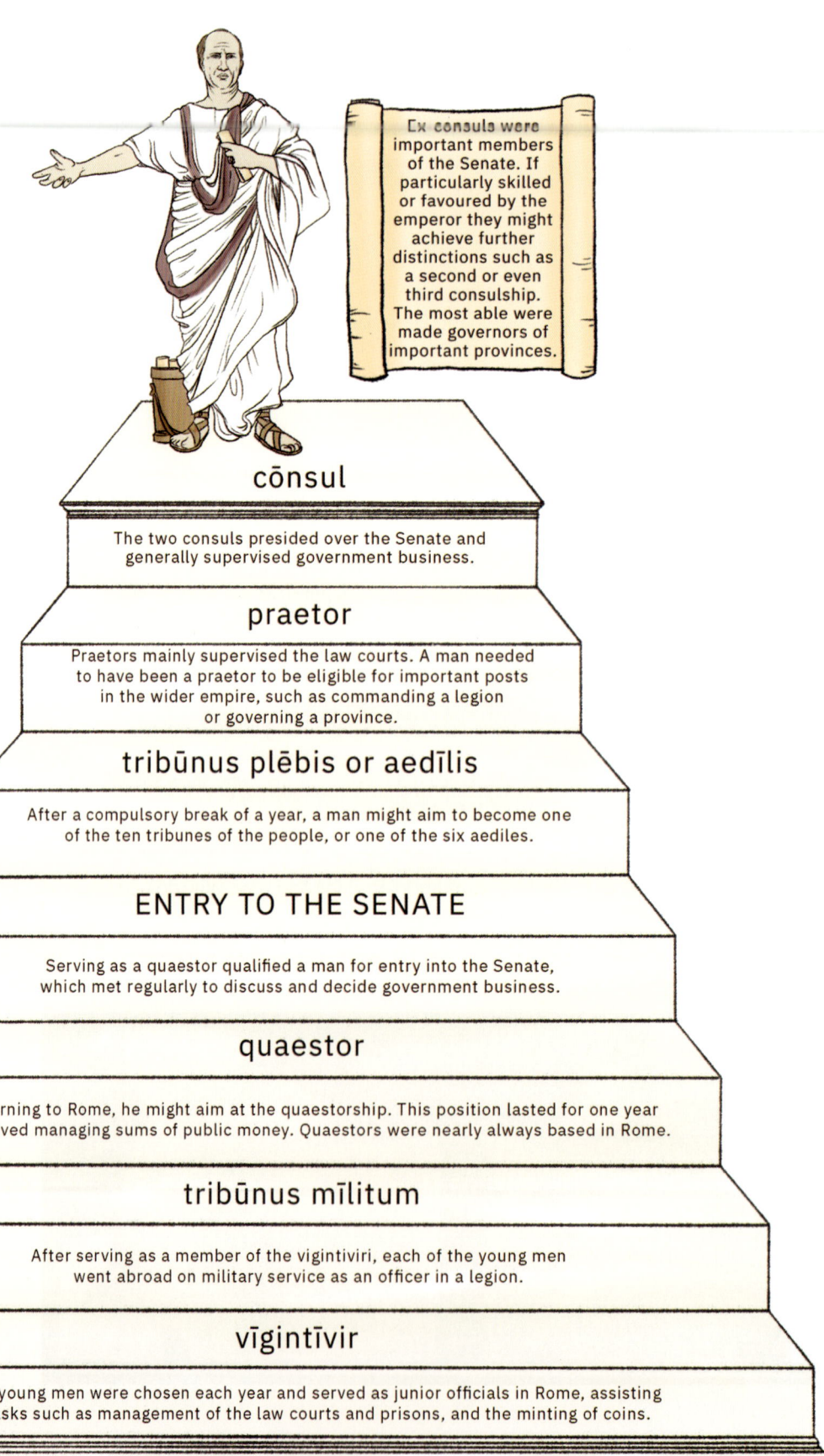

Ex consuls were important members of the Senate. If particularly skilled or favoured by the emperor they might achieve further distinctions such as a second or even third consulship. The most able were made governors of important provinces.

cōnsul
The two consuls presided over the Senate and generally supervised government business.

praetor
Praetors mainly supervised the law courts. A man needed to have been a praetor to be eligible for important posts in the wider empire, such as commanding a legion or governing a province.

tribūnus plēbis or aedīlis
After a compulsory break of a year, a man might aim to become one of the ten tribunes of the people, or one of the six aediles.

ENTRY TO THE SENATE
Serving as a quaestor qualified a man for entry into the Senate, which met regularly to discuss and decide government business.

quaestor
On returning to Rome, he might aim at the quaestorship. This position lasted for one year and involved managing sums of public money. Quaestors were nearly always based in Rome.

tribūnus mīlitum
After serving as a member of the vigintiviri, each of the young men went abroad on military service as an officer in a legion.

vīgintīvir
Twenty young men were chosen each year and served as junior officials in Rome, assisting with tasks such as management of the law courts and prisons, and the minting of coins.

Agricola's early life and career

Our main source regarding Agricola's life is the biography written by Agricola's son-in-law, the historian Tacitus. He tells us that Agricola was born in southeast Gaul in AD 40. His father had been made a senator by Emperor Tiberius, but later fell out of favour with Emperor Gaius Caligula and was executed shortly after Agricola was born.

Agricola went to school in Massilia (Marseilles), which was the cultural and educational centre of southern Gaul. He followed the normal curriculum for the young sons of upper-class Roman families, including public speaking and philosophy.

Thinking point 3: You learned about Roman education in Book I, Stage 10. As well as public speaking and philosophy, what else might Agricola have studied? How might this education have helped him during his career?

'I remember that Agricola often told us that when he was young, he was more enthusiastic about philosophy than a Roman senator was expected to be, and his mother thought it wise to restrain such a passionate interest.'

(Tacitus, *Agricola* 4)

At the age of 18, Agricola served in the Roman army in Britain as a military **tribūnus** (a high-ranking officer) under Suetonius Paulinus, governor of Britannia from AD 59 to 61.

'Agricola was not careless like those young men who treat soldiering as a game. Neither was he lazy, he never used his tribune's rank or his inexperience as a reason to escape from duty and enjoy himself. Instead, he tried to learn about the province and got to know the men in the army. ...

Britain had never been more troubled, or in a more critical condition. Veteran soldiers had been massacred, colonies burned, and armies cut off from their bases. One moment might bring victory, the next a fight for survival. Although all this happened under someone else's leadership (the glory of winning back the province belonged to the general who was in command), the young officer still gained skill, experience and ambition.'

(Tacitus, *Agricola* 5)

Thinking point 4: Tacitus describes Britannia as in 'critical condition' during the governorship of Suetonius Paulinus. What rebellion was responsible for the burning of colonies and massacre of soldiers mentioned by Tacitus?

Agricola returned to Rome to continue his political career and in the civil war of AD 69 took the side of the future Emperor Vespasian. In AD 70, he returned to Britain to take command of the undisciplined and troublesome Twentieth Legion, stationed at Viroconium (Wroxeter) in the west of England.

Thinking point 5: According to Tacitus, what was Agricola like as a young man and early in his career?

An antefix (a kind of roof tile) made by the Twentieth Legion. The boar was their symbol.

'At that time Vettius Bolanus was governor of Britannia. He was too gentle a ruler for such an unstable province. Under his leadership, Agricola restrained his own energy and enthusiasm, as he had been trained to obey his superiors and think about practicalities as well as glory. A short time later, Petilius Cerealis was appointed governor and Agricola had more opportunities to show his skills. ... To test his abilities, Cerealis frequently entrusted Agricola with part of his army, and due to his success, sometimes enlarged the forces under his command.'

(Tacitus, *Agricola* 8)

Thinking point 6: What is Tacitus' opinion of Vettius Bolanus as governor of Britannia? How does he portray Agricola's experience of working with him and then with Petilius Cerealis?

Agricola's success in handling this command was rewarded by promotion to the governorship of Aquitania (the central region in modern France) in Gaul. He then became consul in Rome and in AD 78 returned to Britain for a third time, this time as **prōpraetor** (governor) of the province.

Thinking point 7: What experience and qualities did Agricola have that would have made him seem a good choice as governor of Britannia?

Governing Britannia

A governor appointed by the emperor was normally given instructions or **mandāta** regarding the work he was to do in the province. By the reign of Emperor Vespasian, the Romans considered their control of the southeast of Britain to be reasonably secure, so the mandata given to governors of Britannia appointed by Vespasian included expanding control into modern Wales and the north of the island.

A governor's first and most important duty is a military one: to protect his province against attack from outside and rebellion from inside, using the troops under his command. He might, like Agricola, use these troops to conquer further territory, but he can also use them, if necessary, to deal with problems such as bandits or pirates. A small number of soldiers serve as officials on the governor's staff, but soldiers should not otherwise be used for jobs that can be done by ordinary people.

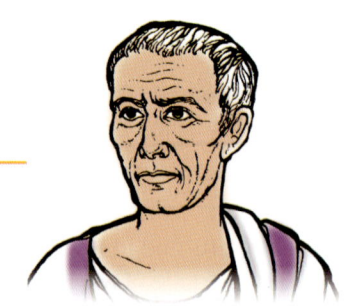

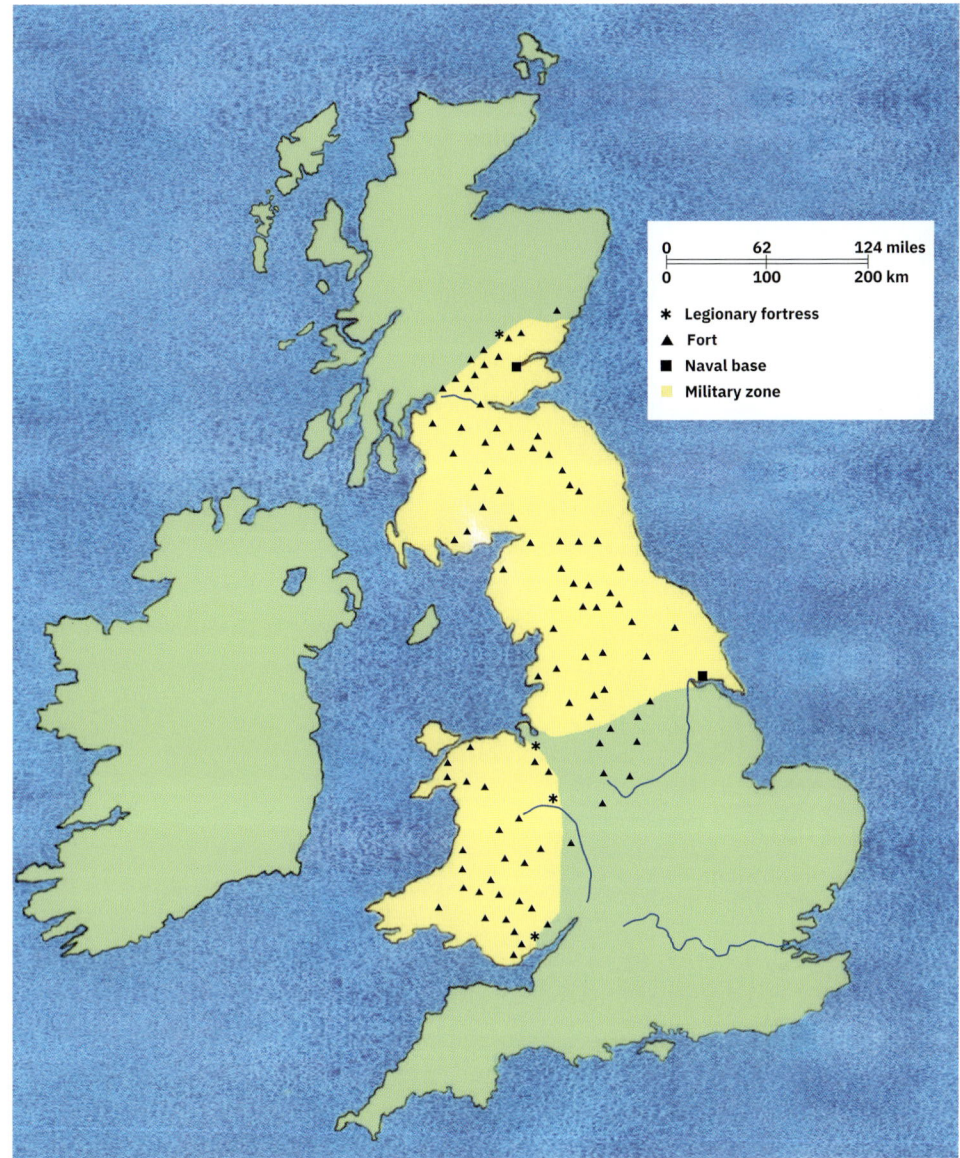

Thinking point 8:
How does this map support the claim that the Romans considered their control of the southeast to be secure?

Legend:
* Legionary fortress
▲ Fort
■ Naval base
▨ Military zone

Scale:
0 — 62 — 124 miles
0 — 100 — 200 km

Britain between AD 70 and 85.

Agricola was the third governor of Britannia appointed by Vespasian. He completed the conquest of what is now Wales and then fought a series of successful campaigns in modern Scotland, culminating in his victory at Mons Graupius in the north of the Grampian mountains. He extended the network of roads and forts across the north of Britannia and established the legionary fortress at Chester.

'Experts remarked that no general had ever shown greater skill in the choice of good sites than Agricola; none of his forts were destroyed by storms or surrendered to the enemy. Troops could march out frequently because they had enough supplies to survive a twelve-month siege … each garrison could defend itself and the enemy were helpless and driven to despair.'

(Tacitus, *Agricola* 22)

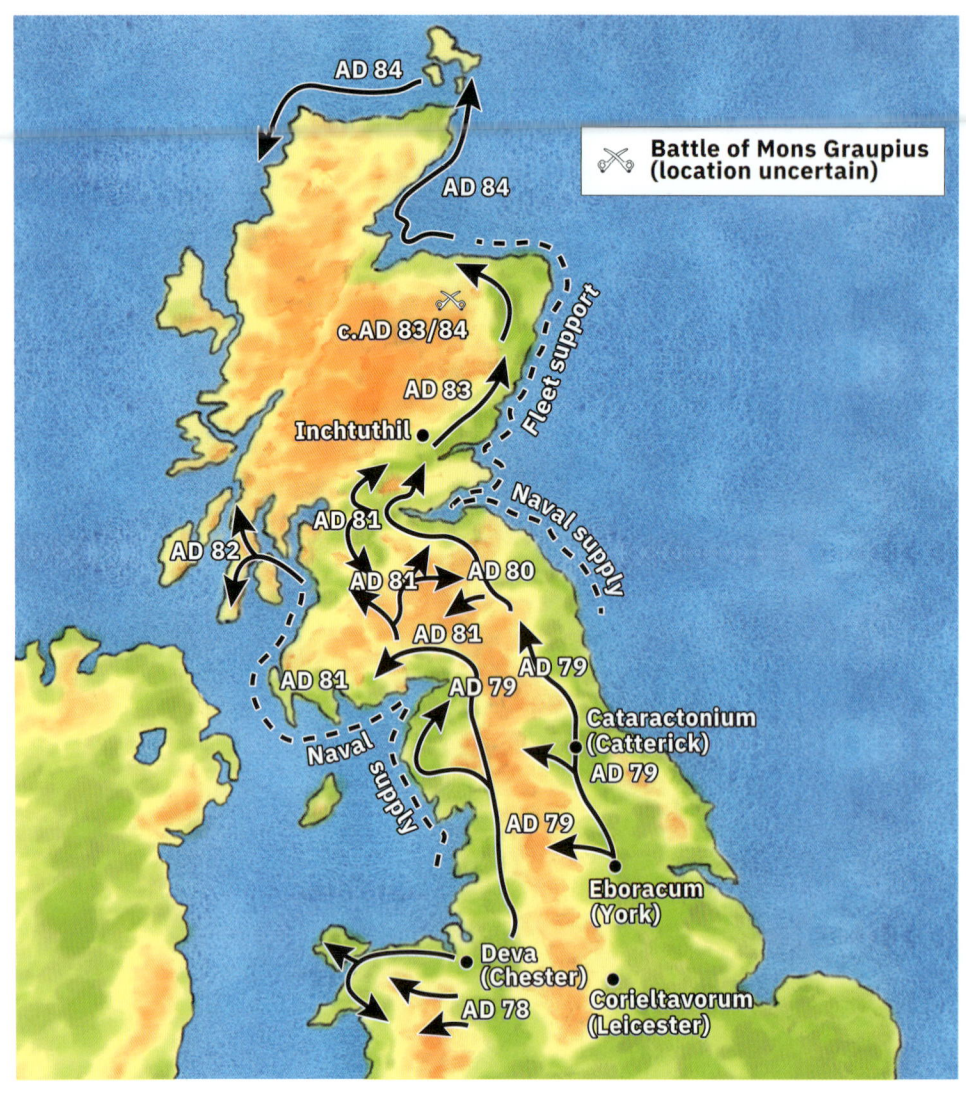

Map of Agricola's campaigns in Britain.

The earthworks of Chew Green in Northumberland, one of the camps built by Agricola on his way to try to conquer the Caledonians of Scotland.

In addition to military duties, the governor also had an important role in the provincial justice system. As the empire grew and became more complicated to run, however, this combination of military and administrative duties became more difficult to handle. Emperor Vespasian therefore created a new post, the **lēgātus iūridicus**.

Governors are expected to travel around their province and act as judge in the towns' law courts. As well as appeals, all cases involving the death penalty or large sums of money have to be heard by the governor. Sometimes, governors like Agricola are too busy with military tasks to administer the law. When this happens, the emperor can send out another official to handle the law courts. This is the position I hold in Britannia; I act as legatus iuridicus in the south while Agricola is busy campaigning in the north.

Thinking point 9: Explain the role of the legatus iuridicus. Why might a governor like Agricola have benefited from the support of a man in this position?

This inscription dedicated to Salvius found near Urbs Salvia in Italy mentions his posting as iuridicus in Britain as well as membership of the Arval Brotherhood.

Salvius held an important priesthood as one of the twelve Arval Brothers. The records of the Arval Brotherhood show long periods in which Salvius did not attend meetings, implying that he was not in Rome. Historians infer that some of these absences are due to Salvius being posted to the provinces. It is suggested that Salvius was sent as iuridicus to Britain around AD 80 during the governorship of Agricola. He clearly had a close relationship with several emperors. As a reward for his services, he received the consulship from Emperor Domitian.

Tacitus records that Agricola tried to introduce the Britons to the Roman way of life, encouraging the building of temples, fora and houses in the Roman style.

He also apparently arranged for the sons of British chiefs to receive a Roman education. Tacitus also claims that Agricola took great care to rule fairly, putting a stop to corruption and abuses in tax collection. His aim, so Tacitus claims, was to convince the Britons that it was better to live peacefully and obey the Romans than to rebel against them.

> '[Agricola] had learned from others' experience that little is gained by conquest if it is followed by injustice.
>
> … he made peace shine brightly when the indifference or arrogance of previous governors had made it seem just as dreadful as war.'
>
> (Tacitus, *Agricola* 19–20)

Agricola was governor of Britannia for seven years, an unusual length of time and longer than any other imperial Roman governor. During this time the area under direct Roman control nearly doubled. Agricola was recalled from Britain in AD 85. Tacitus says this was because of the jealousy of Domitian; however, Tacitus often tries to make Domitian appear paranoid and cruel. His portrayal of Agricola might be seen as a way to highlight the shortcomings of the emperor who recalled him.

When he returned to Rome, Agricola was given the honours due to a successful general, but this was the end of his career. He retired and held no other public offices until his death in AD 93.

Thinking point 10: How much longer was Agricola's term of office than that usually served by imperial governors? Why do you think he was governor of Britannia for such a long time?

A lead water pipe (above) found at Chester. The inscription tells us that the pipe was made when Vespasian and Titus were consuls and Agricola was governor of Britannia (AD 79). Agricola's name also appears in an inscription (below) from the basilica of the forum in Verulamium (St Albans), but only fragments of this survive. These two references might have been almost all we knew about Agricola, if Tacitus had not written his biography.

Thinking point 11: Summarise the evidence that we have about Agricola's governorship of Britannia. How useful are the different sources for finding out about his governorship?

Agricola encouraged the building of Roman-style fora in Britannia's towns; this is an artist's impression of that built in Verulamium (St Albans) in c.AD 79. Fora like this would have been important for local government and administration.

Enquiry: What does the life and career of Agricola reveal about how the Romans governed their empire?

You may wish to consider the following:

- types of provincial governor and their roles
- the nature of Britannia as a Roman province
- Agricola's background and status
- his career before he became governor
- his actions as governor of Britannia
- how typical Agricola and Britannia were as a governor and province
- issues arising from the nature of available evidence about Agricola.

Vocabulary checklist 24

arcessō, arcessere, arcessīvī, arcessītus	*summon, send for*
auctōritās, auctōritātis	*authority*
carcer, carceris	*prison*
comes, comitis	*comrade, companion*
comprehendō, comprehendere, comprehendī, comprehēnsus	*arrest, seize*
cum	*when*
dēscendō, dēscendere, dēscendī	*come down, go down*
humī	*on the ground*
intereā	*meanwhile*
minor, *gen.* **minōris**	*smaller, less*
moveō, movēre, mōvī, mōtus	*move*
neque . . . neque	*neither . . . nor*
passus, passa, passum	*having suffered*
retineō, retinēre, retinuī, retentus	*hold back, keep (back)*
saevus, saeva, saevum	*savage, cruel*
secūtus, secūta, secūtum	*having followed*
sub	*under, beneath*
ultimus, ultima, ultimum	*final, last, furthest*
vērum, vērī	*the truth, truth*
vultus, vultūs	*expression, face*

Good roads were crucial for Roman control of the provinces. This modern road follows the course of the Stanegate, thought to have been built under Agricola's governorship to link Corstopitum (Corbridge) in the east and Luguvalium (Carlisle) in the west. The stone on the left is the remains of a Roman milestone.

Dēvae

1   mīles legiōnis secundae per castra ambulābat. subitō iuvenem
latentem prope horreum cōnspexit.
'heus tū,' clāmāvit mīles, 'quis es?'
iuvenis nihil respondit. mīles iuvenem iterum rogāvit quis esset.
iuvenis fūgit.

2   mīles iuvenem petīvit et facile superāvit.
'furcifer!' exclāmāvit. 'quid prope horreum facis?'
iuvenis dīcere nōlēbat quid prope horreum faceret.
mīles eum ad centuriōnem dūxit.

3 centuriō, iuvenem cōnspicātus,
'hunc agnōscō!' inquit. 'est Vercobrix, fīlius prīncipis
Deceanglōrum, quem saepe prope castra cōnspexī.
quō modō eum cēpistī?'
tum mīles explicāvit quō modō Vercobrigem cēpisset.

4 centuriō, ad Vercobrigem conversus,
'cūr in castra vēnistī?' rogāvit.
Vercobrix tamen tacēbat. centuriō, ubi cognōscere nōn poterat
cūr Vercobrix in castra vēnisset, mīlitem iussit eum ad carcerem
dūcere.

Crīspus

cum mīles Vercobrigem ad carcerem dūceret, conturiō optiōnem arcessīvit. eum statim iussit duōs custōdēs ad carcerem mittere.

'nōnne Crīspus et Frontō tālem rem suscipere possunt?' inquit.

optiō, simulatque haec audīvit, per castra contendit. Crīspum, nūper Dēvam regressum, mox cōnspexit. *5*

optiō: heus Crīspe! hūc venī! tibi aliquid dīcere volō. centuriō tē iubet ad carcerem statim festīnāre.

Crīspus: īnsānit centuriō! innocēns sum.

optiō: tacē! centuriō Frontōnem quoque iussit ad carcerem īre.

Crīspus: deōs testēs faciō. innocentēs sumus. nūllum scelus commīsimus. *10*

optiō: caudex! tacē! vōs ambōs carcerem custōdīre iussit centuriō.

Crīspus: nōlī mē vituperāre! rem nunc intellegō. centuriō, vir magnae prūdentiae, nōs vult custōdēs carceris esse. bene! decōrum est centuriōnī nōs ēligere. etiam lēgātus legiōnis scit nōs ambōs esse mīlitēs summae fortitūdinis fideīque. ōlim pontem dēfendimus *15* et tria mīlia hostium occīdimus.

optiō: (susurrāns) difficile est mihi hoc crēdere.

Crīspus: quid dīcis?

optiō: necesse est vōbīs carcerem dīligentissimē custōdīre. nam inter captīvōs est Vercobrix, iuvenis magnae dignitātis, cuius pater *20* est prīnceps Deceanglōrum.

Crīspus: nōlī anxius esse, mī optiō. nōbīs nihil difficile est, quod fortissimī sumus, ut anteā dīxī. ego et Frontō, cum in oppidō Aquīs Sūlis manerēmus, centum latrōnēs, quī fūstēs et alia arma tenēbant, superāvimus. breve erat certāmen. valē! *25*

optiōnem: optiō *optio (officer ranked below centurion)*

castra *camp*

scelus *crime*
commīsimus: committere *commit*

lēgātus *commander*
legiōnis: legiō *legion*

cuius *whose (genitive of quī)*

centum *a hundred*
arma *weapons, arms*
breve: brevis *short, brief*

Tombstone of an optio, from Chester (a copy with the paintings re-created). He holds a staff in one hand and a case of writing-tablets in the other. His sword is slung at his side.

Deva (Chester)

Before the Romans arrived at Deva (modern Chester) there seems to have been a small settlement on the site, possibly a fishing village with farms around it. The good harbour and river crossing may have made it convenient for trade, and it is possible that ships occasionally visited from the western Mediterranean and Gaul.

Precisely when the Romans settled in the area is uncertain. They may have constructed a fort or marching camp here around AD 47/48 to support their campaigns in northeast Wales. In the AD 70s the Romans began to push north under Agricola, and a large fortress was established at Deva to house a legion of soldiers. The harbour provided naval support for Agricola's campaigns, and the fortress itself was well placed to keep watch over some of the newly conquered British tribes.

The fortress initially consisted mainly of timber-framed, wattle-and-daub buildings, although some, such as the baths, were made of stone and concrete. In around AD 102, the wooden sections of the fortress were rebuilt in stone.

Pipes brought water from local springs and distributed it around the fortress. Wastewater and sewage flowed away via channels cut under the main streets. Outside the walls of the fortress was the harbour, a parade ground, baths, hostels and an amphitheatre. A settlement soon developed around the walls, filled with a wide variety of traders, craftspeople, veterans and civilians.

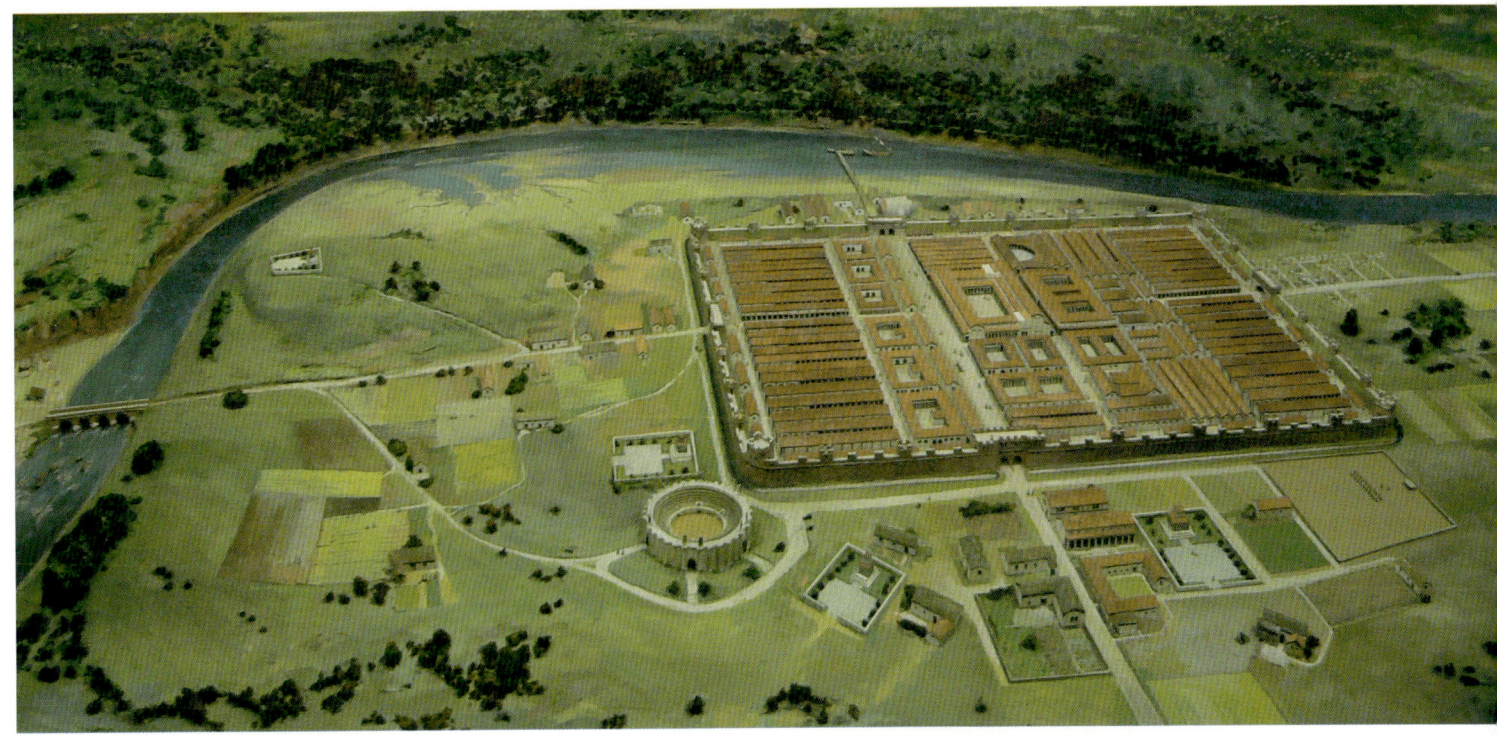

A model showing what the fortress at Deva may have looked like.

in carcere

cum Crīspus Frontōque carcerem custodīrent, tribūnus mīlitum cognōvit
Vercobrigem captīvum esse. centuriōnem igitur arcessīvit.

'dūc mē ad carcerem,' inquit. 'cellās, in quibus captīvī sunt,
īnspicere volō.'

tribūnus et centuriō, carcerem ingressī, custōdēs vocāvērunt. habēbat 5
Crīspus tabulam in quā nōmina captīvōrum scrīpta erant. centuriō eum
rogāvit in quā cellā Vercobrix inclūsus esset. Crīspus, tabulam īnspiciēns,
cognōvit ubi Vercobrix iacēret, et tribūnum ad cellam dūxit Frontō. ille
tamen, cum ad portam cellae advēnisset, cōnstitit tremēns.

tribūnus 'cūr tremis, mīles?' inquit. 'num portam aperīre timēs? 10
sī captīvus vīnctus est, tē laedere nōn potest.'

portam igitur Frontō invītus aperuit.

subitō, dum tribūnus cellam intrat, aliquis exclāmāvit,

'vōbīs nōn decōrum est mē vīnctum in carcere tenēre. mālim in fossā
foedā Britannicā potius quam in cellā sordidā Rōmānā iacēre.' 15

tribūnus, cum haec audīvisset,

'libentissimē tē videō, mī Vercobrix,' inquit. 'nōs tē diū quaerimus.'

iuvenis autem, quod rem graviter ferēbat, īnsolenter respondit.

tribūnus 'sentiō tē esse iuvenem impigrum,' inquit. 'etiam audīvī
tē īnsidiās contrā haec castra parāre. num pater tuus, prīnceps summae 20
fideī, tibi favet?'

Vercobrix 'ōdī Rōmānōs,' inquit. 'pater tamen, sīcut aliī prīncipēs
in hāc parte īnsulae, pugnāre nōn vult. nimis placidus est; mē domī manēre
māvult.'

tribūnus 'aliquandō,' inquit, 'parentēs cōnsilium bonum dant.' 25

tum centuriōnem, iam cellam ingressum, rogāvit cūr fīlius prīncipis
clārissimī in cellā tam parvā et tam sordidā inclūsus esset. centuriō
eī respōnsum bonum dedere nōn poterat. itaque tribūnus Crīspum
et Frontōnem iussit cellam pūrgāre.

tribūnus *tribune*
  (high-ranking officer)

cellās: cella *cell*

cōnstitit: cōnsistere *halt,*
  stop

vīnctus: vincīre *bind, tie up*

dum *while*

fossā: fossa *ditch*

īnsolenter *rudely, insolently*

ōdī *I hate*

pūrgāre *clean*

About the language 1: indirect questions

1   In Book I, you met sentences this:

'quis clāmōrem audīvit?'   'ubi habitat rēx?'
'Who heard the shout?'   *'Where does the king live?'*

In each example, a question is being asked. These examples are known as **direct questions**.

2   In Stage 25, you have met sentences like this:

centuriō nesciēbat **quis clāmōrem audīvisset**.
*The centurion did not know **who had heard the shout**.*

equitēs cognōvērunt **ubi rēx habitāret**.
*The horsemen found out **where the king was living**.*

In each of these examples, the question is referred to, but not asked directly. These examples are known as **indirect questions**. The verb in an indirect question in Latin is subjunctive.

> **subjunctive verbs**: page 197

3   Compare the following examples:

direct questions	*indirect questions*
'quid Vercobrix fēcit?'	mīlitēs intellēxērunt quid Vercobrix fēcisset.
'What has Vercobrix done?'	*The soldiers understood what Vercobrix had done.*
'quis appropinquat?'	rēgīna nesciēbat quis appropinquāret.
'Who is approaching?'	*The queen did not know who was approaching.*
'ubi sunt līberī?'	parentēs cognōvērunt ubi līberī essent.
'Where are the children?'	*The parents found out where the children were.*

4   Further examples of direct and indirect questions:

a   'quis cibum cōnsūmpsit?'

b   nēmō sciēbat quis cibum cōnsūmpsisset.

c   'ubi pecūniam invēnērunt?'

d   iūdex mē rogāvit ubi pecūniam invēnissent.

e   Vitelliānus nesciēbat cūr Quīntus rēgem adiuvāret.

f   Togidubnus cognōvit quō modō Cephalus venēnum comparāvisset.

g   Rūfilla scīre voluit quid in templō esset.

h   Salvius tandem intellēxit quō Quīntus et Dumnorix fūgerent.

In each of the indirect questions state whether the subjunctive is imperfect or pluperfect.

Frontō custōs

I

dum tribūnus centuriōque ad aliam partem castrōrum prōcēdunt, Crīspus et Frontō miserī labōrem dēplōrābant.

'vīsne mē ad culīnam īre et nōbīs aquam quaerere?' tandem rogāvit Frontō. 'et paulum cibī coquere? hominibus miserrimīs cibus spem semper affert.'

'optimum cōnsilium est!' inquit alter. 'quam sapiēns es! tū tamen hīc manē. melius est mihi ipsī ad culīnam īre, quod coquus decem dēnāriōs mihi dēbet.'

haec locūtus, ad culīnam statim cucurrit.

intereā Frontō, ad cellam Vercobrigis lentissimē prōgressus, portam paulātim aperuit. in angulō cellae iacēbat Vercobrix, graviter dormiēns. Frontō, cum eum vīdisset, gladium dēstrīnxit et ad mediam cellam cautē prōcēdit. subitō arānea, ē tectō cellae lapsa, in caput Frontōnis incidit et trāns ōs cucurrit. Frontō, ab arāneā territus, ē cellā fūgit, vehementer clāmāns gladiumque dēiciēns.

Vercobrix, ā mīlite perterritō excitātus, unum oculum aperuit. gladium humī relictum cōnspexit.

5   **affert: afferre** *bring*
     hīc *here*

10   **angulō: angulus** *corner*
     lapsa *having fallen*
     trāns *across*
15   **ōs** *face*
     relictum: relinquere
        leave behind

II

Crīspus, ēgressus ē culīnā ubi cēnam optimam cōnsūmpserat, ad carcerem lentē redībat.

dum carcerī appropinquat, portam apertam vīdit. permōtus,

'dī immortālēs!' inquit. 'Frontō, num portam carceris apertam relīquistī? num captīvōs līberāvistī? in exercitū Rōmānō umquam fuit mīles neglegentior quam tū?' 5

carcerem ingressus, portās omnium cellārum apertās invēnit. cum hoc vīdisset,

'ēheu!' inquit. 'omnēs portae apertae sunt! nunc rem tōtam intellegō. cum ego cēnam in culīnā cōnsūmerem, captīvī īnsidiās parāvērunt. 10 ē cellīs ēlāpsī, Frontōnem oppugnāvērunt. iam fūgērunt!'

Crīspus rem anxius cōgitāvit. nesciēbat enim quō captīvī fūgissent; intellegere nōn poterat cūr Frontō abesset.

'quid facere dēbeō? nēmō nisi ignāvus fugit. sed perīculōsum est hīc manēre ubi mē optiō invenīre potest. ēheu! mihi necesse est hinc effugere. 15 ō Frontō, Frontō! es amīcus minimae fideī. coēgistī mē statiōnem dēserere. sānē captīvīs cessistī. sed deōs testēs faciō. invītus statiōnem dēserō.'

apertam: apertus *open, unlocked*
dī immortālēs!
heavens above!

statiōnem: statiō *post*

III

Crīspus, haec locūtus, subitō conitum audīvit. aliquis magnum gemitum dedit et cellam, in quā Vercobrix iacuerat, exīre temptābat!

Crīspus, cum hoc audīvisset, ad portam cellae cucurrit et clausit.

'Vercobrix, tibi necesse est in cellā manēre!' clāmāvit Crīspus. 'euge! nōn effūgit Vercobrix! eum captīvum habeō! euge! nunc mē neque optiō neque 5 centuriō vituperāre potest, quod fīlium prīncipis Deceanglōrum, captīvum summae dignitātis, in carcere retinuī.'

Crīspus autem anxius manēbat; nesciēbat enim quid Frontōnī accidisset.

'ō Frontō! nēmō īnfēlīcior est quam ego. nam tē amābam sīcut pater fīlium. heus! Vercobrix, mē audī! sī forte Frontōnem meum necāvistī, 10 poenās dare dēbēs.'

dēnique tacuit vōcemque nōtam audīvit.

vōx: Crīspe! mī Crīspe! nōnne mē agnōscis? Frontō sum, quem tū
          amās sīcut pater fīlium.

Crīspus: Frontō? Frontō! num vīvus es? cūr vīvus es? sceleste! furcifer! 15
          unde vēnistī? ubi sunt captīvī quōs custōdiēbās?

Frontō: fūgērunt armātī, Crīspe. mē dēcēpērunt. cum tū aquam
          quaererēs, gladium dīligenter poliēbam. sed iste Vercobrix,
          quī catēnās solvere poterat, gladium rapuit et coēgit mē portās
          omnium cellārum aperīre. 20

Crīspus: ēheu! quid facere dēbēmus? adventum optiōnis timeō.

Frontō: (ē cellā ēgressus) ego custōs fidēlis fuī. tū tamen optiōnī id quod
          in culīnā faciēbās explicāre dēbēs.

Crīspus: (amīcum amplexus) ō Frontō! ō, quam īnfēlīx sum!

armātī: armātus *armed*
poliēbam: polīre *polish*
catēnās: catēna *chain*
solvere *undo, loosen*

adventum: adventus *arrival*

Lead was an important commodity in the Roman world. It was used in the production of bronze and pewter, as well as in manufacturing a wide range of objects including pipes. By the time of our stories, Britain was the main source of lead for the Roman Empire and maintaining this supply was an important aim of the occupation.

This lead ingot weighs almost 7 kilograms (15 pounds) and is stamped with the letters DECEANG, which shows that it came from the territory of the Deceangli tribe. It was discovered near a Roman road and may have fallen from a wagon as it was being transported south.

Resisting the Romans

Resisting or rebelling against the Romans was a dangerous business. The Romans rarely used long prison sentences; a prisoner like Vercobrix would have been held until they were executed or subjected to some other form of severe, possibly very cruel, punishment.

Despite the dangers, people continued to resist Roman rule. Provinces under Roman control often took a long time to settle down and become relatively stable. Some, like Britannia, never really did. Gaul became part of the empire in the first century BC but experienced rebellions well into the first century AD. At the time of our stories, Roman control in Britannia was less than fifty years old.

The Romans faced fierce resistance in their attempts to conquer and control the people of Britannia. Julius Caesar writes that the British chieftain Cassivellaunus led the defence against his invasion in 54 BC. Cassivellaunus apparently used his knowledge of the land and the speed of his chariots to hound Caesar's army, making it hard for the soldiers to find food and supplies. Caratacus, leader of the Catuvellauni, held out against the Romans from AD 43 to 51 until he was betrayed by Cartimandua, queen of the Brigantes, and taken captive by the Romans. Tacitus names Calgacus as the leader of the Caledonii who fought Agricola and his army at Mons Graupius in c.AD 83/84 (although historians have debated whether this fierce warrior actually existed).

> **Thinking point:** Boudica was one of the most famous Britons to rise up against the Romans. What can you remember about her and her rebellion?

The island of Mona, off the coast of Wales, was an important site for the religious practices of the druids and a centre of resistance against the Romans. In AD 60, Roman governor Suetonius Paulinus led a force across the water to crush the opposition:

> 'On the shore stood the enemy in a dense, armed mass. Between the ranks dashed women, with black clothing and messy hair like the Furies, waving torches. All around, the druids lifted up their hands to heaven, and screamed dreadful curses. Scared by this strange sight, the soldiers stood as though they were paralysed, making them an easy target.'
>
> (Tacitus, *Annals* 14.30)

The Romans overcame their shock and went on to win a brutal victory. They had to abandon their occupation of Mona, however, to march east and tackle Boudica's rebellion. The island remained free of Roman control for another sixteen years until it was captured once more by Agricola in AD 77.

About the language 2: more about the imperfect and pluperfect subjunctive

1 In Stages 24 and 25, you have met the 3rd person singular ('he', 'she', 'it', 'they' singular) and plural ('they' plural) of the imperfect and pluperfect subjunctive. For example:

nēmō sciēbat ubi Britannī **latērent**.
*Nobody knew where the Britons **were lying hidden**.*

centuriō, cum hoc **audīvisset**, saeviēbat.
*When the centurion **had heard** this, he was furious.*

2 Now study the forms of the 1st person ('I', 'we') and the 2nd person ('you' singular and plural) of the imperfect and pluperfect subjunctive.

Singular	IMPERFECT	PLUPERFECT
1st person	portārem	portāvissem
2nd person	portārēs	portāvissēs
3rd person	portāret	portāvisset

Plural		
1st person	portārēmus	portāvissēmus
2nd person	portārētis	portāvissētis
3rd person	portārent	portāvissent

3 Translate the following examples:

    a   custōdēs nōs rogāvērunt cūr clāmārēmus.

    b   nesciēbam quō fūgissēs.

    c   cum in Britanniā habitārem, oppidum Aquās Sūlis saepe vīsitāvī.

    d   cum cēnam tuam cōnsūmerēs, centuriō tē quaerēbat.

    e   rēx nōbīs explicāvit quō modō vītam suam servāvissētis.

    f   cum nōmina recitāvissem, hospitēs ad rēgem dūxī.

    g   amīca mea cognōscere voluit ubi habitārētis.

    h   puella nōs rogāvit cūr rem tam difficilem suscēpissēmus.

In each sentence state whether the subjunctive is 1st or 2nd person singular or plural and whether it is imperfect or pluperfect.

Building words: adjectives and nouns

1   Study the form and meaning of the following adjectives and nouns:

adjective		noun	
probus, proba	*honest*	probitās	*honesty*
līber	*free*	lībertās	*freedom*
gravis	*heavy, serious*	gravitās	*heaviness, seriousness*

2   Now work out the words that are missing from this table:

benignus, benigna	*honest*	benignitās	. . . .
līberālis	. . . .	līberālitās	*generosity*
fēlīx	*lucky, happy*	fēlīcitās	. . . .
celer	. . . .	celeritās	*speed*
immortālis	. . . .	immortālitās	. . . .
suāvis	. . . .	. . . .	. . . .
crūdēlis	. . . .	crūdēlitās	. . . .
tranquillus, tranquilla	*calm, peaceful*	. . . .	. . . .
pauper	*poor*	. . . .	*poverty*
callidus, callida	. . . .	. . . .	. . . .

3   Many of the nouns in paragraphs 1–2 can be translated by an English derivative ending
    in *-ity* or *-ty*. Where you have not done so already, and using an English dictionary to help you
    if you want, give an English meaning ending in *-ity* or *-ty* where one exists for these words.

To attack the druids, the Romans would have had to cross the Menai Strait from the mainland (modern Wales on the right) to the
shores of Mona (left). Although it can be forded at low tide, the currents are treacherous. The Romans used rafts to carry their troops
across, whilst the cavalry rode or swam.

Practising the language

in portū

An inhabitant of Chester receives worrying news.

cum diēs illūscēreret, fēmina sōla ē vīcō discessit. mox ad rīpam
flūminis prope castra pervēnit, ubi nāvis, quae ad portum modo
advēnerat, dēligāta erat. vīdit vēla nāvis esse scissa, mālum frāctum.
nautae, ā magistrō iussī, nāvem iam reficiēbant.

fēmina, magistrum cōnspicāta, celerius prōcēdit. cognōscere   5
cupiēbat unde nāvis vēnisset. magister, ad fēminam conversus,
explicāre coepit quid accidisset.

'cum prope īnsulam Monam nāvigārēmus, tempestās vēnit. statim
vēla subdūximus antennāsque dēmīsimus; amphorās frūmentumque in
mare dēiēcimus. ita ad salūtem pervenīre et nāvem servāre potuimus.   10
sed ventus validus alteram, quae plēna mīlitum erat, in lītus impulit.'

fēmina, cum dē naufrāgiō audīvisset, maximē commōta,

'ēheu!' inquit, lacrimāns. 'mīles, quem illa nāvis īnfēlīx vehēbat,
mihi mātrimōnium nūper prōmīsit. sī forte mortuus est, līberī meī
patrem āmīsērunt.'   15

'nōlī dēspērāre!' respondit magister. 'fortasse ille tūtus est. multī
mīlitēs, cum in mare dēsiluissent, ad terram natāre poterant.'

fēmina, domum regressa, laeta adventum mīlitis exspectābat.

illūscēreret: illūscērere
grow bright, dawn
vīcō: vīcus *settlement*
modo *just now, recently*
vēla: vēlum *sail*
mālum: mālus *mast*

Monam: Mona
Ynys Môn, Anglesey
subdūximus: subdūcere
draw up, raise
antennās: antenna *yardarm*
ventus *wind*

dēsiluissent: dēsilīre
jump down

---

1   Explore the story

a   **cum diēs illūscēreret, fēmina sōla ē vīcō discessit** (line 1): what are we told
about the woman who left the settlement?

b   Look at lines 1–3: **mox ad rīpam ... mālum frāctum**.

   i   Where was the recently arrived ship moored?

   ii   What did the woman notice about the ship?

c   **nautae, ā magistrō iussī, nāvem iam reficiēbant** (line 4): what had the ship's
captain ordered the sailors to do?

d   Look at lines 5–6: **fēmina, magistrum cōnspicāta ... unde nāvis vēnisset**.

   i   What did the woman do when she caught sight of the ship's captain?

   ii   What did the woman want to find out?

e   **magister, ad fēminam conversus, explicāre coepit quid accidisset** (lines 6–7):
what did the ship's captain start to explain to the woman?

f   Look at lines 8–10: **cum prope īnsulam ... in mare dēiēcimus**.

   i   When did the storm at sea arrive?

   ii   What was the immediate reaction of the ship's captain and his crew?

   iii What items of cargo did they throw into the sea?

g Look at lines 10–11: **ita ad salūtem … in lītus impulit**.

  i What were the ship's captain and his crew able to do?

  ii What happened to the other ship that was full of soldiers?

h Look at lines 12–15: **fēmina, cum dē naufrāgiō audīvisset … patrem āmīsērunt**.

  i What did the woman say had been promised her by one of the soldiers travelling in the other ship?

  ii Who did she say her children would have lost if he had died?

i **'nōlī dēspērāre!' respondit magister. 'fortasse … ad terram natāre poterant'** (lines 16–17): how did the ship's captain attempt to reassure the woman that the soldier might be safe?

j **fēmina, domum regressa, laeta adventum mīlitis exspectābat** (line 18): what did the woman do after she had returned home?

2 Explore the language

Authors often use the sounds of words to bring parts of their stories to life, repeating those sounds in different words. Sometimes the sounds of the words will mimic the sounds in the story. How is sound being used in these lines of the story?

a (line 3) **vīdit vēla nāvis esse scissa, mālum frāctum**.

b (lines 5–6) **fēmina, magistrum cōnspicāta, celerius prōcēdit. cognōscere cupiēbat unde nāvis vēnisset**.

c (line 11) **sed ventus validus alteram, quae plēna mīlitum erat, in lītus impulit**.

d (lines 13–15) **'ēheu!' inquit, lacrimāns … āmīsērunt.'**

3 Explore further

In Roman literature storms and shipwrecks are a common setting. They are often used to create a moment of drama, tension and uncertainty.

In the stories you have read there have also been common settings and many have involved nature.

What common settings have you noticed? What kind of moments do you think they have been used to create?

Deva was founded at the highest point on the River Dee that seagoing ships could reach. Part of the Roman quayside can still be seen today.

Reviewing the language Stage 25: page 218

The Roman army was divided into legions, each of which was made up of over 5000 professional soldiers. The number of legions varied over time, but in the first century AD there were approximately thirty, stationed across the Roman Empire.

A full military career usually lasted twenty-five years, after which the soldier could retire with an honourable discharge. Some careers were much shorter, though. A soldier who had been wounded in battle and could no longer fight would usually be given an honourable discharge, regardless of how long he had served, and of course many men did not live to see retirement.

There were two different classes of soldier in the Roman army: legionaries and auxiliaries.

Legionary soldiers are Roman citizens. We are paid more than auxiliaries and when we retire we are given a sum of money or some land as a reward. Auxiliary soldiers are not Roman citizens. Their salary is usually about a third of what a legionary soldier is paid and when they retire they are rewarded with Roman citizenship for themselves and their children.

Thinking point 1: What do the differences between legionary and auxiliary soldiers suggest about the importance of citizenship in Roman society?

Recruitment

If a young man wanted to join the Roman army as a legionary, he would bring a letter of recommendation from a respectable person to a group of investigators. The investigators would check whether the recruit was a Roman citizen and then would proceed to give him a medical exam to ensure he was fighting fit. In the fourth century AD the author Vegetius wrote a military manual which included advice about the recruitment of suitable soldiers:

'A young soldier should have alert eyes and hold his head upright. The recruit should be broad-chested with powerful shoulders and strong arms. His fingers should be long rather than short. He should not be pot-bellied or have a fat bottom. His calves and feet should not be flabby; instead they should be all muscle.

In choosing or rejecting recruits, it is important to find out what trade they have been following ... smiths, carpenters, butchers and hunters of deer and wild boar are the most suitable kind of recruit. The whole well-being of the Roman state depends on the kind of recruits you choose; so you must choose men who are outstanding not only in body but also in mind.'

(Vegetius, *de re militari* 1.6)

Thinking point 2: According to Vegetius, what is the ideal Roman recruit like? Do you agree that such a man would make a good soldier? Are there any qualities you think Vegetius has missed out?

If a recruit passed his initial examination, he would be assigned to a legion and given money to pay for his journey, which was often hundreds of miles over both land and sea. Some legionaries may have served close to home, but auxiliary soldiers were not usually allowed to serve in the province of their birth. This policy was intended to reduce the chances of rebellion, but it had another consequence: it encouraged migration of young men across the empire, resulting in increased diversity in the army. A Latin inscription found in Cumbria in the north of England tells us that between AD 253 and 258 a group of soldiers from the province of Mauretania (modern Morocco and West Algeria) were stationed in the area.

This figure, found in London, shows a horseman from Mauretania. His circular shield sits in front of him on his horse's back, although the horse itself has been lost. Cavalry from Mauretania were famous for their skills and were deployed as specialist units in the Roman army.

The first recorded African community in Britain guarded a Roman fort on this site

3rd century AD

A BBC HISTORY PROJECT

Memorial plaque in Burgh by Sands, Cumbria.

Training

To be a Roman soldier you have to be really physically fit and strong. Training for recruits focuses on improving strength, stamina and agility and includes running, jumping, swimming and marching over long distances carrying a heavy pack. New recruits also use a wooden sword and wicker shield and fight dummy targets to work on their technique before they are allowed to use real weapons. All of this initial training takes place within the safety of the fortress at which the recruit is based.

Daily life for soldiers was hard. They rarely had time to relax, even during peacetime, and the constant training and physical work took a toll on their bodies. The skeleton of a 24–28-year-old soldier found in modern Serbia showed pressure marks on the shoulder blades, pelvis, ankles and knees, while another aged between 25 and 30, with considerable damage to his spine and right arm, was found in Velsen in the Netherlands. These injuries were probably caused by wearing heavy armour and equipment for long periods of time, and no doubt many soldiers suffered from long-term pain and mobility issues.

When a recruit could handle his weapons competently and was physically fit, he was ready to leave the fortress and train in the open countryside. This would begin with a route march, on which he carried not only his armour and weapons, but also a heavy pack (around 40 kilograms, or 88 pounds) containing a warm cloak, dishes, water bottle, several days' food and equipment for making an overnight camp, including an axe and a basket for moving earth. It was vital that soldiers were able to construct a camp at the end of a long day's march for protection against the weather as well as potential attacks. Several practice camps and forts have been found in Britain.

Remains of a temporary Roman camp known as Haltwhistle Burn 1 located near Hadrian's Wall on the Stanegate road.

Soldiers marching with their equipment; each one has a pack (sarcina) carried on a pole (furca).

An important aspect of a soldier's training would have been the mental preparation necessary for fighting in battle. Vegetius reminds leaders to pay attention to the mental state of their men as well as their physical fitness:

'It is natural for men in general to be affected by some sense of fear at the beginning of a battle, but there are definitely some who have nervous natures and panic at the very sight of the enemy. To reduce these concerns, before venturing out on an engagement frequently draw up your army in order of battle while in a safe situation, so that your men may become used to the sight and appearance of the enemy. ... Things with which we are familiarised are no longer able to inspire terror in us.'

(Vegetius, *de re militari* 3.12)

Thinking point 3: Explain how the training of Roman legionaries helped them to be effective soldiers.

Armour and weapons

Legionary soldiers were almost always infantry (soldiers who fight on foot). They were well protected by armour which was tough but allowed them to move easily. The metal helmet was padded on the inside, to prevent it from moving around in battle. Separate cheek-guards were attached to the helmet, providing some protection to the side of the soldier's face. The body was protected by a **lōrīca segmentāta**, a piece of armour consisting of a breastplate and backplate made from metal strips, which let the soldier twist his body in combat. A skirt made from leather straps and leather sandals offered some protection to the lower half of his body, but his legs and arms were relatively unprotected. He would therefore also need to use his **scūtum** (a large, rectangular, slightly curved shield) to deflect enemy attacks.

This statuette is wearing armour typical of a legionary soldier.

Thinking point 4: Look at the statuette. Can you identify some of the armour mentioned in the information above? What legionary armour or equipment is not shown in this source?

The Ermine Street Guard is a society that studies the Roman army's equipment and makes replicas for re-enactments. This member is wearing a full set of segmented armour and carrying a javelin and scutum.

Each legionary was equipped with three weapons: a **pīlum**, a **gladius** and a **pugiō**. The pilum was a wooden javelin with a heavy metal spearpoint. At the start of a battle, a soldier would hurl his pilum at the enemy from a distance of about 25 metres (82 feet). If the pilum pierced an enemy shield, the spear tip would usually bend, making it impossible to pull out. The shield was then useless and the pilum could not be thrown back.

The legionary soldier's main weapon was the gladius, a short sword used for stabbing. If the legionary lost or broke his gladius, he could resort to using his pugio, a short dagger.

Thinking point 5:
How might historical re-enactment enrich our understanding of the past? What are its limitations and problems?

'Further, they learned to strike not with the edge of their swords, but with the point. The Romans did not only find it easy to beat those fighting with the edge of their swords, but even made jokes about them. A cut made with the edge of the sword, however forceful, rarely kills, because the vital parts of the body are protected by both armour and bones. But a stab driven in just two inches is usually fatal, as it will almost always hit something vital.'

(Vegetius, *de re militari* 1.12)

Auxiliary soldiers' weapons and armour would vary depending on the job they did in battle. Some were infantry soldiers, and their equipment would be similar to that of a legionary. Others had more specialised roles, such as archers (equipped with bows and arrows) and slingers (equipped with slingshots and stone or metal bullets), as well as cavalry (equipped with short lances, javelins, long swords and sometimes even bows and arrows). The Roman army tried to make use of the special skills of auxiliaries from different regions. For example, archers were usually from places such as Arabia, where there was a long cultural tradition of archery.

Soldiers carved (sometimes very rude) messages into the pellets they fired from their slingshots. This one has the soldier's name on it, perhaps so that his victim would know who shot him.

Image from Trajan's Column of auxiliaries crossing a river. They are carrying oval shields rather than the rectangular ones carried by legionaries.

The people the Romans fought were often armed very differently and used different battle tactics. For example, one soldier stationed in Britain wrote:

'… the Britons are unprotected by armour. There are very many cavalry. The cavalry do not use swords nor do the wretched Britons get on their horses in order to throw javelins …'

(Vindolanda Tablet 164 – translation)

Vindolanda Tablet 164.

Tombstone of Titus Flavius Bassus, a cavalry auxiliary. The inscription reads:

'Titus Flavius Bassus, son of Mucala, of the Dansala tribe, cavalryman of the ala Noricorum, in Fabius Pudentis' unit, lived 46 years, served 26, his heir had this set up.'

Thinking point 6: What can we learn about Titus Flavius Bassus from his tombstone?

Life and work of a soldier

Once a province had been conquered, the army could be used to deal brutally with any resistance to Roman rule. Often, however, just the presence of a Roman legion in an area was enough to intimidate the locals into submission without the need for actual fighting. A fully trained soldier therefore did not spend all or even most of his time on combat duty.

You can learn some useful skills being a soldier. A legion has to be self-sufficient and needs people trained in jobs such as engineering, architecture, carpentry, farming, blacksmithing, medicine, record-keeping and accounting. When we are not on combat duty we will often do things such as farming, guard duty and constructing bridges, buildings and roads.

Thinking point 7: Think of some situations in which it might be essential for a legion to have people such as engineers and architects available. What sort of complex structures might they need to design and build?

A carving of a legionary soldier, employed on harvesting duties.

In this scene from Trajan's Column we can see auxiliary soldiers standing guard in the foreground, while legionary soldiers do engineering work in the background.

Soldiers rotated between jobs, probably to ensure that the most difficult jobs were shared and to ease any potential boredom. A papyrus document, containing a duty roster, survives from a legion stationed in Egypt. It lists the names of thirty-six soldiers from the same unit and details the jobs they were each assigned for the first ten days in October. Among the jobs were guard duty, staffing the armoury and caring for the bath house (probably stoking the furnace to heat the water).

Pay and promotion

Whether it was war or peacetime, Roman soldiers were given the same rate of pay. In the first century BC, Julius Caesar set the pay for legionary soldiers at 225 denarii per year. Emperor Domitian (AD 81–96) raised legionary pay to 1 200 denarii per year.

One of the things that attracted me to a career in the army was the promise of regular pay; there are few other jobs where I could be guaranteed to earn money reliably the way I do as a soldier. Money is deducted from my pay to cover the cost of food, clothing and equipment, however, and lots of us also put some aside for the future in the military savings bank. After all these deductions, I only actually have a small proportion of my pay available to spend each month: enough to visit a tavern or two and play a bit of dice, though.

If a soldier wanted to improve his rate of pay, he could try to get promoted. There were plenty of specialist roles and management positions in each legion to which an ambitious soldier could aspire. These roles tended to come with an increase in pay, and some came with other perks as well.

Each legion was divided into ten units called cohorts. Each cohort was made up of smaller units called centuries. A century usually contained eighty soldiers and was led by an officer called a **centuriō**, assisted by a second-in-command called an **optiō**. Any legionary soldier could work his way up to become a centurion, in which case his life would change significantly. On the pre-Domitian salary scale he would be paid around 1500 denarii per year – more than six times his previous salary – and would be exempted from many of the daily duties performed by the ordinary soldiers. Instead, he would be responsible for the training and discipline of his century. Most centurions earned promotion by displaying extraordinary courage and ability over several years as an ordinary soldier.

Each century also had a **signifer**, who carried the century's standard (a kind of banner) into battle, and a **tesserārius**, who was responsible for organising the guards and distributing the passwords. A **cornicen** was a horn player, who would play musical signals to send instructions both on and off the battlefield. There would also be one or two clerks doing administrative tasks.

The tombstone of Lucius Duccius Rufinus was found in York. The inscription tells us that he was a signifer for the Ninth Legion and that he was 28 when he died. The sculpture shows Rufinus holding his century's standard.

Thinking point 8: What does this tombstone suggest were Lucius Duccius Rufinus' feelings about his role as signifer?

This member of the Ermine Street Guard is dressed as a centurion, with decorative armour and a transverse (side-to-side) plume on his helmet.

Trajan's Column image of a cornicen player.

Cornicen mouthpiece found in Vindolanda.

Diagram of a legion

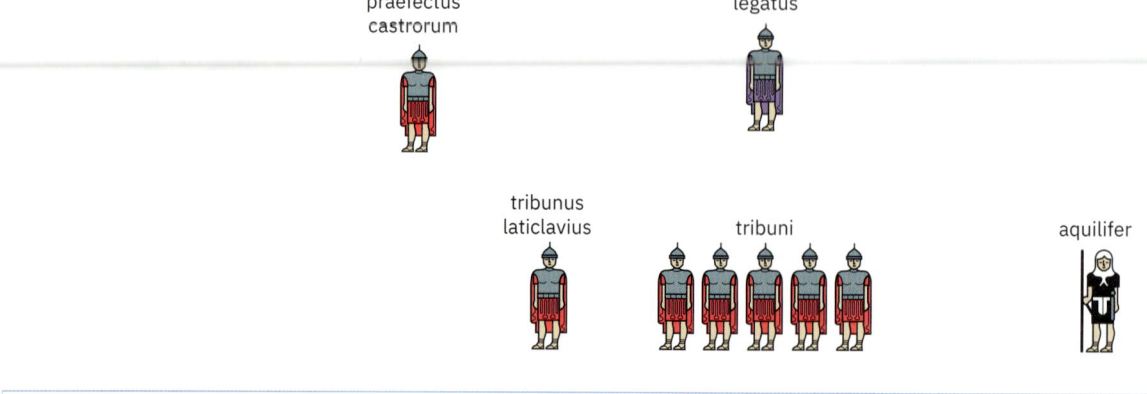

praefectus castrorum · legatus · tribunus laticlavius · tribuni · aquilifer

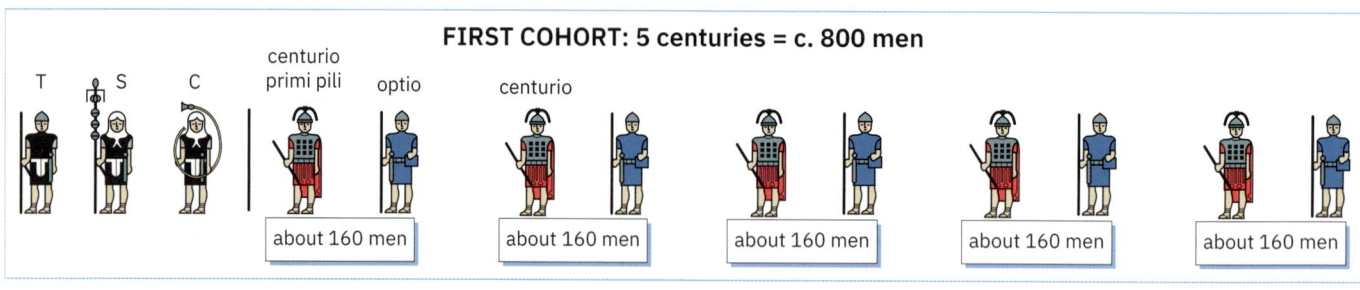

FIRST COHORT: 5 centuries = c. 800 men

T · S · C · centurio primi pili · optio · centurio

about 160 men · about 160 men · about 160 men · about 160 men · about 160 men

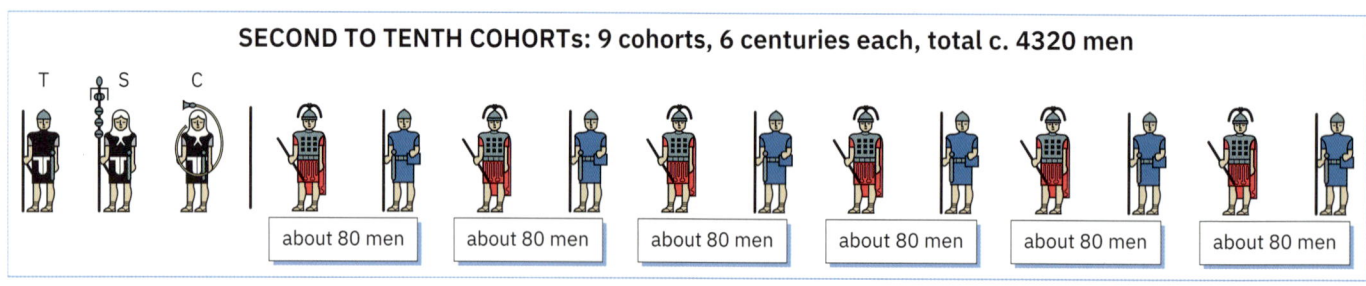

SECOND TO TENTH COHORTs: 9 cohorts, 6 centuries each, total c. 4320 men

T · S · C

about 80 men · about 80 men · about 80 men · about 80 men · about 80 men · about 80 men

HORSEMEN: about 120

> **Thinking point 9:** How might the structure of a Roman legion have helped to make it effective?

If a soldier was highly capable and ambitious, he might be able to rise above his century and take on a job managing the whole legion. For example, the most senior centurion in the legion was called the **prīmus pīlus**. He would have been a centurion for a long time and at least 50 years old. He was highly respected for his experience and practical wisdom and so he was invited to join senior war councils.

> The primus pilus holds office for just one year, then he can retire with a large payment. Some men progress even higher and become the **praefectus castrōrum** (commander of the camp). This is the highest-ranking position that a career soldier like me could achieve: you never know, maybe one day. The overall commander of a legion is the **lēgātus**, but men with this rank are not professional soldiers; they are politicians from high-ranking families. No matter how dedicated, able and ambitious a legionary soldier like me might be, we will never be given command of a whole legion.

Life after retirement

In the first century AD, soldiers in the Roman army stood a good chance of surviving until they were eligible for retirement. Legionary soldiers would be paid a cash lump sum of 3000 denarii or given a plot of land to help set them up for their retirement. If the soldier wanted to return to his birthplace, he would typically take the money and might use it to buy a farm. Otherwise, it was common for retired soldiers to settle in **colōniae**, towns founded specifically for veterans, where they were given plots of land to farm to support their families. Gloucester, Colchester and Lincoln are all examples of British towns that were founded as Roman coloniae.

When they retired, auxiliary soldiers were granted Roman citizenship for themselves and their children. As proof of their service, they were given a military diploma, which provided the auxiliary soldiers with verification of their new status.

Leaving the army and setting up a new life as a civilian could be hard. Veterans had to adapt to a new way of life without the army's strict rules and routines. A retired soldier might earn extra money by setting up a business, perhaps using some of the skills he developed while in the army, such as blacksmithing or construction.

The Romans acknowledged the toll that serving in the military took on the minds and bodies of soldiers. Disabled people often faced discrimination and prejudice in the Roman world, but attitudes may have been less harsh towards those who had fought in the army. For example, some Roman laws seem to have made exceptions for soldiers and ex-soldiers suffering from physical or mental distress caused by their service. In some people's eyes, injuries and scars were to be celebrated as evidence of the soldier's bravery in battle, but this was not a universal view. Some veterans were afraid of being ridiculed, pitied or shamed because of their war-wounds. This uncertainty about their status and the reactions of their fellow citizens may have made it harder for some ex-soldiers to transition to civilian life.

The challenges of adapting to life outside of the army possibly contributed to the decision of many soldiers to settle in coloniae. The shared experiences of the veterans and their families may have provided a sense of community and familiarity.

Military diplomas like this one were inscribed on bronze and given to honourably discharged soldiers as proof of their service to the Roman army.

> **Thinking point 10:** A retiring soldier would have needed to set up home and earn a living after leaving the army. What challenges and experiences might have been faced by those who had acquired disabilities during their military service? Try to consider a wide range of disabilities and impairments, including both physical and mental, as well as visible and unseen.

Enquiry: Why might some people have found a career in the Roman army appealing?

You may wish to consider the following:

- the rewards given to soldiers during their service and upon retirement
- the training and experiences that soldiers had
- the status of soldiers and possibilities for promotion
- the level of risk involved
- the different circumstances of citizens and non-citizens.

Vocabulary checklist 25

aliquis	*someone*
aperiō, aperīre, aperuī, apertus	*open*
brevis, breve	*short, brief*
captīvus, captīvī	*prisoner, captive*
castra, castrōrum	*camp*
cōgō, cōgere, coēgī, coāctus	*force, compel*
contrā	*against*
dignitās, dignitātis	*importance, prestige, dignity*
ēligō, ēligere, ēlēgī, ēlēctus	*choose*
hīc	*here*
labor, labōris	*work*
līberō, līberāre, līberāvī, līberātus	*free, set free*
mālō, mālle, māluī	*prefer*
minimus, minima, minimum	*very little, least*
nescio, nescīre, nescīvī	*not know*
nisi	*except, unless*
oculus, oculī, m.	*eye*
poena, poenae	*punishment*
poenās dare	*pay the penalty, be punished*
umquam	*ever*
vīvus, vīva, vīvum	*alive, living*

A Roman soldier's dagger.

AGRICOLA

Stage 26

mīlitēs legiōnis secundae, quī Dēvae in castrīs erant, diū et dīligenter labōrābant. nam lēgātus legiōnis adventum virī clārī exspectābat. mīlitēs, ā centuriōnibus iussī, multa et varia faciēbant: aliī arma poliēbant; aliī aedificia pūrgābant; aliī plaustra reficiēbant.

post trēs diēs lēgātus mīlitibus adventum Agricolae nūntiāvit. mīlitēs, cum hoc audīvissent, maximē gaudēbant quod Agricolam dīligēbant.

1   tertia hōra erat. lēgātus sibi dīxit, 'mīlitibus decōrum est Agricolam salūtāre.'
itaque mīlitēs in ōrdinēs longōs īnstrūxit ut Agricolam salūtārent.
mīlitēs, cum Agricolam castra intrantem vīdissent, magnum clāmōrem sustulērunt:
'iō, Agricola! iō, iō, Agricola!'

2 Agricola, ā mīlitibus ita salūtātus, ad lēgātum sē vertit.
'prīmō mīlitibus pauca verba dīcere volō,' inquit.
tum Agricola tribūnal cōnscendit ut mīlitibus pauca dīceret.

3 dum Agricola cōnsīdit, lēgātus silentium postulāvit.
'tacēte vōs omnēs!' clāmāvit. 'tacēte vōs,
sī Agricolam audīre vultis!'
omnēs statim tacuērunt ut Agricolam audīrent.
Agricola 'gaudeō,' inquit, 'quod hodiē vōs rūrsus
videō. nūllam legiōnem fidēliōrem habeō, nūllam
fortiōrem. virtūtem vestram magnopere laudō.'

4 posteā Agricola, ad lēgātum conversus,
'nunc mīlitēs īnspicere volō,' inquit. 'dūc mē
tēcum per ōrdinēs.'
Agricola per ōrdinēs ita prōcessit ut mīlitēs
īnspiceret.

in prīncipiīs

When you have read this story, answer the questions at the end.

Agricola, cum mīlitēs legiōnis secundae īnspexisset, ad prīncipia prōcessit ut sermōnem cum lēgātō habēret.

Salvius ipse paulō prius ad castra advēnerat. iam in prīncipiīs sedēbat, adventum Agricolae anxius exspectāns. sollicitus erat quod in epistulā, quam ad Agricolam mīserat, multa falsa scrīpserat. in prīmīs Togidubnum sēditiōnis accūsāverat. in animō volvēbat num Agricola sibi crēditūrus esset. Belimicum sēcum dūxerat ut testis esset.

subitō Salvius, Agricolam intrantem cōnspicātus, ad eum festīnāvit ut salūtāret. deinde commemorāvit ea quae in epistulā scrīpserat. Agricola, cum haec audīvisset, diū tacuit. dēnique maximē commōtus,

'quanta perfidia!' inquit. 'quanta īnsānia! id quod mihi patefēcistī, vix intellegere possum. īnsānīvit rēx. īnsānīvērunt prīncipēs Rēgnēnsium. numquam barbarīs crēdere dēbēmus; semper nōs prōdunt.'

haec locūtus, ad lēgātum legiōnis sē vertit.

'necesse est nōbīs rēgem prīncipēsque Rēgnēnsium quam celerrimē opprimere. ī nunc; dūc duās cohortēs tēcum.'

lēgātus, ē prīncipiīs ēgressus, centuriōnibus mandāta dedit. dum eōs iubet cohortēs parāre, Agricola plūra dē rēgis perfidiā rogāre coepit. Salvius eī respondit,

'ecce Belimicus, vir ingeniī optimī summaeque fideī, quem iste Togidubnus corrumpere temptābat. Belimicus autem, quī blanditiās rēgis spernēbat, omnia mihi patefēcit.'

'id quod Salvius dīxit vērum est,' inquit Belimicus. 'rēx Rōmānōs ōdit. Rōmānōs ē Britanniā expellere tōtamque īnsulam occupāre cupit. crēdō rēgem nāvēs comparāre et mīlitēs exercēre. etiam bēstiās saevās colligit Togidubnus. nūper bēstiam in mē impulit ut mē interficeret.'

Agricola tamen, hīs verbīs diffīsus, Salvium dīligentius rogāvit quae indicia sēditiōnis vīdisset. cognōscere voluit quot essent mīlitēs, num Britannī cīvēs Rōmānōs interfēcissent, quās urbēs dēlēvissent.

fuit subitō clāmor imprōvīsus. omnēs vīdērunt per iānuam prīncipiōrum intrāre hominem claudicantem. quī ad Agricolam magnā cum difficultāte praeceps cucurrit genibusque eius haesit.

'cīvis Rōmānus sum,' inquit. 'Quīntum Caecilium Iūcundum mē vocant. multās iniūriās passus, hūc tandem advēnī. hoc ūnum dīcere volō. Togidubnus est innocēns.'

haec locūtus, ad pedēs Agricolae prōcubuit exanimātus.

prīncipia *headquarters*

prius *earlier*

falsa: falsum *lie, untruth*
in prīmīs *in particular*
sēditiōnis: sēditiō *rebellion*
in animō volvēbat: in animō volvere *wonder, turn over in the mind*
num *whether*
crēditūrus *going to believe*

prōdunt: prōdere *betray*

opprimere *crush*
cohortēs: cohors *cohort*

corrumpere *corrupt*
blanditiās: blanditiae *flattery*
spernēbat: spernere *despise, reject*

diffīsus *having distrusted*
indicia: indicium *sign, evidence*
quot *how many*
imprōvīsus *unexpected, unforeseen*
haesit: haerēre *cling*

5

10

15

20

25

30

35

Questions

1 Look at lines 3–6: **iam in ... sēditiōnis accūsāverat**.

   a Why was Salvius in the headquarters?

   b Why is Salvius described as **sollicitus**?

   c What accusation had Salvius previously made?

2 **Belimicum sēcum dūxerat ut testis esset** (line 7): why had Salvius brought Belimicus with him?

3 **Agricola, cum haec audīvisset, diū tacuit** (lines 9–10): why do you think that Agricola did not reply immediately to what Salvius had said?

4 **'quanta perfidia! ... nōs prōdunt.'** (lines 11–13): do these words tell us that Agricola believed what Salvius was telling him, or not? Give a reason for your answer.

5 Look at lines 15–16: **'necesse est nōbīs rēgem prīncipēsque Rēgnēnsium quam celerrimē opprimere. ī nunc; dūc duās cohortēs tēcum.'**

   a What did Agricola tell the legionary commander that they must do?

   b What two orders did Agricola give the legionary commander?

6 **dum eōs iubet cohortēs parāre, Agricola plūra dē rēgis perfidiā rogāre coepit** (lines 17–18): what did Agricola try to find out?

7 Look at lines 20–22: **'ecce Belimicus ... mihi patefēcit.'**

   a How did Salvius describe Belimicus' character?

   b What did Salvius say that Belimicus had done to help him?

8 **'id quod ... mē interficeret.'** (lines 23–26): from the information given by Belimicus, choose one detail that Agricola might have believed and one thing about which he might have had doubts. Explain your choices.

9 **cognōscere voluit quot essent mīlitēs, num Britannī cīvēs Rōmānōs interfēcissent, quās urbēs dēlēvissent** (lines 28–29): what three things did Agricola want to find out about the rebellion Salvius was accusing Togidubnus of making?

10 **fuit subitō clāmor imprōvīsus. omnēs vīdērunt per iānuam prīncipiōrum intrāre hominem claudicantem** (lines 30–31): what caused the unforeseen uproar?

11 **quī ad Agricolam magnā cum difficultāte praeceps cucurrit genibusque eius haesit** (lines 31–32): what two things did the newly arrived man do?

12 **'cīvis Rōmānus ... est innocēns.'** (lines 33–35): which three Latin words from these lines explain what happened in line 36 (**ad pedēs Agricolae prōcubuit exanimātus**)?

About the language 1: purpose clauses

1 Study the following examples:

mīlitēs ad prīncipia convēnērunt **ut Agricolam audīrent**.
*The soldiers gathered at the headquarters **in order that they might hear Agricola**.*

per tōtam noctem labōrābat medicus **ut vulnera mīlitum sānāret**.
*The doctor worked all night **in order that he might treat the soldiers' wounds**.*

The groups of words in **bold** are known as **purpose clauses**, because they indicate the purpose for which an action was done. The verb in a purpose clause in Latin is always subjunctive.

> **imperfect and pluperfect subjunctive**: page 198

2 Further examples:

   a omnēs cīvēs ad forum contendērunt ut senātōrem spectārent.

   b Catia stilum et cērās postulāvit ut epistulam scrīberet.

   c dēnique ego ad patrem rediī ut rem explicārem.

   d rēx iter ad fontem fēcit ut auxilium quaereret.

   e equōs celeriter cōnscendimus ut ex oppidō fugerēmus.

   f vīllam intrāvistī ut pecūniam nostram caperēs.

3 Instead of translating **ut** and the subjunctive as *in order that I (you, etc.) might ...*, it is often possible to use a simpler form of words:

mīlitēs ad prīncipia convēnērunt ut Agricolam audīrent.
The soldiers gathered at the headquarters in order to hear Agricola.
Or, simpler still:
The soldiers gathered at the headquarters to hear Agricola.

Being a Roman citizen (or not) often affected how you were treated. When Paul (later a Christian saint) was arrested by Roman soldiers in Jerusalem, he was bound and almost whipped before he declared '**cīvis Rōmānus sum**'. The Roman commander was very worried about the possibility of mistreating a citizen. Therefore when tensions escalated, he chose to send Paul to present his case to his superior, the governor of Judaea.

tribūnus

Agricola, priusquam Salvius aut Belimicus respōnsum daret, custōdēs iussit Quīntum auferre medicumque arcessere. tum ad tribūnum mīlitum, quī adstābat, sē vertit.

'mī Rūfe,' inquit, 'propter prūdentiam tuam optimus es omnium tribūnōrum quōs habeō. tē iubeō hunc hominem summā cum cūrā interrogāre.' 5

Salvius, cum Rūfus exiisset, valdē commōtus,

'omnia explicāre possum,' inquit. 'nōtus est mihi hic homō Pompēiānus. nūper in vīllā mē vīsitāvit, quamquam nōn invītāveram. porrō, nesciēbam quālis esset gēns eius. per tōtam hiemem apud mē mānsit, opēs meās 10 dēvorāns. duōs tripodas argenteōs habēbam, quōs abstulit ut Togidubnō daret. sed eum nōn accūsāvī, quod hospes erat. ubi tamen ad oppidum Aquās Sūlis mēcum advēnit, scelus pessimum committere temptāvit. venēnum parāvit ut Memorem, haruspicem Rōmānum, necāret. postquam rem nōn effēcit, mē ipsum accūsāvit. nōlī eī crēdere. multō perfidior est 15 quam Britannī. nōnne cōnsentīs omnēs Pompēiānōs esse mendācēs?'

haec cum audīvisset, Agricola tantum respondit,

'sī haec fēcit, perīre dēbet.'

tum Agricola Salviusque in silentiō exspectābant dum redīret Rūfus. tandem revēnit tribūnus valdē attonitus. 20

'Quīntus Caecilius,' inquit, 'est iuvenis summae fideī et virtūtis. patrem meum, quem Alexandrīae relīquī, bene nōverat. hoc prō certō habeō quod Quīntus hanc epistulam mihi ostendit, ā patre ipsō scrīptam. iter longum et perīculōsum fēcit dum mē invenīret.'

priusquam Salvius quicquam dīcere posset, Agricola Quīntum ad sē 25 vocāvit, cēterōsque dīmīsit. Salvius, Quīntum dētestātus, anxius exiit. Agricola cum Quīntō sermōnem longissimum habēbat.

---

priusquam *before*

adstābat: adstāre *stand in attendance*
propter *on account of, because of*
interrogāre *question*

gēns *family*
opēs *money, wealth*
dēvorāns: dēvorāre *devour, eat up*

dum *until*

Alexandrīae *at Alexandria*
prō certō habeō: prō certō habēre *know for certain*

dētestātus *having cursed*

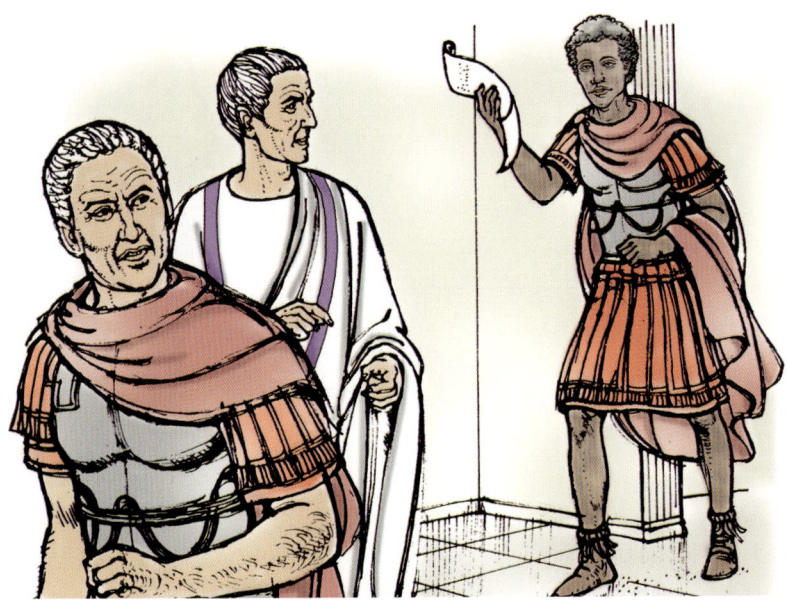

Senior soldiers in the Roman army

Tho officor who commandod a legion was called a legatus. He would have been a member of the Senate in Rome and usually in his mid-thirties. The legatus was assisted by six military tribunes (for a diagram of the hierarchy of a Roman legion, see page 114). Of these tribunes, one was usually a young man of noble birth, serving in the military before starting a political career. After holding civilian posts in Rome or one of the provinces, such a man might be appointed as legatus himself and spend three or four years commanding his legion. He would then usually resume his civilian career (for the stages of a Roman political career, see page 82).

The other five tribunes were usually also in their thirties and members of a slightly lower social class. They were generally able, wealthy and educated men, often aiming at important posts in the imperial administration. Some of them returned to the army later to command auxiliary cavalry units. The senior officers usually spent only short periods in the army, unlike the centurions and the legionaries, who served for the whole of their working lives. The officers therefore relied heavily on the advice and expertise of the experienced centurions. The army was highly trained and well organised, so the appointment of relatively inexperienced officers rarely affected the success of its operations.

Some officers, such as Agricola, proved themselves to be extremely capable and were promoted to become governors of provinces such as Britannia where military skill and strong leadership were required.

> **Thinking point:** Think back to Stage 24. When and where did Agricola serve as a military tribune? Which of the two sorts of tribune was he?

Senior soldiers could bring their households with them on their posting. This altar (discovered in modern York) is dedicated to Fortune and was set up by Sosia Juncina, wife of the legatus Quintus Antonius Isauricus.

The god Mars, wearing the helmet, breastplate and greaves of a senior officer.

About the language 2: priusquam and dum, and the imperfect subjunctive

1   From Stage 24 onwards, you have met sentences with **cum** and the imperfect subjunctive.

cum and the imperfect subjunctive: page 75

  cum Dēvam iter facerent, ad pontem sēmirutum vēnērunt.
  When *they were travelling to Chester, they came to a weak bridge.*

  captīvus, **cum** in cellā iaceret, dē vītā dēspērābat.
  When *the prisoner was lying in the cell, he was in despair of his life.*

2   Now study the following examples:

  priusquam rēx vīnum biberet, Quīntus pōculum ē manibus eius rapuit.
  Before *the king might drink the wine, Quintus grabbed the cup from his hands.*

  Or, in more natural English:

  Before *the king drank the wine, Quintus grabbed the cup from his hands.*

  intentē audiēbāmus **dum** rem intellegerēmus.
  *We listened carefully **until** we understood the truth.*

  In these sentences, the imperfect subjunctive is being used with **priusquam** (meaning *before*) and **dum** (meaning *until*).

3   Further examples:

  a   priusquam lēgātus signum daret, mīlitēs magnum clāmōrem sustulērunt.

  b   equus cautissimē flūmen trānsībat dum ad alteram rīpam pervenīret.

  c   Rūfilla, priusquam rēgīnae respondēret, Vitelliānum appropinquantem vīdit.

  d   longē nāvigābant dum terram cōnspicerent.

contentiō

Agricola, cum Quīntum audīvisset, Salvium furēns arcessīvit, immōtus in sellā sedēbat dum Salvius advenīret. quī, simulatque intrāvit, aliquid dīcere coepit. Agricola tamen, cum silentium iussisset, surrēxit ut Salvium vehementer accūsāret.

'dī immortālēs! Togidubnus est innocēns, tū perfidus. Quīntus Caecilius, 5
ā tē maledictus, mihi patefēcit quid accidisset. multa eum rogāvī ut vērum
cognōscerem. cūr tam īnsānus eram ut tibi crēderem? simulatque ad hanc
prōvinciam vēnistī, amīcī mē dē calliditāte tuā monuērunt. nunc rēs ipsa
mē docuit. num imperātor Domitiānus hanc tantam perfidiam ferre potest?
ego sānē nōn possum. in hāc prōvinciā summam potestātem habeō. iubeō 10
tē hās inimīcitiās dēpōnere. iubeō tē ad Togidubnī aulam īre, veniamque
ab eō petere. praetereā imperātōrī ipsī rem explicāre dēbēs.'

haec ubi dīxit Agricola, Salvius īrātus,

'quam caecus es!' clāmāvit. 'quam longē errās! nōnne rem intellegis?'

sed priusquam Agricola eī respondēret, Salvius 15

'tū ipse imperātōrī Domitiānō id quod in Britanniā facis explicāre dēbēs,'
inquit. 'tū enim in ultimīs Britanniae partibus bellum geris et victōriās
inānēs ē Calēdoniā refers; sed imperātor pecūniam opēsque accipere
cupit. itaque rēgnum Togidubnī occupāre cōnstituit. tū sānē nescīs
imperātōrem Calēdoniam nōn cūrāre. in magnō perīculō es, sī cōnsilium 20
meum spernis. nōn sōlum mihi sed etiam imperātōrī ipsī obstās.'

cum hanc contentiōnem inter sē habērent, subitō nūntius prīncipia
ingressus exclāmāvit,

'mortuus est Togidubnus!'

maledictus: maledīcere *insult, slander*
prōvinciam: prōvinciam *province*

inimīcitiās: inimīcitia *feud, quarrel*

victōriās: victōria *victory*
inānēs: inānis *empty, meaningless*
Calēdoniā: Calēdonia *Scotland*
cōnstituit: cōnstituere *decide*

Building words: verbs and nouns

1   Some verbs and nouns are closely connected. For example:

Quīntus omnēs familiārēs **amāre** nōn poterat. **amor** omnia vincit.
Quintus was not able to love all his relatives. Love conquers all.

mīlitēs **clāmāre** volēbant. Agricola **clāmōrēs** audīvit.
The soldiers wanted to shout. Agricola heard the shouts.

2   Further examples:

verbs		nouns	
favēre	*to favour*	favor	*favour*
terrēre	*to terrify*	terror	*terror*
tremere	*to shake*	tremor	*shaking*

3   Now work out the words that are missing from this table:

timēre	*to fear*	timor	. . . .
dolēre (1)	*to hurt, to be in pain*	dolor (1)	. . . .
dolēre (2)	*to grieve*	dolor (2)	. . . .
honōrāre	. . . .	honor	*honour*
furere	. . . .	furor	*rage*
labōrāre	. . . .	. . . .	. . . .

These Roman leather shoes were found at the Bar Hill Roman Fort in modern Scotland. The three different sizes were probably for a man, a woman and a child.

Practising the language

amor omnia vincit

Quintus helps Rufus come to terms with his feelings of guilt.

Rūfus ad legiōnis secundae valētūdinārium, in quō Quīntus iacēbat
īnfirmus, cotīdiē veniēbat. multa dē patre suō rogāvit, prope lectum
sedēns. quamquam epistulam Barbillī identidem lēgerat,
vix intellegere potuit cūr pater veniam petīvisset.

'cum apud Graecōs sōlus manērem,' inquit tribūnus trīstis,   5
'ad Aegyptum redīre voluī ut veniam ā patre peterem. fortūna tamen
coēgit mē invītum per tōtum orbem errāre, sīcut Ulixēm. nam deī, quī
nōbīs imperium lātissimum dedērunt, mē ad hanc īnsulam bellicōsam
procul in marī dūxērunt. ēheu! sine dubiō decōrum est mihi poenās
dare. propter stultitiam meam māter vītam āmīsit, et pater uxōrem.'   10

cum Rūfus haec dīxisset, Quīntus bracchium tetigit et respondit,

'quis fortūnae resistere potest, mī amīce? cotīdiē nōbīs imminet
mors. id quod Plōtīnae accidit tua culpa nōn fuit. praetereā poēta
quīdam dīxit amōrem omnia vincere. ita Barbillus, multōs cāsūs
passus, ā tē veniam petīvit. ad fīnem parentēs maximē amābāmus,   15
et illī nōs.'

amor *love*

valētūdinārium *hospital*

identidem *repeatedly*

orbem *world*
errāre *wander*
Ulixem: Ulixēs *Ulysses
(Roman name for
Odysseus)*
bellicōsam: bellicōsus
warlike
bracchium *arm*
imminet: imminēre
hang over, threaten
culpa *fault*
cāsūs: cāsus *misfortune*
ad fīnem *to the end*

---

1 Explore the story

   a **Rūfus ad legiōnis secundae valētūdinārium … cotīdiē veniēbat** (lines 1–2):
      what are we told about Quintus here?

   b **multa dē patre suō rogāvit** (line 2): whom was Rufus asking Quintus about?

   c Look at lines 3–4: **quamquam epistulam … veniam petīvisset**.

      i   What had Rufus been reading repeatedly?

      ii Despite what he had read, what was Rufus struggling to understand?

d **cum apud Graecōs … ā patre peterem** (lines 5–6): what had Rufus wanted to do when he was staying in Greece on his own?

e Look at lines 6–9: **fortūna tamen … in marī dūxērunt**.

   i How did Rufus compare his fate to the fate of Ulysses?

   ii What did Rufus say the gods had given him and his fellow Romans?

   iii Where was the location of the island that the gods had led Rufus to?

f Look at lines 9–10: **ēheu! sine dubiō … et pater uxōrem**.

   i What outcome was Rufus suggesting he had deserved?

   ii What losses was he blaming on his own foolishness?

g Look at lines 11–13: **cum Rūfus haec dīxisset … imminent mors**.

   i In response to Rufus, what does Quintus say about destiny?

   ii What did Quintus suggest was a daily threat?

h **id quod Plōtīnae accidit tua culpa nōn fuit** (line 13): what did Quintus say was not Rufus' fault?

i **praetereā poēta quīdam dīxit amōrem omnia vincere** (lines 13–14): what was the original line of poetry that Quintus was quoting?

j Look at lines 14–16: **ita Barbillus … et illī nōs**.

   i What are we told about Barbillus here?

   ii What are we told about the relationship between children and their parents?

2 Explore the language

In this story, Quintus and Rufus are talking about serious things and they choose their language carefully to reflect how important these events are to them.

Think carefully about how each character uses serious-sounding words and phrases. Identify two examples from each of their speeches and explain why you think they have chosen these words.

3 Explore further

In this story, both Rufus and Quintus refer to famous poems to try to explain their thoughts to one another. Rufus says that he was like the Greek hero Ulysses when he was forced to wander the world. Quintus quotes the Roman poet Virgil when he talks about love.

Think about why someone might use quotations or well-known references when talking to another person. What kind of impression are they trying to make? How might sharing these things help someone to build a relationship with another person?

Reviewing the language Stage 26: page 220

The legionary fortress

If the legion itself was like a miniature army, the fortress in which it lived when not on campaign could be compared to a fortified town. The fortress had to accommodate and defend the legion and provide facilities for the daily life of its inhabitants. Remains of legionary fortresses exist all over Europe. No two are identical, but all follow a similar pattern and include most of the same features. When the army moved into new territory, it needed to construct a fortress quickly. Therefore, fortresses tended to be made from wood at first, as this was relatively quick and easy. Over time, however, they would usually be rebuilt in stone.

> **Thinking point 1:**
> Why do you think legionary fortresses all followed a similar design?

The left picture shows a reconstruction of a wooden gate at a fort in central England (seen from the inside). Right is a reconstructed stone gateway at a fortress used as a supply base for Hadrian's Wall.

> **Thinking point 2:** What are the advantages of a stone fortress over a wooden fortress?

When a soldier approached his fortress for the first time, he might have felt reassured by the impressively tall walls and 6-metre-wide (20-foot) ditch around the entire perimeter, designed to slow down potential attackers. Towers – one on each corner of the fortress and spaced along the sides – enabled lookouts to spot hostile troops before they could get too close. The only way in or out of the fortress was through one of four gates, which would have been easy to defend.

'Also, take care that gates cannot be burned by fires lit near them. To protect against this, cover them with animal skins and iron.'

(Vegetius, *de re militari* 4.4)

Entering through the main gate, the soldier would walk along a straight road called the **via praetōria**, to the headquarters of the legion, the **prīncipia**. The principia was a large and impressive building at the heart of the fortress. A visitor would first enter a courtyard surrounded on three sides by a colonnade and storerooms. On the far side of the courtyard was a large **basilica** or a great hall, where the legatus worked with his officers, interviewed important local people and administered military justice. There were also offices where clerks would do administrative work, such as organising the pay for the soldiers.

The principia also included a small temple **(sacellum)**, which housed the **aquila,** the legion's battle standard. The aquila was an image of an eagle perched with outspread wings on the top of a pole. It was made of gold and in its talons it clutched a bundle of golden darts that represented the thunderbolts of Jupiter. The aquila represented the spirit of the legion; to lose it in battle was the worst possible disgrace.

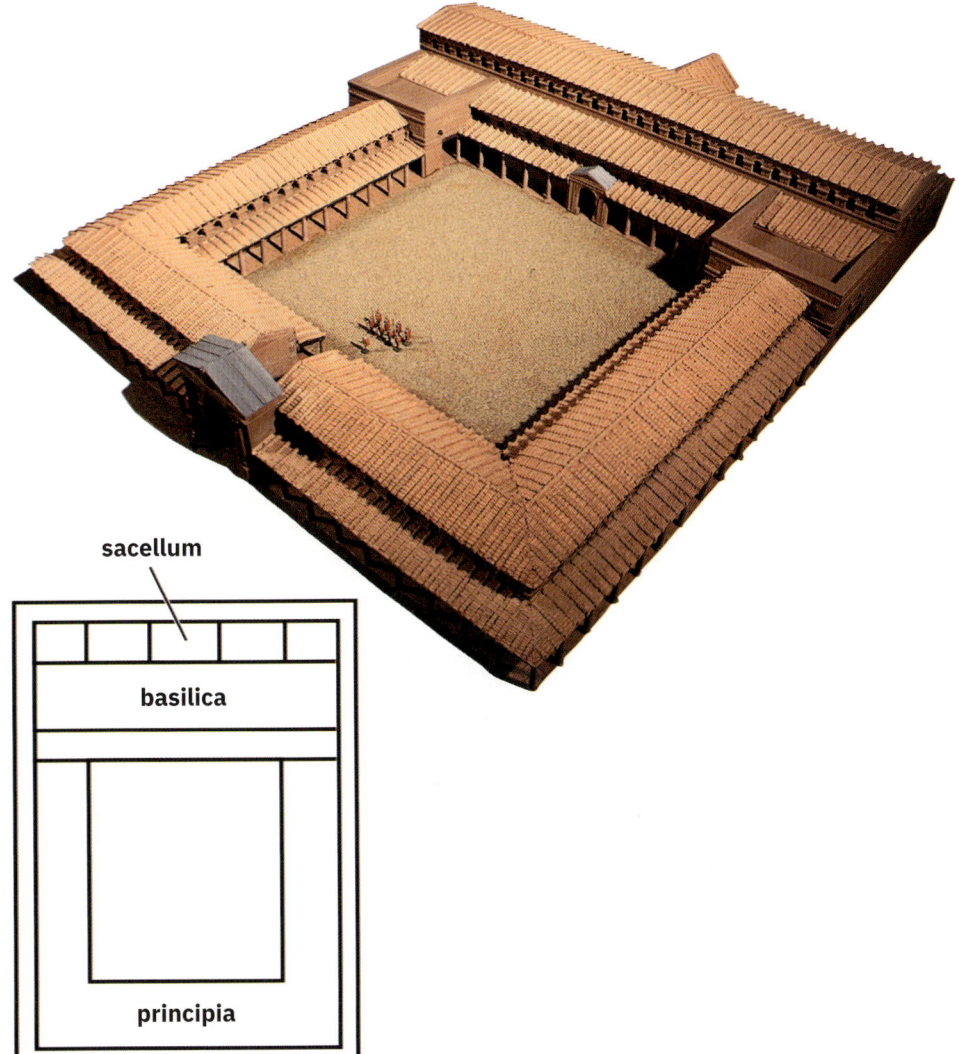

sacellum

basilica

principia

Model and plan of the principia at Deva (Chester).

At the Battle of Carrhae in 53 BC the Parthian army defeated the Romans and took several aquilae. In 20 BC the Romans were able to negotiate the return of the aquilae. This was cause for much celebration and is commemorated by this statue of Emperor Augustus.

Thinking point 3: Why do you think the principia was located where it was in the fortress?

Clustered around the principia were other buildings that were important for the day-to-day running of the legion.

Horses are valuable, so need to be protected by the walls of the fort. The stables keep them safe, fed and sheltered.

We practise fighting techniques in the large drill hall.

Workshops are used to build things we need, including weapons, armour, furniture and other day-to-day items.

Grain is the main staple of a legionary soldier's diet, and granaries (**horrea**) keep it dry and safe. A fortress might have several granaries, often arranged side by side in pairs, containing stocks of grain sufficient for at least one year, possibly two. Good ventilation protects against rot, and cats are good for dealing with rats and other vermin.

The small prison sometimes houses valuable hostages or prisoners of war. Sometimes unruly legionaries might end up there, but it isn't for long prison sentences; very badly behaved legionaries are punished by having their wages cut, being beaten or even being killed!

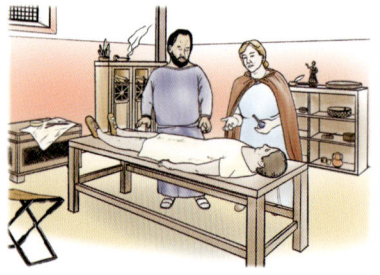

There is a hospital building (**valētūdinārium**) for treating the sick and wounded. The most common illnesses are stomach problems and eye issues. This building isn't equipped to deal with long-term recovery, though; anyone seriously injured is usually discharged from the army. The medics are well respected and have a lot of opportunity to study the human body; I think they are often actually better than civilian doctors.

Near to the principia was the **praetōrium**, where the legatus lived. Unlike ordinary soldiers, senior officers such as the legatus were allowed to marry, and their families would have lived with them in the fortress. We can see evidence of their presence in letters and tombstones. The accommodation of the legatus was designed like a luxury villa, including gardens, central heating and a private bathing complex. The legatus would entertain important local people in his home, and the comfortable accommodation was a show of wealth that could presumably impress or intimidate, depending on the situation.

Thinking point 4:
What sort of people would have made up the household of the legatus?

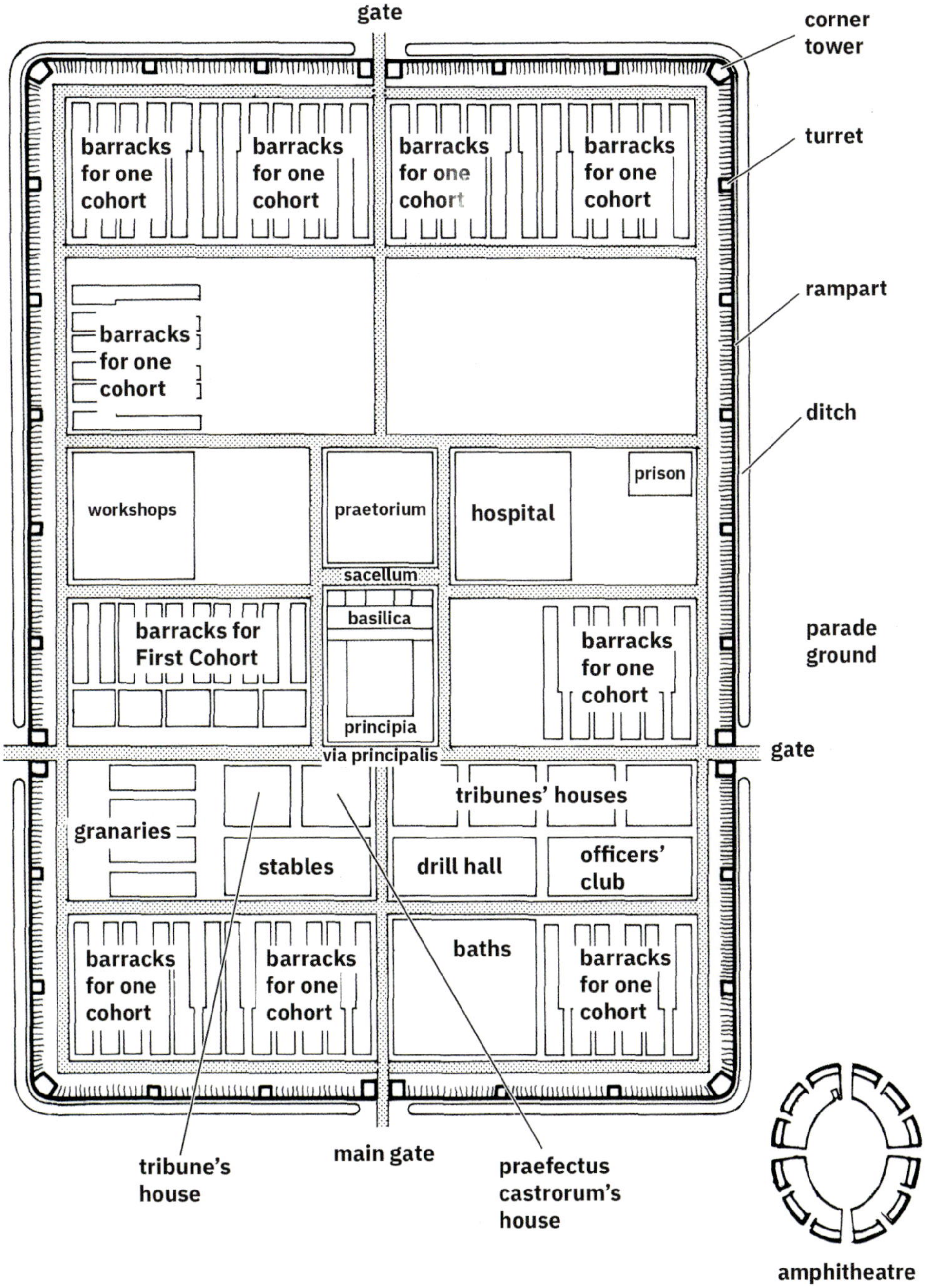

A tiny leather baby boot from c.AD 100 found in the praetorium at Vindolanda fort.

Plan of a legionary fortress.

(Plan labels: gate; corner tower; turret; barracks for one cohort (×4 at top); barracks for one cohort; rampart; ditch; prison; workshops; praetorium; hospital; sacellum; basilica; barracks for First Cohort; barracks for one cohort; parade ground; principia; via principalis; gate; granaries; stables; tribunes' houses; drill hall; officers' club; baths; barracks for one cohort (×4 at bottom); tribune's house; main gate; praefectus castrorum's house; amphitheatre)

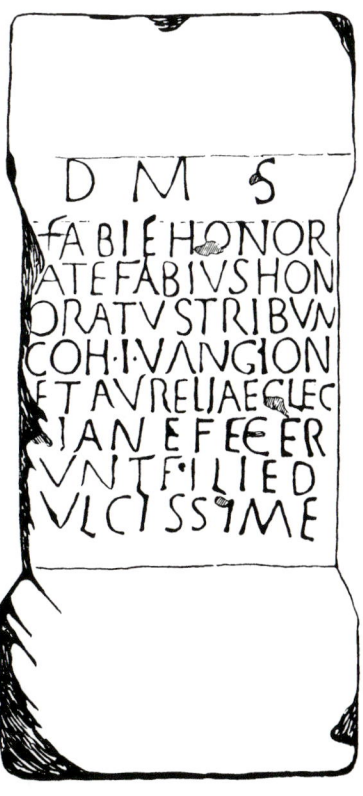

A drawing of the tombstone of Fabia Honorata, the young daughter of Aurelia Eglectiane and her husband, Fabius Honoratus, a tribune stationed at Deva in the late second century.

Moving further away from the centre of the fortress, the soldier would find his barracks. A legion was made up of 5000–6000 men, each of whom needed somewhere to rest; it is no surprise therefore that the barracks took up most of the fortress. Barracks were arranged by cohort, then by century, then by **contubernium** (a unit of eight men; there were ten contubernia in a century). Legionaries trained, fought and lived alongside their contubernium, so it is likely that soldiers came to regard them as family.

> **Thinking point 5:** What do you think a Roman soldier might have liked about living in the barracks? What might he not have enjoyed about it?

Each contubernium shared two rooms: a bedroom and a communal space which acted as a living room and kitchen. This reconstruction is from the National Roman Legion Museum at Caerleon in Wales.

> **Thinking point 6:** Why do you think the legatus lived in the praetorium rather than in the barracks?

We tribunes have our houses on the **via prīncipālis**, opposite the principia. They're not quite as big or as pleasant as the legatus' house, but they're not too shabby either! Mine is organised around a courtyard that I use for entertaining guests or when I just want a bit of peace and quiet from the rest of the fortress. My house is much better than the barracks that most of the soldiers live in. I sometimes hear them grumbling about how cramped it can be. I think it's a good way to motivate them to work hard – if they earn a promotion to centurion or a member of the first cohort then they can move into nicer accommodation. Not quite as good as mine, of course!

Every fortress also had a bath house. This might have been inside the fortress, or outside by a river or stream. Bathing was important for hygiene, but it also gave the soldiers somewhere to relax. The social aspect of bathing was an important part of Roman culture and a daily trip to the bath house with his friends might have helped a Roman soldier to feel connected to his cultural identity, even if he was stationed hundreds or even thousands of miles from home.

Thinking point 7: Almost all Roman baths throughout the empire were heated in the same manner. Think back to Book I: can you remember how the Romans usually heated their baths?

The remains of a fortress bath house were found in the cellar of a pub in York (Roman Eboracum). The bath house was originally built sometime between AD 71 and AD 122 by the Ninth Legion.

An archaeologist inspecting the Roman sewer which served the legionary bath house at Eboracum. Objects such as small glass and bone playing counters, gold beads and gemstones from rings were found in the soil of these sewers: probably lost by people using the baths.

Poor sanitation and failure to clean up toilet waste could lead to disease, not to mention unpleasant smells! Therefore, there were toilets positioned throughout the fortress. These resembled benches containing holes; they were positioned above running water to 'flush' the waste away.

The remains of the toilets at Housesteads Roman Fort on Hadrian's Wall. The men might have sat side by side, maybe having a chat, and rather than toilet roll many used (and shared!) a sponge on a stick that was washed between uses.

Outside the fortress walls would be an amphitheatre, very similar to those one might find in a Roman town. This provided a space for ceremonial parades, or for the legatus to address the entire legion with a speech. It could also be used to demonstrate tactics and for weapon training. The amphitheatre at Deva is the largest known in Britain.

> **Thinking point 8:**
> Why might the amphitheatre be located outside of the fortress?

> **Thinking point 9:** How do you think local civilians might have felt about the presence of a legionary fortress nearby?

Enquiry: The Roman army was crucial for the conquest and control of the Roman Empire. How did legionary fortresses contribute to this?

You may wish to consider the following:

- the standardised design of fortresses and their construction
- defensive features
- the living conditions and locations for different types of soldiers and officers
- facilities and amenities.

The amphitheatre at Chester today.

Vocabulary checklist 26

amor, amōris	*love*
auferō, auferre, abstulī, ablātus	*take away, carry off, steal*
bellum, bellī	*war*
commōtus, commōta, commōtum	*alarmed, excited, upset*
doceō, docēre, docuī, doctus	*teach*
dum	*while; until*
lēgātus, lēgātī	*commander; governor*
legiō, legiōnis	*legion*
magnopere	*greatly, very much*
nōtus, nōta, nōtum	*famous, well known*
num	*whether*
patefaciō, patefacere, patefēcī, patefactus	*reveal*
quantus, quanta, quantum	*how big, how great*
quot?	*how many?*
referō, referre, rettulī, relātus	*carry, bring back, tell, relate*
sī	*if*
testis, testis	*witness*
ut	*that, in order that*
vester, vestra, vestrum	*your (plural)*
virtūs, virtūtis	*courage, virtue*

Roman soldiers carrying an eagle and other standards.

EXTRA MUROS

Stage 27

1 'mitte plūrēs custōdēs ad portās!'
   lēgātus et centuriō sermōnem gravem habēbant.
   lēgātus centuriōnem monēbat ut plūrēs custōdēs ad portās mitteret.

2 'custōdīte portās castrōrum cum summā dīligentiā!'
   prō prīncipiīs centuriō mīlitibus mandāta dabat.
   centuriō mīlitibus imperābat ut portās castrōrum cum summā dīligentiā custōdīrent.

3 'castra Rōmāna oppugnāte! horrea incendite!'
in silvā proximā Vercobrix ōrātiōnem apud Britannōs habēbat.
Vercobrix Britannōs incitābat ut castra Rōmāna oppugnārent et horrea incenderent.

4 'tabernam intrāte! āleam lūdite!'
in vīcō caupōna mīlitēs salūtābat.
caupōna mīlitibus persuādēbat ut tabernam intrārent et āleam lūderent.

patrēs et līberī

Rūfus, ab Agricolā dīmissus, medicō imperāvit ut Quīntum in valētūdināriō optimē cūrāret. Quīntus ibi trēs diēs quiescēbat dum convalēsceret; quārtō diē ad vīcum, ubi Aventīna Vilbiaque manēbant, īre cōnstituit. eīs valedīcere volēbat.

Agricola, cum hoc audīvisset, Rūfō monuit ut ad vīcum cum Quīntō īret. Rūfus igitur, ā prīncipiīs profectus, Quīntum per portam castrōrum dūxit. quī, plūrēs custōdēs quam anteā cōnspicātus, tribūnum rogāvit cūr tot mīlitēs castra custōdīrent.

Rūfus: crēdimus hostēs īnsidiās aut aliam fraudem parāre. nūper dux
               eōrum haec castra clam intrāvit ut horrea īnspiceret.

Quīntus: quis est ille dux?

Rūfus: est fīlius prīncipis Deceanglōrum, nōmine Vercobrix, iuvenis
               vīgintī annōrum. porrō, quamquam in carcere inclūsus fuerat,
               ē manibus custōdum effugere potuit.

Quīntus: sānē iuvenis magnae calliditātis est.

Rūfus: et obstinātus. Vercobrix putat sē Caratacum alterum esse,
               imperātōrem Britannicum summae audāciae. nam bellam
               ōrātiōnem habēre Britannōsque incitāre potest. prīnceps tamen
               fīliō imperāvit ut arma dēpōneret.

Quīntus: ēheu! contentiōnēs cum parentibus habēre solent līberī.

Rūfus: vērum dīcis. nunc autem propter mortem Togidubnī dē pāce
               inter Britannōs et Rōmānōs anxius sum.

Quīntus: nōlī dēspērāre! hostibus nōn facile est nōs superāre. praetereā
               rēgīna Catia, quae rēgnum Togidubnī nunc possidet, est fēmina
               summae fideī.

Rūfus: mī amīce, esne ignārus fortūnae Catiae?

Quīntus: tē ōrō, Rūfe. dīc mihi: quid novī?

Rūfus amīcō dīxit Vitelliānum in aulā Togidubnī Catiam retinēre. Quīntus tam attonitus erat ut prīmō nihil dīcere posset. tandem tribūnum ōrāvit ut omnia explicāret. nam 'nōn crēdō,' inquit, 'Vitelliānum perfidum esse.' Rūfus magnā cum difficultāte Quīntō persuāsit ut sibi crēderet.

imperāvit: imperāre *order, command*
trēs diēs *for three days*
convalēsceret: convalēscere *get better, recover*
quārtō diē *on the fourth day*
valedīcere *say goodbye*
monuit: monēre *advise*
profectus *having set out*
dux *leader*

imperātōrem: imperātor *general, commander*
audāciae: audācia *boldness, audacity*
bellam: bellus *pretty*
ōrātiōnem habēre *make a speech*

ignārus *not knowing, unaware*

This small piece of leather made to look like a mouse, with markings representing fur and eyes, was found in a bag of leather scraps in an officer's residence at Vindolanda. It may have been a child's toy.

About the language 1: indirect commands

1 In Book 1, you met sentences like this:

'redīte!'   'pecūniam trāde!'
'Go back!'   *'Hand over the money!'*

In each example, an order or command is being given.
These examples are known as **direct commands**.

imperatives: page 199

2 In Stage 27, you have met sentences like this:

lēgātus mīlitibus imperāvit **ut redīrent**.
*The commander ordered his soldiers **that they should go back**.*

Or, in more natural English:

*The commander ordered his soldiers **to go back**.*

fūrēs mercātōrī imperāvērunt **ut pecūniam trāderet**.
*The thieves ordered the merchant **that he should hand over the money**.*

Or, in more natural English:

*The thieves ordered the merchant **to hand over the money**.*

In each of these examples, the command is not being given directly, but is being reported or referred to. These examples are known as **indirect commands**.

The verb in an indirect command in Latin is usually subjunctive.

imperfect and pluperfect subjunctive: page 198

3 Compare the following examples:

direct commands	*indirect commands*
'contendite!'	iuvenis amīcīs persuāsit ut contenderent.
'Hurry!'	*The young person persuaded their friends to hurry.*
'dā mihi aquam!'	captīvus custōdem ōrāvit ut aquam sibi daret.
'Give me water!'	*The prisoner begged the guard to give him water.*
'fuge!'	mē monuit ut fugerem.
'Run away!'	*She warned me to run away.*

4 Further examples of direct and indirect commands:

a 'tacē!'

b centuriō mihi imperāvit ut tacērem.

c ad templum venīte!

d sacerdōs nōs ōrābat ut ad templum venīrēmus.

e nēmō puellae persuādēre poterat ut fībulam trāderet.

f rēgīna iuvenibus imperāvit ut equum in āream dūcerent.

g vōs saepe monēbam ut Rōmānīs pārērētis.

h mīlitēs mercātōrem monuērunt ut ab oppidō celeriter discēderet.

Vercobrix

dum Quīntus miser sēcum cōgitat, Rūfus 'ecce Vercobrix!' clāmāvit.
'dux hostium vīcum intrat!'

    sine morā nōnnūllī mīlitēs, ā tribūnō missī, ad vīcum festīnāvērunt
Vercobrigemque quaerere coepērunt. multitūdō tamen in vīcō erat dēnsa.
tot hominēs pecudēsque per vīcum prōcēdēbant ut mīlitibus obstārent.   *5*

    intereā medium ad vīcum pervēnit Vercobrix. clāmor ubīque erat: fabrī
labōrantēs, puerī lūdentēs, agricolae cibum vēndentēs. tantus erat clāmor
ut tōtum vīcum complēret.

    ūnum ex agricolīs iuvenis rogāvit in quā casā habitāret ferrārius.

    'ferrārius?' inquit agricola. 'quī Rōmānōs semper dēplōrat? haud procul   *10*
est. vōmerem meum frāctum nūper refēcit. adeō gaudēbam ut eī duōs
saccōs frūmentī grātīs darem.'

    in illā casā Vilbia sōla manēbat. subitō vōcem ignōtam audīvit.

    'ferrārius adest?'

    Vilbia, cum vōx esset ignōta, erat tam perterrita ut prīmō immōta   *15*
stāret. tandem cautē sē vertit Vercobrigemque vīdit. quī, priusquam Vilbia
exclāmāret, 'nōlī timēre!' inquit. 'amīcus sum.'

morā: mora *delay*

pecudēs: pecus *farm animal*

haud *not*
vōmerem: vōmer *ploughshare
(the blade of a plough)*
gaudēbam: gaudēre
be pleased, rejoice
saccōs: saccus *bag, sack*
ignōtam: ignōtus *unknown*
cum *since*

About the language 2: result clauses

1 In Stage 27, you have met sentences like this:

tanta erat multitūdō **ut tōtum vīcum complēret**.
*So great was the crowd **that it filled the whole settlement**.*

Quīntus tam attonitus erat **ut nihil dīcere posset**.
*Quintus was so astonished **that he was not able to say anything**.*

The groups of words in **bold** are known as **result clauses**, because they indicate a result.

The verb in a result clause in Latin is always subjunctive. ⎯⎯ **imperfect and pluperfect subjunctive**: page 198

2 Further examples:

  a tam longa erat fābula ut omnēs hospitēs obdormīrent.

  b tantus erat clāmor ut nēmō iussa centuriōnum audīret.

  c Agricola tot mīlitēs ēmīsit ut hostēs fugerent.

  d centuriōnem adeō timēbam ut ad castra redīre nōn audērem.

  e tot amīcōs habēbās ut eōs numerāre nōn possēs.

  f medicae tam dīligenter labōrābant ut eās saepe laudārēmus.

Notice that in the first part of each sentence there is a word that signals that a result clause is coming. For example, study the first sentence in paragraph 1. **tanta**, *so great*, is a signal for the result clause **ut tōtum vīcum complēret**.

In sentences **d–f** in paragraph 2, what are the signal words? What do they mean?

Vilbia Vercobrigem excipit

I

Vercobrigem, casam ingressum, Vilbia rogāvit unde vēnisset, quid quaereret, num mīlitēs per vīcum ruentēs vīdisset. quī, cum vērum patefacere nōn timēret, eī hoc respōnsum dedit.

'vah! quālēs sunt hī Rōmānī? scīsne? pācis Britannicae neglegēntēs sunt, mōrum Britannōrum ignārī. tanta erat arrogantia eōrum ut lūcōs sacrōs dēlērent Druidāsque caederent. ōdī Rōmānōs. cum cōpiae Boudicae urbī Londiniō appropinquārent, Rōmānī adeō crūdēlēs erant ut fēminās ac līberōs sine praesidiō relinquerent. quanta fuit clādēs? tōta urbs ardēbat. patrem meum incitāvī ut exercitum Rōmānum opprimeret. ego, Vercobrix, legiōnēs in mare pellere velim.'

iuvenis, haec locūtus, tacuit; Vilbia tam permōta erat ut quoque tacēret. subitō vōcem Aventīnae extrā casam audīvērunt. Vilbia statim surrēxit ut amitam acciperet; Vercobrix ē cōnspectū in angulō casae sē cēlāvit. tum intrāvērunt nōn sōlum Aventīna sed etiam Quīntus. ubi Vilbia, Quīntum cōnspicāta, pallēscēbat, Aventīna attonita

'mea lūx!' inquit. 'num Quīntum nostrum timēs?'

'minimē, amita!' eī respondit puella. 'pallida sum … quod nōn cēnāvī. id parvī mōmentī est. quid quaeritis?'

'iuvenis quīdam in vīcō latet,' inquit Quīntus. 'duās hōrās mīlitēs eum quaerunt.'

Vilbia, pallidior quam anteā, 'Vercobrigem haud vīdī,' dīxit. 'sōla patrem exspectō.'

Aventīna, falsum suspicāta, puellam rogāvit num vērum dīceret. sed priusquam plūra dīcere posset Vilbia, Vercobrix ē tenebrīs prōsiluit, pugiōnem vibrāns.

excipit: excipere *take in, receive*

5

vah! *ugh!*
mōrum: mōs *custom, practice*
lūcōs: lūcus *grove, small wood*
Druidās: Druidae *Druids*

pellere *drive*

10

cōnspectū: cōnspectus *sight, view*

15

pallida *pale*
mōmentī: mōmentum *importance*

20

tenebrīs: tenebrae *darkness*

25

While some aspects of metalworking have changed significantly since the first century AD, blacksmiths like Vilbia's father would recognise many of the tools and techniques used today. The image on the right is the grave marker of a Roman blacksmith. It shows his forge hearth on the left and the blacksmith himself on the right, gripping a heated piece of metal in a set of tongs and using a hammer to shape it on his anvil. The modern metalworker (left) is employing a similar set of tools to create a horseshoe.

II

Quīntus, simulac pugiōnem vīdit, 'cavēte, omnēs!' clāmāvit. 'perfidus est hīc iuvenis!'

Vercobrix, ā Quīntō valdē vexātus,

'prō certō habēs mē perfidum esse?' inquit. 'nūllī perfidiōrēs sunt quam Rōmānī ipsī!' 5

'iuvenis magnae fortitūdinis es,' Vercobrigī respondit Quīntus, 'sed parvae prūdentiae. lēgātus plūrēs mīlitēs mīsit ut portās castrōrum custōdīrent. cēterīs imperāvit ut diem noctemque hostēs cavērent. mihi crēde: nūlla spēs manet.'

cum Vercobrix cōnsisteret, Vilbia 'cūr tū perstās in eādem sententiā?' 10
inquit. 'Quīntus Caecilius est vir summae fideī virtūtisque.'

'cum istum audīrem,' respondit iuvenis, 'adeō saeviēbam ut vix mē continēre possem.'

haec ubi dīxit Vercobrix, Aventīna respondit permōta,

'satis! satis fraudum! satis īnsidiārum! et Dumnorix et Togidubnus mortuī 15
sunt. Vercobrix, volō tē hanc īram dēpōnere. nimium mortis iam vīdimus.'

Quīntus tamen, quī Rūfī vōcem extrā casam audīverat, ad Vercobrigem versus,

'mē hūc secūtus, tribūnus mīlitum adest!' inquit susurrāns. 'tibi tūtius est pugiōnem remittere quam frūstrā resistere!' 20

simulac iuvenis ad iānuam casae sē vertit, Quīntus prōsiluit ut pugiōnem Vercobrigis raperet.

cum Quīntus pugiōnem tenēret, Vilbia sollicita,

'clēmēns estō!' clāmāvit. 'victōribus decōrum est victīs parcere!'

'verba inānia dīcis,' respondit Vercobrix. 'nōtī sunt mihi hī Rōmānī. nōn 25
sōlum Regnēnsēs sed etiam cēterās gentēs Britannicās dēvorāre cupiunt.'

Quīntus, cum haec audīvisset, haesitāvit. multa dē Togidubnō ac Dumnorige in animō volvēbat. ita Vercobrix, ē manibus Quīntī ēlāpsus, per fenestram casae fūgit praeceps.

 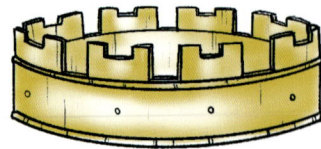

postrīdiē Quīntus tribūnō dīxit Aventīnam ad vīllam in oppidō Aquīs Sūlis 30
redīre, et Vilbiam cum patre ad oppidum Eborācum iter facere.

tum Rūfus amīcum rogāvit num ad Aegyptum aut Ītaliam redīre cōnstituisset.

'Rōmam īre dēbeō,' respondit Quīntus, 'ubi Lūcia apud familiārēs manet.'

perstās: perstāre *persist, stand firm*
eādem *the same*

continēre *contain*

et ... et *both ... and*

clēmēns estō! *be merciful!*
victīs: victī *the conquered*
parcere *spare*

haesitāvit: haesitāre *hesitate*

fenestram *window*

Eborācum *York*

Explore further

Think about the different ways the characters react in this tense situation, and the arguments they put forward for their own behaviour or opinions.

Now think about Quintus' reaction in lines 27–28: **Quīntus, cum haec audīvisset, haesitāvit. multa dē Togidubnō ac Dumnorige in animō volvēbat**.

Which arguments do you think have influenced Quintus' actions here?

Building words: adjectives and nouns

1 Study the form and meaning of the following adjectives and nouns:

adjectives		nouns	
longus, -a	*long*	longitūdō	*length*
sollicitus, -a	*worried*	sollicitūdō	*worry, anxiety*
altus, -a	*deep*	altitūdō	*depth*

2 Now work out the words that are missing from this table:

sōlus, -a	*alone, lonely*	sōlitūdō	. . . .
magnus, -a	. . . .	magnitūdō	. . . .
lātus, -a	*wide*	. . . .	. . . .
mānsuētus, -a	*tame*	mānsuētūdō	. . . .
fortis	*brave*	. . . .	. . . .
pulcher, pulchra	. . . .	pulchritūdō	. . . .
multus, multa	*much*	multitūdō	. . . .

3 Many of the nouns in paragraphs 1–2 can be translated by an English word ending in *-tude*. Where you have not done so already, and using an English dictionary to help you if you want, give an English meaning ending in *-tude* where one exists for these words.

4 Notice some slightly different examples:

cupere	*to desire*	cupīdō	*desire*
		Cupīdō	*Cupid, the god of desire*
valēre	*to be well*	valētūdō	*health*
			(1) *good health*
			(2) *bad health*

The imperative of **valēre** has a special meaning which you have met before:

valē *be well*, i.e. *farewell, goodbye*

Practising the language

Vilbia

Newly settled in York, Vilbia makes a decisive break with the past.

Vilbia, ex oppidō Eborācō ēgressa, per arborēs contendit ut amīcīs obviam īret. locum sēcrētum in rīpā flūminis nōverat ubi amīcae convenīre solēbant. ibi sōla manēbat, dum cēterae venīrent. et vōtum argenteum tenēbat, quod pater eius ē fibulā Belimicī fēcerat.

subitō Vilbia audīvit tubam sonantem. simul vīdit agmen longum 5
per portam castrōrum lentē prōcēdere.

'ēheu!' sibi dīxit puella. 'Ebōrācum, sīcut Dēva, est plēnum mīlitum.'

haec cum dīxisset, ūnam ex amīcīs cōnspexit accurrentem.
quae, priusquam Vilbia surgere posset, 10

'audīvistīne nūntium?' inquit. 'aliī dīcunt senātōrem Rōmānum ā Britannīs pecūniam extorquēre. nōnnūllī prīncipēs, ā senātōre adductī, eī auxilium dant. prīmus inter eōs est prīnceps Cantiacus, vir ingeniī malī et summae avāritiae.'

dum amīca haec dīcit, Vilbia surrēxit. vōtum argenteum tenēns, 15
manūs ad caelum sustulit ut auxilium ā deō peteret. amīca attonita Vilbiam rogāvit quid faceret. quae autem, Belimicum dētestāta, vōtum in flūmen, quod erat altum et lātum, iniēcit.

sēcrētum: sēcrētus *secret*
vōtum *votive offering*

extorquēre *extort*
adductī: addūcere *lead (on),*
urge (on)
avāritiae: avāritia *greed*

---

1 Explore the story

a **Vilbia, ex oppidō Eborācō ēgressa, per arborēs contendit ut amīcīs obviam īret** (lines 1–2): whom had Vilbia been hurrying to meet?

b Look at lines 2–3: **locum sēcrētum ... dum cēterae venīrent**.

  i Where was the secret location that Vilbia knew about for the gathering?

  ii What did Vilbia then wait on her own for?

c **et vōtum argenteum tenēbat, quod pater eius ē fibulā Belimicī fēcerat** (lines 3–4): what had Vilbia's father made her silver votive offering from?

d Look at lines 5–6: **subitō Vilbia ... lentē prōcēdere**.

  i What did Vilbia hear all of a sudden?

  ii What did she see at the same time through the camp gate?

e **haec cum dīxisset, ūnam ex amīcīs cōnspexit accurrentem** (line 9): what did Vilbia then see?

f Look at lines 10–12: **quae, priusquam Vilbia ... pecūniam extorquēre**.

  i What question was Vilbia asked before she had time to get up?

  ii What were some people saying was happening to the Britons?

g Look at lines 12–14: **nōnnūllī prīncipēs … summae avāritiae**.

    i Who was being helped by a number of chieftains?

    ii Who was the leading chieftain among them?

    iii What are we told about this chieftain?

h Look at lines 15–16: **dum amīca haec dīcit … ā deō peteret**.

    i What did Vilbia do while her friend was talking?

    ii Why did she raise her hands towards the sky?

i **amīca attonita Vilbiam rogāvit quid faceret** (lines 16–17): what did Vilbia's friend ask her?

j **quae autem, Belimicum dētestāta, vōtum in flūmen, quod erat altum et lātum, iniēcit** (lines 17–18): what did Vilbia do before throwing the votive offering into the river?

2 Explore the language

In this story, Vilbia does not say much about how she is feeling. Instead, her emotions are shown through her actions.

Read through the story again carefully, thinking about what she is doing. How do you think she is feeling at the following points in the story?

a When she is waiting for her friends (lines 3–4).

b When she is looking at the column of soldiers (lines 7–8).

c When she reacts to her friend's news (lines 15–18).

3 Explore further

Sometimes all that survives of a person from the ancient world is a tiny clue about their life, a tool, a ring, a votive offering. More often, there is nothing at all. Written evidence is often very limited indeed, but it can give us much more information about people's opinions and feelings.

Think about the different characters you have met in this book. Which characters are most likely to have their opinions and thoughts recorded? Which characters are most likely to be missing from any written records?

A small silver plaque (about 14.5 cm, or nearly 6 inches) dedicated to the goddess Senuna by a man named Servandus Hispani. It was found near Baldock in Hertfordshire.

Reviewing the language Stage 27: page 221

Towns in Britannia

During the Roman occupation of Britain many settlements were founded, grew, disappeared or otherwise changed. Many factors influenced what these places were like including: who was in charge; if it was formally planned or allowed to develop gradually over time; and whether the area was mainly used for military, farming or industrial activities. Some important Roman settlements developed in places where the Britons had already built thriving communities.

For all the Romans talk about the importance and civilised nature of their towns, living as a community in a large, well-organised settlement was not a Roman innovation. For example, the large town they call Calleva Atrebatum was important to the Atrebates tribe long before the Romans arrived. The buildings may have looked very different, but the settlement created by the Britons was almost as big as the later Roman one. It had defences in case it was attacked, and the buildings were organised into a street plan. This town was a crucial part of a trading network that stretched not only across southern Britain but across the sea to Gaul and further south to the Mediterranean.

Location of some Roman towns which were also major settlements during the late Iron Age.

Reconstruction of the late Iron Age town at Silchester.

Roman towns were assigned a category which had implications for things such as taxes and how they were run. A colonia (town created to house retired soldiers) had an almost entirely Roman population, while a **mūnicipium** often had more of a mix of Roman citizens and non-Romans. Both, however, were obliged to recognise and follow Roman law. The settlements known as **cīvitātēs** had a role in local government and administration but were not 'official' Roman towns, and therefore could apply more local customs and laws. A town's status often changed over time as it developed.

Roman Silchester (Calleva Atrebatum) as it may have looked in the third century AD.

Thinking point 1: The best (indeed sometimes the only) way to find out what towns and their surrounding areas were like is to use archaeological evidence. Many Roman towns are still settlements today (for example, London, St Albans and York). Why might this make studying them particularly difficult?

Towns also often grow up around Roman forts and fortresses. Soldiers get regular wages and often have more money to spend than most ordinary people. A large community of soldiers also creates demand for a variety of goods and services. To take advantage of this people build shops, houses and workshops close to the forts and fortresses. The fortress here at Deva provides some excellent business opportunities, especially as it has a good harbour. I'm sure merchants can always find a buyer for the goods they import.

Roman Britain's second largest town was Corinium Dobunnorum (modern Cirencester). Unlike in Calleva, no town existed in this location before the Roman invasion, but the ruler of the Dobunni tribe was probably based at a settlement nearby. The Romans set up a fort to guard an important road junction, and within a decade a trading centre had developed to the northwest. The population living in the original Dobunni settlement shrank as the one near the fort grew, eventually disappearing altogether.

When Roman troops left the fort in about AD 70, Corinium was chosen as the administrative base for the area. A new grid of streets was built on top of the fort and the settlement around it. The town was in an excellent position on the road network and had well-established industries because of its relationship with the fort. Trade with soldiers was easily replaced by trade from farther afield. Corinium remained an important centre for trade and local government for over three centuries.

Thinking point 2: Look at the map on page x in the introduction to the book. Which roads met in Corinium? Why was this junction important?

Thinking point 3: What factors influenced Corinium Dobunnorum's development into an important Roman town?

Part of the wall which surrounded Corinium Dobunnorum. This was over 3 kilometres (2 miles) long and enclosed an area of 97 hectares (240 acres; one hectare is about the size of an international rugby pitch).

This very fine bowl decorated with vines and leaves was found in Cirencester (Roman Corinium Dobunnorum). This kind of pottery was very expensive and mainly made in Gaul.

Life in and around Deva

Living close to a fort like Deva means a steady supply of work. The army has its own smiths and crafters, but there are plenty of jobs to go around. Sometimes soldiers will bring me their equipment to repair or recycle into something else. Craftspeople and traders around here rely on the army for much of their income.

There is relatively little evidence for what life was like in the community surrounding Deva, but there is more from other, similar settlements. In about AD 71 a Roman fortress was established at Eboracum (York) in the north of England. Archaeological evidence shows that by the second century AD Eboracum, like Deva, was surrounded by a thriving settlement with a great deal of industry and crafting. This included iron smithing, copperwork and leatherworking, all of which would have been important to the military.

Many off-cuts of leather and pieces of shoes have been found in York, some stamped with their makers' marks.

This sword blade was possibly brought to a smith in the civilian settlement around Eboracum to be repaired or recycled.

This decorative tombstone of a blacksmith (found near York) shows how profitable metal work could be.

It was not only crafters, traders and workers who lived in these settlements; these communities were made up of whole households. People of all ages, genders and statuses – free and enslaved – lived in the shadow of the forts and fortresses, all making their own contributions to their community.

Technically, ordinary soldiers were not allowed to marry, but the evidence suggests that many had long-term, stable relationships and children who were recognised as their heirs. Rather than living in the forts and fortresses like those of officers, these families probably followed the soldiers on their postings and lived and worked in the nearby communities. When the soldier retired, he might choose to settle down with his family in one of these communities.

A lot of retired soldiers live around Deva. Unlike many other towns, Deva is still under direct military control, so it's a good choice if you want to be near your former comrades and like life to have a more military flavour.

This inscription was found in Caerleon in Wales, the site of the Roman fortress of Isca Silurum. It is a memorial for a soldier, set up by his wife:

'To the spirits of the departed; Julius Julianus, soldier of the Second Legion Augusta, of 18 years' service, aged 40, lies buried here; Amanda, his wife, was in charge of this work.'

Any large community needs a reliable supply of food to survive; especially one with a lot of hungry soldiers! Bread is essential, of course, so like all Roman towns we need access to bakers, the ability to mill flour and a reliable supply of grain.

Providing enough meat to feed the soldiers stationed here is a huge undertaking. Farms provide meat from ox, sheep, goats, pigs, chicken, ducks and geese, while hunting brings in wild game such as deer, boar, pheasant and swan. Preparing all this meat keeps the butchers busy, and I get work making and mending tools for them, the farmers and the hunters. The butchers also have a good relationship with the local leather tanners; once the meat is butchered the skins can be used to make leather.

 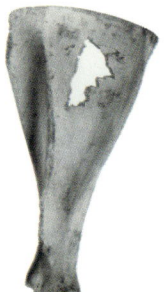 

By the late second century AD a butchery in Eboracum was processing meat on a huge scale. This iron meat cleaver was found in the same area as many bones from shoulders of beef, all with holes in roughly the same place. These holes were probably made so the meat could be hung up and smoked.

Thinking point 4: Why do you think meat was such an important part of a Roman soldier's diet?

Deva is on the coast, so seafood is easy to get and very popular; it's lucky I like oysters and mussels. You don't have to live near the sea to enjoy such things, though – the road and river network makes transporting food and other goods around Britannia very straightforward and reliable. Back in Aquae Sulis oysters and mussels were popular with customers and easy to get despite the town being inland.

Foods such as olives, grapes, wine and figs have to be imported from elsewhere in the empire, so they are always a bit more expensive and harder to come by. Such goods come into Deva's harbour on ships and fetch a good price. For some people they are a new luxury to try, for others they are a taste of home.

People in Eboracum ate a lot of brown crabs and Atlantic herring, probably caught about 50–65 kilometres (30–40 miles) away. Both are still caught in this area today.

Also imported were aspects of the Roman way of life. Buildings such as theatres, amphitheatres and bath houses were constructed in towns all over the empire, and Britain was no exception. In addition to the first century AD fortress baths you learned about in Stage 26, Eboracum had another bath house in the civilian settlement, built in the second or third century AD. In Deva, to the west of the fortress are the remains of what appears to have been a set of large, luxurious baths which were in use from the early second century AD.

The fortress and surrounding community at Deva also had access to the large amphitheatre. When it was built in about AD 70 it had a simple earthen bank as seating, but when it was re-modelled in about AD 100 it was made far grander, including wooden seating for at least 7000 people. There is also evidence of food and souvenir stalls around the outside.

Reconstruction of the amphitheatre at Deva.

The amphitheatre outside the fortress walls is used for military purposes such as parades and weapons demonstrations, but everyone needs a break sometimes and we Romans love a show. I have always enjoyed going to watch gladiator fights, and in Deva there is enough space for a big, lively audience. I can even buy myself a souvenir if I want, just like back home.

These archaeologists are working on a site in York which was part of a large cemetery on the outskirts of Eboracum, across the river from the legionary fortress. It has been suggested that the eighty men whose graves have been excavated might have been gladiators.

People living near the location of the first legionary fortress in Britain at Camulodunum (Colchester) could even enjoy one of the oldest and most popular Roman sports: chariot racing. Camulodunum was probably the first Roman town to be established in Britain and it became one of the largest and most important. It was founded in AD 49 on the site of an earlier, pre-Roman settlement, as a community for veterans. The circus (an arena for holding races) was probably built in around AD 100 and could hold between 12 500 and 15 000 people. It would also have been used for other spectator sports, including boxing and maybe gladiator fights.

Glass beakers decorated with scenes of chariot races are called circus-beakers. They may have been sold as souvenirs commemorating popular charioteers. This one was found in Colchester (Camulodunum).

> **Thinking point 5:** Why do you think it important to the Romans to make sure towns in the provinces had access to things such as baths, amphitheatres, circuses and theatres?

Enquiry: 'Deva's main importance was as a military base.' To what extent do you agree with this statement?

You may wish to consider the following:

- the various roles Deva played in the lives of different types of people
- Deva's location and resources
- the significance of Roman towns in maintaining Roman rule and spreading Roman culture
- the economic and social life of the community at Deva
- how Roman settlements developed, including those close to Roman military bases.

You may find information from previous Stages, especially Stage 26, to be useful in exploring this question.

What the circus at Colchester may have looked like.

Vocabulary checklist 27

adeō	*so much, so greatly*
animus, animī	*soul, spirit, mind*
arma, armōrum	*weapons, arms*
cōpiae, cōpiārum	*forces, troops*
exercitus, exercitūs	*army*
gaudeō, gaudēre	*be pleased, rejoice*
gēns, gentis	*family, tribe, race, people*
hostis, hostis	*enemy*
imperō, imperāre, imperāvī, imperātus	*order, command*
incendō, incendere, incendī, incēnsus	*burn, set on fire*
lātus, lāta, lātum	*wide*
opprimō, opprimere, oppressī, oppressus	*crush, overwhelm*
oppugnō, oppugnāre, oppugnāvī, oppugnātus	*attack*
ōrō, ōrāre, ōrāvī	*beg, beg for*
prīmō	*at first*
propter	*on account of, because of*
proximus, proxima, proximum	*nearest*
quālis, quāle	*what sort of*
tantus, tanta, tantum	*so great, such a great*
tot	*so many*

Very little is known of the numerous temples and shrines which undoubtedly existed in and around Deva. This shrine was set up in a Roman quarry. The carving is thought to be of Minerva.

post mortem Togidubnī, Salvius rēgnum eius occupāvit Catiamque expellāvit. pecūniam ā Britannīs extorquēre statim coepit. Salvium adiuvābat Belimicus, prīnceps Cantiacōrum.

prope aulam habitābat agricola Britannicus, quī Salviō pecūniam trādere nōluit. Salvius igitur mīlitibus imperāvit ut casam agricolae dīriperent. centuriō manum mīlitum ad casam dūxit.

1 mīlitēs, gladiīs hastīsque armātī, casam agricolae oppugnāvērunt.

2 agricola, gladiō centuriōnis vulnerātus, exanimātus dēcidit.

3 līberī, clāmōribus territī, fūgērunt.

4 uxor agricolae, fūste armāta, frūstrā restitit.

5 Belimicus, spē praemiī adductus, mīlitēs Rōmānōs adiuvābat et incitābat.

6 mīlitēs casam intrāvērunt et arcam, pecūniā complētam, abstulērunt.

7 deinde mīlitēs captīvōs, catēnīs vīnctōs, ad castra dūxērunt.

8 postrēmō mīlitēs casam incendērunt. flammae, ventō auctae, casam celeriter cōnsūmpsērunt.

9 pāstōrēs, quī prope casam habitābant, immōtī stābant, spectāculō attonitī.

casam vīdērunt, flammīs cōnsūmptam.

uxōrem agricolae vīdērunt, hastā graviter vulnerātam.

agricolam ipsum vīdērunt, gladiō centuriōnis interfectum.

tandem abiērunt, īrā commōtī, Belimicum Rōmānōsque vituperantēs.

testāmentum

ego, Tiberius Claudius Togidubnus, rēx magnus Britannōrum, morbō gravī
afflīctus, hoc testāmentum fēcī.

ego Titum Flāvium Domitiānum, optimum imperātōrum, hērēdem meum
faciō. mandō T. Flāviō Domitiānō rēgnum meum cīvēsque Rēgnēnsēs.
iubeō cīvēs Rēgnēnsēs lēgibus pārēre et vītam quiētam agere.

dō lēgō Cn. Iūliō Agricolae statuam meam, ā fabrō Britannicō factam.
sīc Agricola mē per tōtam vītam in memoriā habēre potest.

dō lēgō C. Salviō Līberālī, fidēlissimō amīcōrum meōrum, duōs tripodas
argenteōs. Salvius vir summae prūdentiae est.

dō lēgō L. Marciō Memorī vīllam splendidam prope Aquās Sūlis sitam.
L. Marcius Memor, ubi aeger ad thermās vēnī, ut auxilium ā deā Sūle
peterem, benignē mē excēpit.

dō lēgō Dumnorigī, prīncipī Rēgnēnsium, quem sīcut fīlium amāvī, mīlle
aureōs aulamque meam. sī forte Dumnorix mortuus est, haec C. Salviō
Līberālī lēgō.

dō lēgō Belimicō, prīncipī Cantiacōrum, quīngentōs aureōs et nāvem
celerrimam. Belimicus enim mē ab ursā ōlim servāvit, quae per aulam
meam saeviēbat.

mandō C. Salviō Līberālī cūram fūneris meī. volō Salvium corpus meum
sepelīre. volō eum mēcum sepelīre gemmās meās, paterās aureās, omnia
arma quae ad bellum vēnātiōnemque comparāvī.

mandō C. Salviō Līberālī hoc testāmentum, manū meā scrīptum
ānulōque meō signātum. dolus malus ab hōc testāmentō abestō!

5

lēgibus: lēx *law*
agere *lead*
sīc *thus, in this way*
in memoriā habēre
    keep in mind, remember

10

benignē *kindly*

mīlle *a thousand*

15

20

sepelīre *bury*
ad *for (the purpose of)*

dolus ... abestō!
    trickery, be gone!

in aulā Salviī

When you have read this story, answer the questions at the end.

Salvius, cum dē morte Togidubnī audīvisset, ē castrīs discessit. per prōvinciam iter fēcit ad aulam quam ē testāmentō accēperat. ibi novem diēs manēbat ut rēs Togidubnī administrāret. decimō diē, iterum profectus, pecūniam opēsque ā Britannīs extorquēre incēpit. nōnnūllī prīncipēs, avāritiā et metū corruptī, Salvium adiuvābant.   5

Belimicus, quamquam multa praemia honōrēsque ā Salviō accēpit, haudquāquam contentus erat. rēx enim Rēgnēnsium esse cupiēbat. hāc spē adductus, cum paucīs prīncipibus coniūrātiōnem facere coepit. quī tamen, Belimicō diffīsī, rem Salviō rettulērunt.

Salvius, audāciā Belimicī incēnsus, eum interficere cōnstituit. Rūfillae,   10
cui nōn cōnfīdēbat, nihil dīxit; illa in animō volvēbat num Catia moritūra esset. Salvius igitur Vitelliānum ad sē vocāvit; eum in tablīnum ingressum rogāvit quō modō mortem Belimicō īnferret.

'venēnum,' inquit fīlius, 'Belimicō, hostī īnfestō, aptissimum est.'

'sed quō modō tālem rem efficere possumus?' inquit Salvius. 'est nēmō   15
prūdentior Belimicō.'

'hunc homunculum dēcipere nōbīs facile est,' inquit ille. 'garum venēnō mixtum virōs callidiōrēs Belimicō fallere potest. et ignis omnia indicia sceleris cēlāre potest.'

'euge!' inquit Salvius, cōnsiliō fīliī dēlectātus. 'facillimum est mihi illum   20
ad cēnam sūmptuōsam invītāre. necesse est mihi epistulam blandam ad eum mittere. verbīs enim mollibus ac blandīs resistere nōn potest.'

Salvius igitur Belimicum ad aulam sine morā invītāvit. quī, epistulā mendācī dēceptus neque ūllam fraudem suspicātus, ad aulam nōnā hōrā vēnit.

decimō: decimus *tenth*

metū: metus *fear*

haudquāquam *not at all*

rettulērunt: referre *tell, report*
incēnsus *incensed, angered*

aptissimum: aptus *suitable*

prūdentior Belimicō *more sensible than Belimicus*

mixtum: miscēre *mix*
fallere *deceive*

blandam: blandus *flattering*
mollibus: mollis *soft*

neque *and not*
ūllam: ūllus *any*
nōnā: nōnus *ninth*

Questions

1   **Salvius, cum dē morte Togidubnī audīvisset, ē castrīs discessit** (line 1): where was Salvius when he heard of Togidubnus' death?

2   Look at lines 1–3: **per prōvinciam … Togidubnī administrāret**.

   a   To where did Salvius travel after hearing the news of Togidubnus' death?

   b   How long did Salvius stay there?

   c   Why did Salvius stay there?

3   Look at lines 3–5: **decimō diē … Salvium adiuvābant**.

   a   What did Salvius do after setting out again?

   b   Why did some of the chieftains help Salvius?

4   Look at lines 6–9: **Belimicus, quamquam … Salviō rettulērunt**.

    a   Why would Salvius have expected Belimicus already to be satisfied?

    b   Why did Belimicus start plotting?

    c   Who seemed to support Belimicus in his plot?

    d   How did Salvius find out about Belimicus' plot?

5   Look at lines 10–13: **Salvius, audāciā … Belimicō īnferret**.

    a   What decision did Salvius take when he heard of Belimicus' treachery?

    b   Who did Salvius not confide in?

    c   What question did Salvius put to his son?

6   **'venēnum,' inquit fīlius, 'Belimicō, hostī īnfestō, aptissimum est.'**
    (line 14): what was Vitellianus' advice?

7   **'sed quō modō tālem rem efficere possumus?' inquit Salvius. 'est nēmō
    prūdentior Belimicō.'** (lines 15–16): what problem did Salvius foresee in
    putting this advice into practice?

8   **'hunc homunculum … cēlāre potest.'** (lines 17–19): what details
    did Vitellianus add to the plan?

9   **'facillimum est mihi illum ad cēnam sūmptuōsam invītāre** (lines 20–21):
    what did Salvius say would be very easy to do?

10 Look at lines 21–22: **necesse est … nōn potest.'**

    a   How did Salvius say that he would lure Belimicus into his trap?

    b   Why was Salvius certain that he would succeed?

11 **Salvius igitur Belimicum ad aulam sine morā invītāvit** (line 23):
    which Latin phrase shows that Salvius put his plan in motion quickly?

12 **quī, epistulā … hōrā vēnit** (lines 23–24): what three details are we told
    that show that Belimicus fell into Salvius' trap?

An amphora that brought garum from Spain to Chester.

About the language 1: the ablative case

1   In Book I you met the ablative case used with prepositions in sentences like this:

Metella et Caecilius **cum multīs hospitibus** cēnābant.
*Metella and Caecilius were dining **with many guests**.*

2   In Stage 21, you met the ablative case used with perfect passive participles:

faber, **ab architectō** arcessītus, ad thermās festīnāvit.
*The craftsman, summoned **by the architect**, hurried to the baths.*

3   Study the following sentences:

Britannī, **iniūriā** incēnsī, cōnsilium cēpērunt.
*The Britons, angered **by the injustice**, made a plan.*

iuvenis, **gladiō** armātus, ad castra contendit.
*The young man, armed **with a sword**, hurried to the camp.*

rēgīna, **clāmōre** permōta, ex aulā discessit.
*The queen, disturbed **by the shout**, left the palace.*

arca, **aureīs** complēta, gravissima erat.
*The strongbox, filled **with gold coins**, was very heavy.*

cīvēs, **vōcibus** excitātī, ē lectīs surrexērunt.
*The citizens, awakened **by the voices**, rose from their beds.*

The words in **bold** are also in the ablative case, but there is no preposition before them in Latin. Notice the various ways of translating these words into English.

4   Compare the nominative singular with the ablative singular and ablative plural:

	nominative singular	*ablative singular*	*ablative plural*
first declension	puella	puellā	puellīs
second declension	amīcus	amīcō	amīcīs
	faber	fabrō	fabrīs
	templum	templō	templīs
third declension	mercātor	mercātōre	mercātōribus
	leō	leōne	leōnibus
	vōx	vōce	vōcibus
	nōmen	nōmine	nōminibus

5 Further examples:

    a Salvius, audāciā Belimicī attonitus, nihil dīxit.

    b mīlitēs, mūrō dēfēnsī, hostibus diū resistēbant.

    c mercātor ānulum, gemmīs ōrnātum, vēndidit.

    d spectātōrēs, arte āctōris dēlectātī, plausērunt.

6 From Stage 10 you have met sentences of this kind:

    comparatives: page 188

nēmō callidior est quam iste philosophus.
No one is cleverer than that philosopher.

canis meus maior est quam fēlēs tua.
My dog is bigger than your cat.

You have now met another way of expressing the same idea using the ablative case:

nēmō est prūdentior Belimicō.
No one is wiser than Belimicus.

aula mea est pulchrior vīllā tuā.
My palace is more beautiful than your house.

7 Further examples:

    a quis est īrātior Salviō?

    b nihil est melius amīcitiā.

    c nēmō sapientior tabernāriō in tōtō urbe erat.

    d dōnum pulchrius tuā ūrnā numquam vīdī.

This carving, found in Bo'ness in modern Scotland, shows a victorious Roman cavalryman and four naked, defeated Britons.

cēna Salviī

Belimicum aulam intrantem Salvius benignē excēpit et in trīclīnium
addūxit. ibi sōlī sūmptuōsē atque hilarē cēnābant. Belimicus, Salvium
rīdentem cōnspicātus vīnōque solūtus, audācter dīcere coepit:

'mī Salvī, multa et magna beneficia ā mē accēpistī. postquam effūgērunt
Quīntus et Dumnorix, ego sōlus tē adiūvī; multōs continuōs diēs eōs   5
persecūtus, Dumnorigem occīdī; multa falsa Agricolae dīxī ut Togidubnum
perfidiae damnārem. prō hīs tantīs beneficiīs praemium dignum rogō.'

Salvius, ubi haec audīvit, arrogantiā Belimicī incēnsus, īram tamen
cēlāvit et cōmiter respondit:

'praemium dignum iam tibi parāvī. sed cūr nihil cōnsūmis, mī amīce?   10
volō tē garum exquīsītissimum gustāre quod ex Hispāniā importāvī. serve!
fer mihi et Belimicō illud garum!'

cum servus garum ambōbus dedisset, Salvius ad hospitem versus,

'dīc mihi, Belimice,' inquit, 'quid prō hīs tantīs beneficiīs repetis?
es dīvitior cēterīs prīncipibus Britannicīs.'   15

'iam ē testāmentō Togidubnī,' respondit ille, 'quīngentōs aureōs accēpī.
id haudquāquam satis est. humilior Togidubnō sum? rēgnum ipsum repetō.'

quod cum audīvisset, Salvius 'ego,' inquit, 'nōn Togidubnus, aureōs tibi
dedī. cūr haud satis est?'

'quid dīcis?' exclāmāvit Belimicus. 'hoc nōn intellegō.'   20

'illud testāmentum,' respondit Salvius, 'est falsum. nōn Togidubnus sed
ego scrīpsī.'

sūmptuōsē *lavishly*
atque *and*
hilarē *in high spirits*
solūtus *relaxed*
audācter *boldly*
continuōs: continuus
   continuous, on end
damnārem: damnāre
   condemn
prō *in return for*
īram: īra *anger*
exquīsītissimum: exquīsītus
   special
Hispāniā: Hispānia *Spain*

repetis: repetere *claim*

About the language 2: expressions of time

1 Study the following examples:

lēgātus sermōnem cum Quīntō **duās hōrās** habēbat.
*The commander talked with Quintus **for two hours**.*

quattuor diēs fugitīvus in silvā latēbat.
***For four days**, the fugitive was lying hidden in the wood.*

In these sentences, the words in **bold** indicate how long something went on;
for this, Latin uses the **accusative case**.

2 Now study the following:

tertiā hōrā nūntiī advēnērunt.
***At the third hour**, the messengers arrived.*

decimō diē Agricola pugnāre cōnstituit.
***On the tenth day**, Agricola decided to fight.*

In these sentences, the words in **bold** indicate when something happened;
for this, Latin uses the **ablative case**.

3 Further examples:

   a   hospitēs trēs hōrās cēnābant.

   b   quartō diē revēnit rēx.

   c   Agricola prōvinciam septem annōs administrāvit.

   d   secundā hōrā hostēs castra oppugnāvērunt.

   e   mediā nocte rēgīna cōnsilium cēpit.

   f   sex diēs nāvigābāmus; septimō diē ad portum advēnimus.

Reviewing the language Stage 28: page 223

Belimicus rēx

Belimicus, cum haec audīvisset, adeō attonitus erat ut nihil respondēre posset. Salvius autem haec addidit rīdēns,

'mī amīce, cūr tam attonitus es? tū et Togidubnus semper inimīcī erātis. num quicquam ab illō spērāvistī? nōs autem in amīcitiā sumus. tibi multum dēbeō, ut dīxistī. itaque rēgem tē creāre in animō habeō. sed rēgnum quod tibi dēstinō multō maius est quam Togidubnī. heus! serve! plūs garī!'   5

servus, cui Salvius hoc imperāvit, statim exiit. brevī regressus, garum venēnō mixtum intulit atque in Belimicī pateram effūdit. tam laetus erat ille, ubi verba Salviī audīvit, ut garum cōnsūmeret, ignārus perīculī mortis.

'quantum est hoc rēgnum quod mihi prōmīsistī? ubi gentium est?'   10
rogāvit Belimicus.

Salvius cachinnāns 'multō maius est,' inquit, 'quam imperium Rōmānum.'

Belimicus, hīs verbīs permōtus,

'nimium bibistī, mī amīce,' inquit. 'nūllum rēgnum nōvī maius quam   15
imperium Rōmānum.'

'rēgnum est, quō omnēs tandem abeunt,' respondit Salvius. 'rēgnum est, unde nēmō redīre potest. Belimice, tē rēgem creō mortuōrum.'

Belimicus, metū mortis pallidus, surrēxit. haerēbat lingua in gutture;   20
tintinābant aurēs. ventrem, quī iam graviter dolēbat, prēnsāvit. metū īrāque commōtus exclāmāvit,

'tū mē laedere nōn audēs, quod omnia scelera tua Agricolae dēnūntiāre possum.'

'mē dēnūntiāre nōn potes, Belimice, quod nunc tibi imminet mors. nunc   25
tibi necesse est abīre in rēgnum tuum. avē atque valē, mī Belimice!'

Belimicus, venēnō excruciātus, magnum gemitum dedit et humī cecidit mortuus. servī corpus Belimicī ē trīclīniō extractum in hortō incendērunt. flammae, ventō auctae, corpus celerrimē cōnsūmpsērunt.

sīc Belimicus arrogantiae poenās dedit; sīc Salvius cēterīs prīncipibus   30
persuāsit ut in fidē manērent.

spērāvistī: spērāre
hope (for), expect
amīcitiā: amīcitia *friendship*
creāre *make, create*
dēstinō: dēstināre *intend*
effūdit: effundere *pour out*

ubi gentium est?
where in the world?

gutture: guttur *throat*
tintinābant: tintināre *ring*
aurēs: auris *ear*
ventrem: venter *stomach*
graviter dolēbat: graviter dolēre *be in extreme pain*
prēnsāvit: prēnsāre *clutch, take hold of*
dēnūntiāre *denounce, reveal*
avē *hello*
excruciātus: excruciāre *torture, torment*
auctae: augēre *increase*

Building words: adjectives and nouns

1 Study the form and meaning of the following adjectives and nouns:

adjective		noun	
avārus, -a	*greedy, miserly*	avāritia	*greed*
laetus, -a	*happy*	laetitia	*happiness*
perfidus, -a	*treacherous*	perfidia	*treachery*

2 Now work out the words that are missing from this table:

superbus, -a	*proud*	superbia	. . . .
trīstis	. . . .	trīstitia	. . . .
perītus, -a	. . . .	perītia	*skill, experience*
prūdēns	*shrewd, sensible*	prūdentia	. . . .
sapiēns	. . . .	. . . .	. . . .
ēlegāns	. . . .	ēlegantia	. . . .
. . . .	. . . .	audācia	. . . .
amīcus, -a	*friendly*	amīcitia	. . . .
arrogāns	*arrogant*	. . . .	. . . .
. . . .	. . . .	inimīcitia	. . . .
potēns	*powerful*	. . . .	. . . .
. . . .	. . . .	stultitia	. . . .

A skeleton reclining on a couch and pointing at the Greek motto 'know thyself'.

Enquiry: How accurate is it to describe Britain in the first century AD as 'Roman Britain'?

'Roman' culture and identity

Britannia was a Roman province for around 400 years, but that does not mean that everyone who lived and worked there during this time was 'Roman'. A relatively small number of people may have come from Rome itself; others came from Italy and other areas of the empire, some of which had been under Roman control for hundreds of years. Most people living in Britannia, however, would have lived their entire lives on the island, as many of their ancestors had done. Some would have had Roman citizenship, others would not. Some lived in official Roman towns, most did not.

Thinking point 1: Think back over the previous Stages in this book and back to Book II. Create a list of ways in which people in Britain supported or resisted the Romans.

There are probably countless people across the empire who think of themselves as Roman. Some enthusiastically adopt a Roman lifestyle, as they see it as sophisticated and civilised, a way to increase their influence and make connections. Whatever they may think, in my eyes few of these people will ever be truly Roman.
Other people hold on to their own traditions and lifestyles, but they are still affected by Roman culture or are under the direct control of the Roman state. If you have been conquered by Rome, you cannot escape its influence. Even those who have not been conquered cannot ignore us.

The individuals Salvius may have recognised as Romans would no doubt have been those who were at the top of the social hierarchy. They would have been granted citizenship, meaning they were able to vote, would have received property and business benefits and would have been protected by Roman law. In the first century AD, to be a Roman citizen you either had to be born as one, serve as an auxiliary soldier for twenty-five years, marry a citizen (if you were a woman) or have citizenship granted to you by the emperor. Many very rich individuals who were important in their own communities, perhaps even with roles in local government, would not have had citizenship or the rights that went with it.

Thinking point 2: Consider the characters in our stories. Which of them think of themselves as Roman? Who among them might have had citizenship?

The Romans seem to think that everyone from their new province of 'Britannia' is the same. They call us all 'Britons' and ignore the fact that we are not and never have been a single, unified people. Yes, there are those who are happy to see themselves as Roman subjects; some even abandon our traditions to embrace a more Roman way of life. But not me. If the choice is between calling myself a Briton or a Roman, I will settle for 'a Briton', but I am a proud member of the Deceangli first and foremost.

Roman culture was not totally new to everyone in Britain. Many people would have known of the Romans before the invasion, especially those who lived on the south coast and were engaged in trade with the Roman Empire. It is possible these people had more in common with people on the continent than they did with those who lived further inland in Britain.

Finds in a hilltop shrine in Hallaton, Leicestershire, suggest that the Britons and Romans had a relationship based on trade and diplomacy long before the Roman invasion. These finds include 350 Roman coins, the oldest of which is this one dating from 211 BC.

'It was in the interest of the Romans to encourage a sense of Roman identity across the empire. Tacitus tells us that Agricola supported the building of Roman-style temples, houses and fora; offered Roman education to upper-class Britons; supported the learning of Latin; and encouraged people to adopt elements of Roman culture such as dinner parties and use of public baths.

'In their ignorance they called this civilisation, but in fact it was part of their enslavement.'

(Tacitus, *Agricola* 21)

Thinking point 3: Why was it in the interest of the Romans to encourage adoption of Roman culture across the empire? Why might Tacitus describe this as a part of the 'enslavement' of the Britons?

Adopting Roman culture and customs might have been a good idea for someone who wanted power or wealth, but for people who could not afford to buy luxury goods or climb the social ladder 'being Roman' was probably not an important concern.

To be honest, I rarely have anything to do with the Romans, at least if I can help it. I live in a village in the countryside and rarely travel far from it. My parents taught me how to farm and look after my livestock. If I have any problems, I'll ask one of my neighbours for help. I have no interest in Roman fashions and politics. Now and then I make the journey to the market in the nearest town to get a good price for my sheep, and I see how things have changed. Sometimes I get paid in Roman coins, and I've noticed some wealthier people wearing new styles of clothing and jewellery. The closest I've got to embracing Roman fashions is buying a new type of cooking pot.

All over the empire, aspects of culture such as art and religion had common features which made them distinctly 'Roman', but they also reflected local customs, tastes and traditions. For example, sites which had religious importance to Iron Age Britons continued to be places of worship, but with new Roman-style temples and shrines.

> **Thinking point 4:** Think back to Stage 21. How does the evidence from Aquae Sulis illustrate the interaction between Roman and British customs and culture?

Throughout the Roman occupation of Britain rich and powerful people spent large amounts of money to surround themselves with Roman-influenced art and architecture, including the building of impressive villas.

This tombstone found in Colchester (Camulodonum) is that of Longinus, an auxiliary cavalryman from the area of modern Bulgaria. The carving portrays a Roman auxiliary riding over a cowering, naked figure of an enemy, perhaps a Briton. Longinus is a common Roman name.

This third-century AD mosaic was discovered in Rudston, East Yorkshire. In the centre is Venus winning the golden apple from Paris, a scene from Greco-Roman myth. Some elements, such as the Latin 'stage-names' given to the animals of the arena depicted around Venus, are more usually found in North African mosaics. The artistic style is also unusual, and perhaps distinctly British. Maybe a British mosaicist copied the design from a North African pattern book.

> **Thinking point 5:**
> In what ways does this tombstone suggest Longinus could be described as Roman? Can we infer anything about how he thought about himself? What might someone like Salvius have thought about him?

Fishbourne Palace is one of the most remarkable Roman-style buildings discovered in Britain. What Roman features did it have?

> **Thinking point 6:** What can you remember about the differences between Roman villas and traditional British houses? If you need help, look back at Stage 14 in Book II.

The remains of villas are very useful for inferring how 'Roman' different areas of Britain were. Unlike towns and fortresses, villas were not built by the state to help control the province, they were created by private individuals. These people might have lived their whole life in Britannia or have come from elsewhere in the empire. Perhaps they served in the army and chose to retire in the province, or maybe they came for business reasons. In most cases we have no way of knowing. Whatever their background and motivations, though, these people seem to have wanted to live like Romans.

> **Thinking point 7:** Far more people would have lived in small rural settlements than in or around Roman villas. Such communities have, however, not been studied as much as the villas. Why do you think this might be?

Conquest and control

The majority of villas found in Britain are in the south, particularly the southeast. By the time of Agricola's governorship, the Romans considered these areas to be securely under their control. The governors of Britannia under Vespasian were ordered to push north and west to bring the remaining parts of the island under Roman control. In these areas we find more forts and fortresses.

Remains of Roman villas found in Britain.

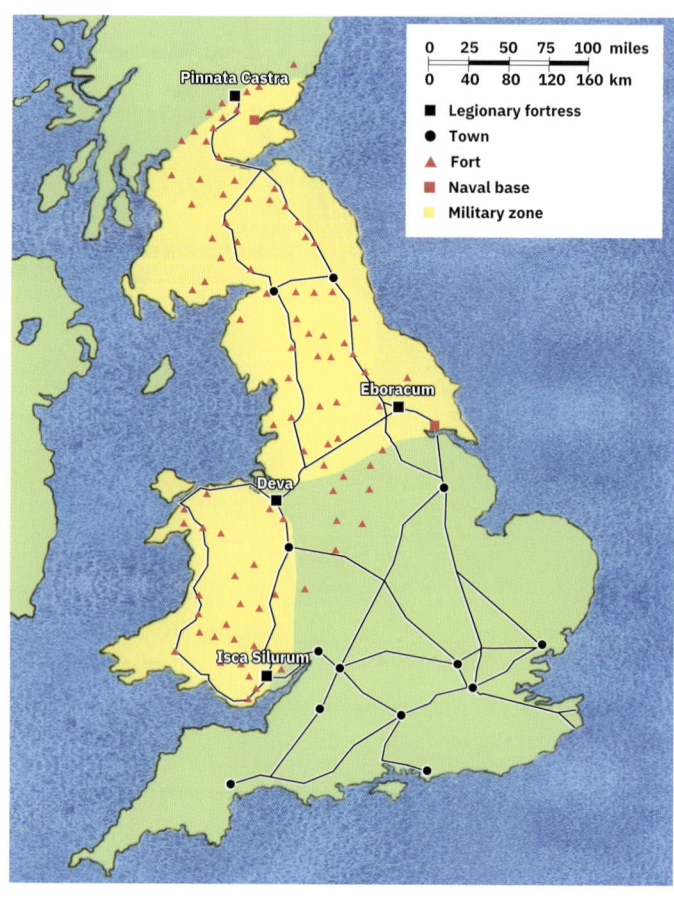

Britain AD 70–85. To support the army in their advance, fortresses were built at Eboracum (York), Isca Silurum (Caerleon), Deva (Chester) and Pinnata Castra (Inchtuthil). In addition, at least eighty new, smaller forts were constructed as well as over 3000 kilometres (over 1800 miles) of new roads.

Before they could be deployed to the north and west of Britain Roman troops had to be released from their duties in the southeast, where they had been used to enforce Roman rule. This meant the Romans needed other ways to keep control of the area. As in other provinces, Roman towns in Britannia became centres for administration and local government. Sometimes these were run by trusted 'client' leaders from the local tribes, for example the Dobunni in Corinium (see Stage 27).

> **Thinking point 8:**
> In Stage 24, you learned about the position of iuridicus, held by Salvius in our stories. What was the purpose of this role and why do you think Vespasian thought one was needed in Britannia?

The Roman plan to conquer the rest of Britain proved to be harder than they may have anticipated. The Silures tribe in what is now southeast Wales had long been a problem for the Romans. The British leader Caratacus encouraged them to violently resist the invasion in the early AD 40s, and while Caratacus was defeated in AD 51 (and then handed over to the Romans by Cartimandua of the Brigantes) the Silures fought on. Tacitus comments that while other tribes settled down once their leaders had been defeated or won over:

'… neither terror nor mercy had the least effect on the Silures; they persisted in war and could be quelled only by legions encamped in their country.'

(Tacitus, *Annals* 12.32)

Eventually the Silures were defeated in AD 74 and the fortress at Isca established in their territory. It was not until AD 78 that Agricola brought the rest of Wales under Roman control. The fortress at Deva became a crucial base for the ongoing military supervision of north and central Wales.

Two Roman towns were established in south Wales and a few villas sprang up nearby, but across much of the rest of the area people seem to have lived in the same settlements they had before the Romans arrived. This pattern can also be seen in the area of modern Cornwall and in the north of England. Even around Eboracum (York) and modern Newcastle, where there were more troops stationed than in any other area of Britain, it seems that rural communities remained relatively unchanged.

Dinas Dinlle hillfort on the northwest Welsh coast near the island of Mona. Finds including Roman coins, jewellery and pottery suggest that it remained occupied during the Roman period. This seems to have been the case for many Iron Age hillforts in Wales.

Thinking point 9: During the Roman occupation the population in the areas of modern Wales, Cornwall and northern England was very spread out and the landscape very rugged. How might these factors have affected the Roman influence on these regions?

Having defeated the British resistance in north Wales, Agricola advanced north and into modern Scotland. Tacitus tells us that in AD 83/84 he won a decisive battle at Mons Graupius. Tacitus depicts this as a last, futile attempt at resistance by the Britons which was crushed by Agricola, bringing his seven-year campaign to a victorious close:

'There were ten thousand enemy dead: on our side three hundred and sixty fell … The following day revealed the extent of the victory: all around was a silent wasteland, deserted hills, smoke was rising from distant houses, and the scouts encountered no one.'

(Tacitus, *Agricola* 38–39)

Thinking point 10: In this extract, how does Tacitus emphasise the magnitude of the Roman victory at Mons Graupius? Why might he have depicted it in this way?

Tacitus gives very few actual details about the battle and its location, despite writing about it at length. He does, however, give an account of a very long (and remarkably anti-Roman) speech given before the battle by the British leader Calgacus:

'Thieves of the world, when the Romans run out of lands to devastate, they ransack the sea. If their enemies are wealthy, they are greedy; if they are poor, they absorb them. Neither the east nor the west has been able to satisfy them. Alone among men they want to take both the rich and poor. Theft, slaughter and plunder they call empire: they make a desert and call it peace.'

(Tacitus, *Agricola* 30)

Interestingly, the only other source for Agricola's campaigns, Dio Cassius, does not mention this battle at all.

Even if Mons Graupius was the great victory that Tacitus claims, it was not the end of the campaign to control Scotland. Forts and roads needed to be built and armies moved into place to control the area. This region had no big settlements or major leaders like Togidubnus who could be used to spread Roman influence. Settlements were smaller and the people very spread out. There was also no history of contact with the Romans: no existing trade relationships or shared culture.

Usually, when they first occupied a region, the Romans stationed troops there and used them to suppress any opposition. Once all resistance was stamped out, a local government would be set up to keep control and the army could be moved to serve elsewhere. In northern Scotland this proved impossible. Many of the military posts established by Agricola were deserted, including the fortress at Inchtuthil which was abandoned before it was even finished. By the reign of Emperor Hadrian in AD 122 the Romans had fallen back even further.

A reconstruction of one of the biggest monumental arches in the Roman Empire, constructed at Rutupiae (Richborough) sometime between AD 85 and AD 150 to celebrate the conquest of Britannia.

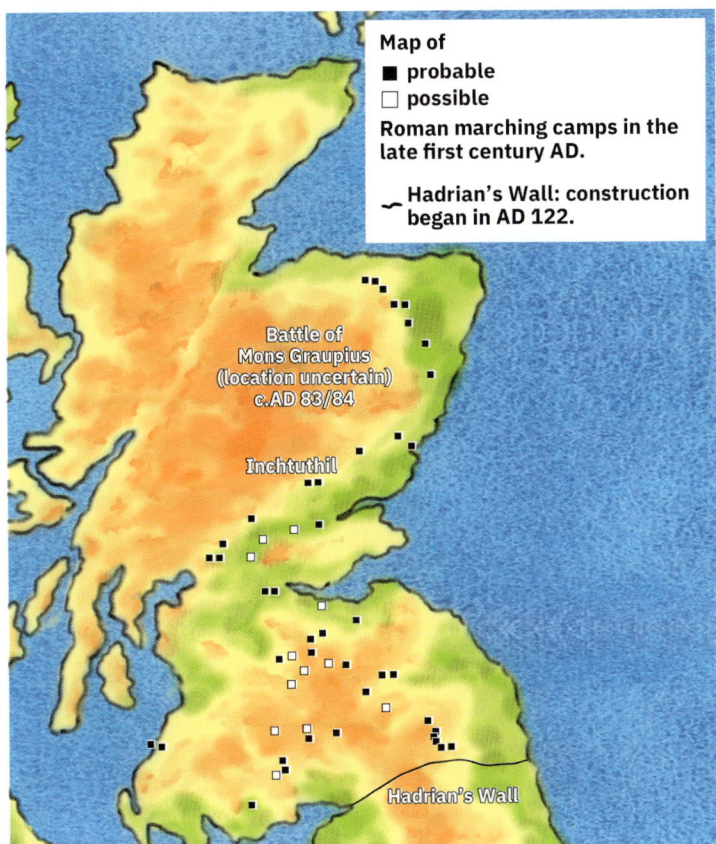

Map of
■ probable
□ possible
Roman marching camps in the late first century AD.

⌒ **Hadrian's Wall: construction began in AD 122.**

Battle of
Mons Graupius
(location uncertain)
c.AD 83/84

Inchtuthil

Hadrian's Wall

The Roman presence in Scotland.

While Rome may have held Britannia for hundreds of years, it remained a fringe province that required a military presence to keep it in line and protect its borders. In the early fifth century AD it ceased to be a Roman province at all. After this time Roman culture disappears from the archaeological record. This is unlike most other provinces, where there is far more continuity. People in these areas seem to have maintained elements of Roman culture. What happened in Britannia is unclear, but it seems that despite nearly 400 years of Roman occupation, the now independent Britons felt little need to keep any sense of Roman cultural identity.

Enquiry: How accurate is it to describe Britain in the first century AD as 'Roman Britain'?

You may wish to consider the following:

- how different people viewed Romanness and the Romans
- how the Romans thought about the Britons and how the Britons may have thought about themselves
- the spread of Roman culture and its interactions with other cultures
- regional differences in Britain
- the difficulties faced by the Romans in Britain.

You may find information from all previous Stages set in Britain to be useful in exploring this question.

Vocabulary checklist 28

ac, atque	and	ūnus	one
cōnstituō, cōnstituere, cōnstituī, cōnstitūtus	decide	duo	two
		trēs	three
corpus, corporis	body	quattuor	four
fidēs, fideī	loyalty, trustworthiness	quīnque	five
forte	by chance	sex	six
ignārus, ignāra, ignārum	not knowing, unaware	septem	seven
īra, īrae	anger	octō	eight
malus, mala, malum	evil, bad	novem	nine
metus, metūs	fear	decem	ten
multō, multum	much	vīgintī	twenty
occīdō, occīdere, occīdī, occīsus	kill	triginta	thirty
		quadrāgintā	forty
opēs, opum	money, wealth	quīnquāgintā	fifty
profectus, profecta, profectum	having set out	sexāgintā	sixty
		septuāgintā	seventy
quicquam (*also spelt* quidquam)	anything	octōgintā	eighty
		nōnāgintā	ninety
rēgnum, rēgnī	kingdom	centum	a hundred
scelus, sceleris	crime	mīlle	a thousand
sīc	thus, in this way	mīlia	thousands
spēs, spēī	hope		
ut	as		
victōria, victōriae	victory		

A replica of a carnyx (a trumpet shaped like a boar's head) found in Scotland. The original dated from between c.AD 80 and 250 and was made from bronze and recycled Roman brass. Tribes all over Europe used carnyces, but this example is typical of metalwork found in northeast Scotland.

Contents

Part One: About the language

Nouns

gender	*first declension* f.	*second declension* m.	m.	n.	*third declension* m.	m.
SINGULAR						
nominative and vocative	puella	amīcus (*voc.* amīce)	faber	templum	mercātor	leō
accusative	puellam	amīcum	fabrum	templum	mercātōrem	leōnem
genitive (of)	puellae	amīcī	fabrī	templī	mercātōris	leōnis
dative (to, for)	puellae	amīcō	fabrō	templō	mercātōrī	leōnī
ablative (by, with)	puellā	amīcō	fabrō	templō	mercātōre	leōne
PLURAL						
nominative and vocative	puellae	amīcī	fabrī	templa	mercātōrēs	leōnēs
accusative	puellās	amīcōs	fabrōs	templa	mercātōrēs	leōnēs
genitive (of)	puellārum	amīcōrum	fabrōrum	templōrum	mercātōrum	leōnum
dative (to, for)	puellīs	amīcīs	fabrīs	templīs	mercātōribus	leōnibus
ablative (by, with)	puellīs	amīcīs	fabrīs	templīs	mercātōribus	leōnibus

gender	*fourth declension* m.	n.	*fifth declension* m.	f.
SINGULAR				
nominative and vocative	manus	genū	diēs	rēs
accusative	manum	genū	diem	rem
genitive (of)	manūs	genūs	diēī	reī
dative (to, for)	manuī	genū	diēī	reī
ablative (by, with)	manū	genū	diē	rē
PLURAL				
nominative and vocative	manūs	genua	diēs	rēs
accusative	manūs	genua	diēs	rēs
genitive (of)	manuum	genuum	diērum	rērum
dative (to, for)	manibus	genibus	diēbus	rēbus
ablative (by, with)	manibus	genibus	diēbus	rēbus

m.f.	f.	f.	n.	gender
				SINGULAR
cīvis	vōx	urbs	nōmen	*nominative and vocative*
cīvem	vōcem	urbem	nōmen	*accusative*
cīvis	vōcis	urbis	nōminis	*genitive (of)*
cīvī	vōcī	urbī	nōminī	*dative (to, for)*
cīve	vōce	urbe	nōmine	*ablative (by, with)*
				PLURAL
cīvēs	vōcēs	urbēs	nōmina	*nominative and vocative*
cīvēs	vōcēs	urbēs	nōmina	*accusative*
cīvium	vōcum	urbium	nōminum	*genitive (of)*
cīvibus	vōcibus	urbibus	nōminibus	*dative (to, for)*
cīvibus	vōcibus	urbibus	nōminibus	*ablative (by, with)*

1   You have now met all the declensions and cases of the noun. For a summary of the ways in which the different cases are used, see **Uses of the cases** page 204.

2   Notice **manus** and **genū** belong to the fourth declension, and **diēs** and **rēs** to the fifth. Compare their endings with those of the other declensions. Notice especially the form and pronunciation of the genitive singular, nominative plural and accusative plural of **manus**.

3   With the help of the table opposite, find the Latin for the words in *italics* in the following sentences:

   a   Seven *days* had now passed.
   b   The priestess raised her *hand*.
   c   They discussed the *matter* secretly.

   d   The child's *knee* was painful.
   e   The man washed his *hands* and face.
   f   It was the sixth hour of the *day*.

4   Translate the following pairs of sentences. State the case, number (i.e. singular or plural), and declension of each noun in **bold**. Use the table of nouns to help you.

   a   fēminae **nōmina** Graeca habēbant.
       puella pauper erat, sed vītam contentam agēbat.
   b   magnus numerus **leōnum** ē silvā ruit.
       mātrōna **fabrum** iussit vīllam magnificam aedificāre.
   c   **amīcī**, ā mīlitibus ēlāpsī, ad portam cucurrērunt.
       Lūcia **frātrī** dōnum dare cōnstituit.
   d   **multitūdō** hominum viās urbis complēbat.
       cīvis, **ānulō** dēlectātus, mercātōrī grātiās ēgit.

Adjectives

1 The following adjectives belong to the first and second declensions:

SINGULAR	*masculine*	*feminine*	*neuter*	*masculine*	*feminine*	*neuter*
nominative and vocative	bonus (*voc.* bone)	bona	bonum	pulcher	pulchra	pulchrum
accusative	bonum	bonam	bonum	pulchrum	pulchram	pulchrum
genitive	bonī	bonae	bonī	pulchrī	pulchrae	pulchrī
dative	bonō	bonae	bonō	pulchrō	pulchrae	pulchrō
ablative	bonō	bonā	bonō	pulchrō	pulchrā	pulchrō

PLURAL						
nominative and vocative	bonī	bonae	bona	pulchrī	pulchrae	pulchra
accusative	bonōs	bonās	bona	pulchrōs	pulchrās	pulchra
genitive	bonōrum	bonārum	bonōrum	pulchrōrum	pulchrārum	pulchrōrum
dative	bonīs	bonīs	bonīs	pulchrīs	pulchrīs	pulchrīs
ablative	bonīs	bonīs	bonīs	pulchrīs	pulchrīs	pulchrīs

2 The following adjectives belong to the third declension:

SINGULAR	*masculine and feminine*	*neuter*	*masculine and feminine*	*neuter*
nominative and vocative	fortis	forte	ingēns	ingēns
accusative	fortem	forte	ingentem	ingēns
genitive	fortis	fortis	ingentis	ingentis
dative	fortī	fortī	ingentī	ingentī
ablative	fortī	fortī	ingentī *or* ingente	ingentī *or* ingente

PLURAL				
nominative and vocative	fortēs	fortia	ingentēs	ingentia
accusative	fortēs	fortia	ingentēs	ingentia
genitive	fortium	fortium	ingentium	ingentium
dative	fortibus	fortibus	ingentibus	ingentibus
ablative	fortibus	fortibus	ingentibus	ingentibus

3 Using paragraphs 1 and 2, find the Latin for the words in *italics* in the following sentences. Remember that adjectives agree with nouns in number, gender and case.

   a The *beautiful* temple stood in the forum.

   b This is the house of a *brave* woman.

   c The craftspeople built three *huge* temples.

   d They put up a statue to the *good* senator.

4 Translate the following sentences.

   a coquus cēnam ingentem celeriter coxit.

   b sacerdōtēs dīs immortālibus sacrificium obtulērunt.

   c amīcus nāvem mercātōris benignī vīdit.

   d fēminae sapientēs pecūniam cēlāvērunt.

   e medicus oculōs mīlitum aegrōrum īnspexit.

   f aedificium ingēns prope flūmen ēmit.

Pick out the noun and adjective pair in each sentence and state its number, gender and case.

Comparatives and superlatives

1   You have met the following comparative and superlative forms of the adjective:

nominative	*comparative*	*superlative*
longus	longior	longissimus
long	*longer*	*very long, longest*
pulcher	pulchrior	pulcherrimus
beautiful	*more beautiful*	*very beautiful, most beautiful*
fortis	fortior	fortissimus
brave	*braver*	*very brave, bravest*
fēlīx	fēlīcior	fēlīcissimus
lucky	*luckier*	*very lucky, luckiest*
prūdēns	prūdentior	prūdentissimus
sensible	*more sensible*	*very sensible, most sensible*

Notice the following example:

facilis	facilior	facillimus
easy	*easier*	*very easy, easiest*

2   Irregular forms:

bonus	melior	optimus
good	*better*	*very good, best*
malus	peior	pessimus
bad	*worse*	*very bad, worst*
magnus	maior	maximus
big	*bigger*	*very big, biggest*
parvus	minor	minimus
small	*smaller*	*very small, smallest*
multus	plūs	plūrimus
much	*more*	*very much, most*

which becomes in the plural:

multī	plūrēs	plūrimī
many	*more*	*very many, most*

3 Translate the following examples:

a 'nēmō fortior est quam Dumnorix,' inquit Quīntus.

b longissima erat pompa, pulcherrima quoque.

c peior es quam fūr!

d Salviī vīlla erat minor quam aula Togidubnī.

e facillimum erat nōbīs urbem capere.

f numquam tabernam meliōrem quam tuam vīsitāvī.

g Memor ad māiōrēs honōrēs ascendere volēbat.

h in mediō oppidō labōrābant plūrimī fabrī, quī templum maximum aedificābant.

4 You have also met another way of translating the superlative:

Rufē, prūdentissimus es omnium amīcōrum quod habeō.
Rufus, you are the shrewdest (or most sensible) of all the friends that I have.

The following examples can be translated in the same way:

a Togidubnus erat divitissimus omnium rēgum quī in Britanniā habitābat.

b omnēs mīlitēs meī sunt fortēs; tū tamen fortissimus es.

c postrēmō Athēnās vīsitāvimus, pulcherrimam omnium urbium.

5 For the use of comparatives with the ablative case, see **Uses of the cases** page 204.

Adverbs

1 Adverbs ending in **-ē** are connected with first and second declension adjectives.

adverb	adjective
laetē *happily*	laetus, laeta, laetum *happy*
pulchrē *beautifully*	pulcher, pulchra, pulchrum *beautiful*

2 Adverbs ending in **-ter** are connected with third declension adjectives.

adverb	adjective
fortiter *bravely*	fortis, fortis, forte *brave*
audācter *boldly*	audāx, audāx, audāx *bold*

3 The comparative form of adverbs is the same as the neuter nominative singular of comparative adjectives.

adverb	adjective
laetius *more happily*	laetior, laetior, laetius *happier*
fortius *more bravely*	fortior, fortior, fortius *braver*

4 The superlative form of adverbs ends in **-ē**.

adverb	adjective
laetissimē *very happily*	laetissimus, laetissima, laetissimum *very happy*
fortissimē *very bravely*	fortissimus, fortissima, fortissimum *very brave*

5 Irregular forms:

bene	melius	optimē
well	*better*	*best, very well*
male	peius	pessimē
badly	*worse*	*worst, very badly*
magnopere	magis	maximē
greatly	*more*	*most, very greatly*
paulum	minus	minimē
little	*less*	*least, very little*
multum	plūs	plūrimum
much	*more*	*most, very much*

6 Superlative forms (of both adjectives and adverbs) are sometimes used with **quam**, meaning '*as … as possible*'.

> quam celerrimē advēnit.
> *She arrived as quickly as possible.*

7 Translate the following examples.

a nēmō vīllās dīligentius custōdit quam tū.

b Vercobrix Rūfō breviter respondit.

c rēgīna tōtam īnsulam occupāre perfidē cupit.

d Belimicus maiōra praemia audācius postulābat.

e hīs iuvenibus quam minimē crēdere dēbēmus.

f fūrēs in cubiculum tacitē intrāvērunt, ē cubiculō timidē fūgērunt.

Pronouns I: ego, tū, nōs, vōs, sē

1   **ego** and **tū** (*I, you*, etc.)

	SINGULAR		PLURAL	
nominative	ego	tū	nōs	vōs
accusative	mē	tē	nōs	vōs
genitive	meī	tuī	nostrum	vestrum
dative	mihi	tibi	nōbīs	vōbīs
ablative	mē	tē	nōbīs	vōbīs

mēcum = *with me*　　　　**nōbīscum** = *with us*
tēcum = *with you* (singular)　　**vōbīscum** = *with you* (plural)

2   **sē** (*herself, himself, itself, themself, themselves*, etc.)

	SINGULAR	PLURAL
nominative	(no forms)	(no forms)
accusative	sē	sē
genitive	suī	suī
dative	sibi	sibi
ablative	sē	sē

sēcum (*with himself*, etc.) is formed like **mēcum**, **tēcum**, etc.
Notice some of the ways it can be translated:

> senātor multōs equitēs sēcum habēbat.
> *The senator had many horsemen with him.*

> Britannī arma sēcum ferēbant.
> *The Britons were bringing weapons with them.*

> rēgīna sēcum cōgitābat.
> *The queen was thinking with herself.*

Or, in more natural English:

> *The queen thought to herself.*

3   Translate the following sentences:

a   nōs, ā tē monitī, perīculum ēvītāvimus.
b   agricola, quod Rōmānī fundō appropinquābant, sē cēlāvit.
c   vīsne mēcum īre?
d   mātrōnae, quod diūtius manēre nōlēbant, domum sine vōbīs rediērunt.
e   Salvius, cum ad aulam prōcēderet, multōs amīcōs sēcum habēbat.
f   sorōrem rogāvī num stolās novās sibi comparāvisset.

Pronouns II: hic, ille, is, ipse

1 **hic** (*this, these*, etc.)

	SINGULAR			PLURAL		
	masculine	*feminine*	*neuter*	*masculine*	*feminine*	*neuter*
nominative	hic	haec	hoc	hī	hae	haec
accusative	hunc	hanc	hoc	hōs	hās	haec
genitive	huius	huius	huius	hōrum	hārum	hōrum
dative	huic	huic	huic	hīs	hīs	hīs
ablative	hōc	hāc	hōc	hīs	hīs	hīs

The various forms of **hic** can also be used to mean *he, she, it, they*, etc.:

> hic tamen nihil dīcere poterat.
> *He, however, could say nothing.*

2 **ille** (*that, those*, etc.; sometimes used with the meaning *he, she, it, they*, etc.)

	SINGULAR			PLURAL		
	masculine	*feminine*	*neuter*	*masculine*	*feminine*	*neuter*
nominative	ille	illa	illud	illī	illae	illa
accusative	illum	illam	illud	illōs	illās	illa
genitive	illīus	illīus	illīus	illōrum	illārum	illōrum
dative	illī	illī	illī	illīs	illīs	illīs
ablative	illō	illā	illō	illīs	illīs	illīs

3 **is** (*he, she, it, they*, etc.)

	SINGULAR			PLURAL		
	masculine	*feminine*	*neuter*	*masculine*	*feminine*	*neuter*
nominative	is	ea	id	eī	eae	ea
accusative	eum	eam	id	eōs	eās	ea
genitive	eius	eius	eius	eōrum	eārum	eōrum
dative	eī	eī	eī	eīs	eīs	eīs
ablative	eō	eā	eō	eīs	eīs	eīs

4 With the help of paragraphs 1–3, find the Latin for the words in *italics* in the following sentences. You may need to use the gender information in the table of nouns on pages 184–185.

a I have never seen *that* girl before.

b Guard *those* men!

c *These* lions are dangerous.

d I hate the noise of *this* city.

e We shall give the prize to *this* boy.

f We soon found *her*.

g Where are the merchants? I want to see *them*.

h Where is the temple? I want to see *it*.

i Where is the city? I want to see *it*.

j I hurried to *his* house.

5 **ipse** (meaning *myself, yourself, himself, themself* etc., depending on the word it is describing):

	SINGULAR			PLURAL		
	masculine	*feminine*	*neuter*	*masculine*	*feminine*	*neuter*
nominative	ipse	ipsa	ipsum	ipsī	ipsae	ipsa
accusative	ipsum	ipsam	ipsum	ipsōs	ipsās	ipsa
genitive	ipsīus	ipsīus	ipsīus	ipsōrum	ipsārum	ipsōrum
dative	ipsī	ipsī	ipsī	ipsīs	ipsīs	ipsīs
ablative	ipsō	ipsā	ipsō	ipsīs	ipsīs	ipsīs

domina **ipsa** lacrimābat.
*The mistress **herself** was weeping.*

fēmina mē **ipsum** accūsāvit.
*The woman accused me **myself**.*

amīcus imperātōris **ipsīus** pecūniam mihi prōmīsit.
*A friend of the emperor **himself** promised money to me.*

nōs **ipsī** latrōnem vīdimus.
*We **ourselves** saw the robber.*

Further examples:

a ego ipse pugnam vīdī.

b nōs ipsī in templō aderāmus.

c subitō rēgem ipsum audīvimus.

d dea ipsa mihi appāruit.

Pronouns III: quī

1 You have now met all the forms of the relative pronoun **quī**:

	SINGULAR			PLURAL		
	masculine	*feminine*	*neuter*	*masculine*	*feminine*	*neuter*
nominative	quī	quae	quod	quī	quae	quae
accusative	quem	quam	quod	quōs	quās	quae
genitive	cuius	cuius	cuius	quōrum	quārum	quōrum
dative	cui	cui	cui	quibus	quibus	quibus
ablative	quō	quā	quō	quibus	quibus	quibus

mātrōna cuius vīlla ardēbat vehementer clāmābat.
The lady whose house was on fire was shouting loudly.

duōs amīcōs habēbam, quōrum alter Graecus, alter Aegyptius erat.
I had two friends, one of whom was Greek, the other Egyptian.

mercātor cui togās vēndidistī hodiē revēnit.
The merchant to whom you sold the togas came back today.

nūntiī, quibus mandāta dedimus, herī discessērunt.
The messengers to whom we gave the instructions departed yesterday.

Further examples of the various forms of **quī**:

a mīlites quōs ēmīsit tandem rediērunt.
b iuvenis, cuius pater in Graeciā aberat, amīcōs ad cēnam sūmptuōsam invītāvit.
c prīnceps fēminās, quae iter longissimum fēcerant, amīcissimē salūtāvit.
d templum, quod in summō monte stābat, saepe vīsitābam.
e epistulam, quam nūntius tulerat, celeriter lēgī.

2 Sometimes the relative pronoun is used at the beginning of a sentence. Study the different ways of translating it:

> Salvius et fīlius īnsidiās Belimicō parāvērunt. **quī**, nihil suspicātus, ad aulam libenter vēnit.
> *Salvius and his son prepared a trap for Belimicus. **He**, having suspected nothing, came willingly to the palace.*

> canis pecūniam custōdiēbat. **quem** cum cōnspexissent, fūrēs fūgērunt.
> *A dog was guarding the money. When they had caught sight of **him** the thieves ran away.*

> Togidubnus 'grātiās vōbīs agō', inquit. **quod** cum dīxisset, cōnsēdit.
> *'Thank you', said Togidubnus. When he had said **this**, he sat down.*

In examples like these, the relative pronoun is said to be used as a **connecting relative**.

Further examples:

a 'cūr mihi nihil dās?' rogāvit fīlius. quod cum audīvisset, mater īrātissima erat.

b mercātor fēminīs pecūniam trādidit. quae, postquam dēnāriōs numerāvērunt, ad vīllam revēnērunt.

c deinde rēx Memorī signum dedit. quī, togam splendidam gerēns, ad āram sollemniter prōcessit.

d multī mīlitēs iam aulam complēbant. quōs cum vīdisset, Catia surrēxit.

Verbs

	first conjugation	*second conjugation*	*third conjugation*	*fourth conjugation*
PRESENT (INDICATIVE)	*I carry, you carry, etc.*	*I teach, you teach, etc.*	*I drag, you drag, etc.*	*I hear, you hear, etc.*
	portō	doceō	trahō	audiō
	portās	docēs	trahis	audīs
	portat	docet	trahit	audit
	portāmus	docēmus	trahimus	audīmus
	portātis	docētis	trahitis	audītis
	portant	docent	trahunt	audiunt
IMPERFECT (INDICATIVE)	*I was carrying*	*I was teaching*	*I was dragging*	*I was hearing*
	portābam	docēbam	trahēbam	audiēbam
	portābās	docēbās	trahēbās	audiēbās
	portābat	docēbat	trahēbat	audiēbat
	portābāmus	docēbāmus	trahēbāmus	audiēbāmus
	portābātis	docēbātis	trahēbātis	audiēbātis
	portābant	docēbant	trahēbant	audiēbant
PERFECT (INDICATIVE)	*I (have) carried*	*I (have) taught*	*I (have) dragged*	*I (have) heard*
	portāvī	docuī	trāxī	audīvī
	portāvistī	docuistī	trāxistī	audīvistī
	portāvit	docuit	trāxit	audīvit
	portāvimus	docuimus	trāximus	audīvimus
	portāvistis	docuistis	trāxistis	audīvistis
	portāvērunt	docuērunt	trāxērunt	audīvērunt
PLUPERFECT (INDICATIVE)	*I had carried*	*I had taught*	*I had dragged*	*I had heard*
	portāveram	docueram	trāxeram	audīveram
	portāverās	docuerās	trāxerās	audīverās
	portāverat	docuerat	trāxerat	audīverat
	portāverāmus	docuerāmus	trāxerāmus	audīverāmus
	portāverātis	docuerātis	trāxerātis	audīverātis
	portāverant	docuerant	trāxerant	audīverant

1 The word indicative is sometimes included in the names of these tenses to distinguish them from, for example, the imperfect subjunctive and pluperfect subjunctive.

2 In Stages 24 and 25, you met two tenses of the *subjunctive:*

IMPERFECT (SUBJUNCTIVE)	*first conjugation*	*second conjugation*	*third conjugation*	*fourth conjugation*
	portārem	docērem	traherem	audīrem
	portārēs	docērēs	traherēs	audīrēs
	portāret	docēret	traheret	audīret
	portārēmus	docērēmus	traherēmus	audīrēmus
	portārētis	docērētis	traherētis	audīrētis
	portārent	docērent	traherent	audīrent
PLUPERFECT (SUBJUNCTIVE)	portāvissem	docuissem	trāxissem	audīvissem
	portāvissēs	docuissēs	trāxissēs	audīvissēs
	portāvisset	docuisset	trāxisset	audīvisset
	portāvissēmus	docuissēmus	trāxissēmus	audīvissēmus
	portāvissētis	docuissētis	trāxissētis	audīvissētis
	portāvissent	docuissent	trāxissent	audīvissent

3 For ways of translating the subjunctive, see **Uses of the subjunctive** pages 207–209.

Infinitives, imperatives and participles

1 You have also met the following forms of the verb:

	first conjugation	*second conjugation*	*third conjugation*	*fourth conjugation*
INFINITIVE	*to carry* portāre	*to teach* docēre	*to drag* trahere	*to hear* audīre
IMPERATIVE *singular* *plural*	*carry!* portā portāte	*teach!* docē docēte	*drag!* trahe trahite	*hear!* audī audīte
PRESENT PARTICIPLE	*carrying* portāns	*teaching* docēns	*dragging* trahēns	*hearing* audiēns
PERFECT PASSIVE PARTICIPLE	*(having been) carried* portātus	*(having been) taught* doctus	*(having been) dragged* tractus	*(having been) heard* audītus

2 You have also met some examples of the **perfect active participle**:

    locūtus *having spoken*   secūtus *having followed*   ingressus *having entered*

These examples all come from a particular group of verbs.
The perfect active participle is the only part of these verbs that you have met so far.

3 For other forms of the present and perfect participles, and for examples of the ways in which they are used, see **Uses of the participle** pages 205–206.

4 The **imperative** is used to give a command.

    Togidubne! **audī** haec verba!   amici! **venīte** ad thermās!
    Togidubnus! **Hear** *these words!*   *Friends!* **Come** *to the baths!*

From Stage 19, you have seen the imperative used with the imperative form of the verb **nōlō** to tell people not to do something:

    puella, **nōlī currere**!   puellae, **nōlīte currere!**
    Girl, **don't run**!   *Girls,* **don't run**!

5 Throughout Books II and III, you have met the **infinitive** used with different verbs and phrases:

a with **volō**, **nōlō** and **possum**:

Vilbia **adiuvāre** vult.　　　　　　　Vercobrix custōdēs **dēcipere** poterat.
*Vilbia wants **to help**.*　　　　　　*Vercobrix was able **to deceive** the guards.*

b with a comparative adverb:

melius est Catiae **fugere**.
*It is better for Catia **to flee**.*

c with **decōrum** and **necesse**:

necesse est mihi Quīntum **adiuvāre**.　　decōrum est vōbīs epistulam **trādere**.
*It is necessary for me **to help** Quintus.*　　*It is right for you **to hand over** the letter.*

d with **iubeō**:

centuriō iubet mīlitem **dēsistere**.
*The centurion orders the soldier **to stop**.*

6 From Stage 24 onwards, you have met the infinitive used in **indirect statements**. Indirect statements are used to state the wish, thought or speech of a person without using quotation. They are expressed by a noun or pronoun in the accusative case and a verb in the infinitive form:

putō senātōrem appropinquāre.
I think that the senator is approaching.

(Compare this with the direct statement: 'senātor appropinquat.')

Rūfilla crēdit multōs Britannōs stultōs esse.
Rufilla believes many Britons are foolish.

(Compare this with the direct statement: 'multī Britannī stultī sunt.')

7 Further examples:

a putō poētam optimē recitāre.
b fīlia crēdit patrem in hortō sedēre.
c nūntius dīcit Agricolam mīlitēs in Calēdoniam dūcere.
d scīmus Aventīnam multās fābulās nārrāre.

8   The indirect statements in paragraphs 6 and 7 are each introduced by a verb in the *present* tense (e.g. **putō**, **crēdit**). Note how the indirect statements in paragraph 6 are translated if they are introduced by a verb in the perfect or imperfect tense.

> putāvī senātōrem appropinquāre.
> *I thought that the senator was approaching.*

> Rūfilla crēdidit multōs Britannōs stultōs esse.
> *Rufilla believed many Britons were foolish.*

9   Further examples:

a   Rūfus putābat amīcum trīstem esse.

b   audīvimus eam optimōs versūs scrībere.

c   scīvistīne Quīntum iter longissimum facere?

d   Vitelliānus dīxit rēgīnam prīncipēs ad aulam invītāre.

Irregular verbs

1 You have now met the following forms of six irregular verbs:

INFINITIVE	*to be*	*to be able*	*to want*	*to bring*	*to go*	*to take*
	esse	posse	velle	ferre	īre	capere
PRESENT (INDICATIVE)	*I am*	*I am able*	*I want*	*I bring*	*I go*	*I take*
	sum	possum	volō	ferō	eō	capiō
	es	potes	vīs	fers	īs	capis
	est	potest	vult	fert	it	capit
	sumus	possumus	volumus	ferimus	īmus	capimus
	estis	potestis	vultis	fertis	ītis	capitis
	sunt	possunt	volunt	ferunt	eunt	capiunt
IMPERFECT (INDICATIVE)	*I was*	*I was able*	*I was wanting*	*I was bringing*	*I was going*	*I was taking*
	eram	poteram	volēbam	ferēbam	ībam	capiēbam
	erās	poterās	volēbās	ferēbās	ībās	capiēbās
	erat	poterat	volēbat	ferēbat	ībat	capiēbat
	erāmus	poterāmus	volēbāmus	ferēbāmus	ībāmus	capiēbāmus
	erātis	poterātis	volēbātis	ferēbātis	ībātis	capiēbātis
	erant	poterant	volēbant	ferēbant	ībant	capiēbant
PERFECT (INDICATIVE)	*I have been, was*	*I have been, was able*	*I (have) wanted*	*I (have) brought*	*I (have) gone, went*	*I have taken, took*
	fuī	potuī	voluī	tulī	iī	cēpī
	fuistī	potuistī	voluistī	tulistī	iistī	cēpistī
	fuit	potuit	voluit	tulit	iit	cēpit
	fuimus	potuimus	voluimus	tulimus	iimus	cēpimus
	fuistis	potuistis	voluistis	tulistis	iistis	cēpistis
	fuērunt	potuērunt	voluērunt	tulērunt	iērunt	cēpērunt
PLUPERFECT (INDICATIVE)	*I had been*	*I had been able*	*I had wanted*	*I had brought*	*I had gone*	*I had taken*
	fueram	potueram	volueram	tuleram	ieram	cēperam
	fuerās	potuerās	voluerās	tulerās	ierās	cēperās
	fuerat	potuerat	voluerat	tulerat	ierat	cēperat
	fuerāmus	potuerāmus	voluerāmus	tulerāmus	ierāmus	cēperāmus
	fuerātis	potuerātis	voluerātis	tulerātis	ierātis	cēperātis
	fuerant	potuerant	voluerant	tulerant	ierant	cēperant

IMPERFECT SUBJUNCTIVE	essem	possem	vellem	ferrem	īrem	caperem
	essēs	possēs	vellēs	ferrēs	īrēs	caperēs
	esset	posset	vellet	ferret	īret	caperet
	essēmus	possēmus	vellēmus	ferrēmus	īrēmus	caperēmus
	essētis	possētis	vellētis	ferrētis	īrētis	caperētis
	essent	possent	vellent	ferrent	īrent	caperent

PLUPERFECT SUBJUNCTIVE	fuissem	potuissem	voluissem	tulissem	iissem	cēpissem
	fuissēs	potuissēs	voluissēs	tulissēs	iissēs	cēpissēs
	fuisset	potuisset	voluisset	tulisset	iisset	cēpisset
	fuissēmus	potuissēmus	voluissēmus	tulissēmus	iissēmus	cēpissēmus
	fuissētis	potuissētis	voluissētis	tulissētis	iissētis	cēpissētis
	fuissent	potuissent	voluissent	tulissent	iissent	cēpissent

2 Give the meaning of the following:

potes; vult; eō; it; fers.

posse; fuī; ībat; capiēbant; tulimus.

cēpistis; fuerāmus; iistis; potuerant; poterant.

3 **capiō** is one of a small group of verbs which belong to the third conjugation but behave in some ways like fourth conjugation verbs. Other common verbs in this group are **accipiō**, **fugiō** and **rapiō**.

Compare the infinitive of **capiō** with the infinitive of **trahō** (third conjugation) on page 199.

Compare the imperfect (indicative) tense of **capiō** with the imperfect (indicative) tense of **audiō** (fourth conjugation) on page 197.

Uses of the cases

1 *nominative*

    fīlius cantābat.   *The son was singing.*

2 *vocative*

    valē, **Quīnte**!   *Goodbye, Quintus!*

3 *accusative*

    a **pontem** trānsiimus.   *We crossed the bridge.*

    b **trēs hōrās** labōrābam.   *I was working for three hours.*

    c per **agrōs**; ad **vīllam**; in **forum**   *through the fields; to the house; into the forum*

4 *genitive*

    a māter **līberōrum**   *the mother of the children*

    b plūs **pecūniae**   *more money*

    c vir **maximae virtūtis**   *a man of very great courage*

5 *dative*

    a **mīlitibus** cibum dedimus.   *We gave food to the soldiers.*

    b **vestrō candidātō** nōn faveō. *I do not support your candidate.*

6 *ablative*

    a **spectāculō** attonitus   *astonished by the sight*

    b **gladiō** armātus   *armed with a sword*

    c **quārtō diē** revēnit.   *He came back on the fourth day.*

    d cum **amīcīs**; ab **urbe**; in **forō**   *with friends; away from the city; in the forum*

    e nēmō est fortior **Quīntō**.   *No one is braver than Quintus.*

7 Further examples of some of the uses listed above:

    a Salvius erat vir summae calliditātis.

    b multōs annōs ibi habitābam.

    c cūr mihi nōn crēdidistī?

    d satis cibī cōnsūmpsistī?

    e decimā hōrā ex oppidō contendimus.

    f prīnceps nōmina iuvenum commemorāvit.

    g Galatēa nōbīs fābulam dē morte Caesaris nārrāvit.

    h Catia, cūr cōnsiliīs meīs obstās?

    i Belimicus, verbīs Salviī dēceptus, cōnsēnsit.

    j uxor senātōris, in ātrium ingressa, statuās pictūrāsque laudāvit.

Uses of the participle

1 In Book II you met the *present participle*:

> parentēs fīliam **cantantem** audīvērunt.
> *The parents heard their daughter **singing**.*

2 In Stage 21 you met the *perfect passive participle*:

> fabrī, ā rēge **iussī**, celeriter rem cōnfēcērunt.
> *The craftspeople, **(having been) ordered** by the king, finished the job quickly.*

3 In Stage 22 you met the *perfect active participle*:

> caupōna, ē tabernā **ēgressa**, mercātōribus vīnum offerēbat.
> *The innkeeper, **having exited** the inn, was offering wine to the merchants.*

4 Translate the following examples. Pick out the participle in each sentence and say whether it is present, perfect passive or perfect active:

a agricolae, in fundō labōrantēs, fessī erant.

b Vilbia, ab Aventīnā iussa, cibum parāvit.

c fēmina, fūrem cōnspicāta, pecūniam celeriter cēlāvit.

d mīlitēs urbem captam incendērunt.

e Rūfus captīvōs, ē carcere ēgressōs, invenīre nōn poterat.

f Salvius in prīncipiīs stābat, saeviēns.

g mātrōna amīcās, ā Graeciā regressās, ad cēnam sūmptuōsam invītāvit.

A participle is used to describe a noun. For example, in sentence **a** above, **labōrantēs** (*working*) describes **agricolae**. Find the nouns described by the participles in sentences **b–g**.

5 A participle agrees with the noun it describes in three ways: case, number and gender.
For example:

nominative	**rēx**, in mediā turbā **sedēns**, dōna accipiēbat.
accusative	Quīntus **rēgem**, in mediā turbā **sedentem**, agnōvit.
singular	**lēgātus**, ad carcerem **regressus**, nēminem ibi invēnit.
plural	**custōdēs**, ad carcerem **regressī**, nēminem ibi invēnērunt.
masculine	**pater**, statim **prōfectus**, ad fundum contendit.
feminine	**māter**, statim **prōfecta**, ad fundum contendit.

6 You have met the following forms of the participles:

a *present participle*. For example: **trahēns** *dragging*:

	SINGULAR		PLURAL	
	masculine and feminine	*neuter*	*masculine and feminine*	*neuter*
nominative and vocative	trahēns	trahēns	trahentēs	trahentia
accusative	trahentem	trahēns	trahentēs	trahentia

Compare the endings of **trahēns** with those of the adjective **ingēns** on page 186.

b *perfect passive participle*. For example: **portātus** *(having been) carried*:

	SINGULAR			PLURAL		
	masculine	*feminine*	*neuter*	*masculine*	*feminine*	*neuter*
nominative and vocative	portātus	portāta	portātum	portātī	portātae	portāta
accusative	portātum	portātam	portātum	portātōs	portātās	portāta

c *perfect active participle*. For example: **ingressus** *(having) entered*:

	SINGULAR			PLURAL		
	masculine	*feminine*	*neuter*	*masculine*	*feminine*	*neuter*
nominative and vocative	ingressus	ingressa	ingressum	ingressī	ingressae	ingressa
accusative	ingressum	ingressam	ingressum	ingressōs	ingressās	ingressa

Compare the endings of **portātus** and **ingressus** with the endings of the adjective **bonus** on page 186.

7 With the help of paragraph 6, find the Latin words for the participles in the following sentences:

a I saw the soldiers dragging the chieftain to prison.

b The boys, having been carried to safety, thanked their rescuers.

c The queen, having entered the atrium, demanded silence.

Uses of the subjunctive

The forms of the imperfect and pluperfect subjunctive are given on page 198. The subjunctive can be used in several different ways, and its translation depends on the way it is being used in a particular sentence. In Book III you have met these uses of the subjunctive:

1 In Stage 24, you met the subjunctive used with **cum** (*when*):

> fabrī, cum pecūniam accēpissent, abiērunt.
> *When the craftspeople had received the money, they went away.*

Further examples:

a Agricola, cum legiōnem īnspexisset, mīlitēs centuriōnēsque laudāvit.

b cum haruspex in templō cēnāret, rex ipse appropinquābat.

Notice in Stage 27 you met an additional meaning of **cum** when used with the subjunctive:

> cum Salvius hostis esset, Catia auxilium quaerēbat.
> *Since Salvius was her enemy, Catia was looking for help.*

2 In Stage 25, you met the subjunctive used in *indirect questions*:

> cognōscere voluimus cūr multitūdō convēnisset.
> *We wanted to find out why the crowd had gathered.*

> (Compare this with the direct question:
> 'cūr multitūdō convēnit?' *'Why has the crowd gathered?'*)

Notice a new meaning of **num** when used with an indirect question:

> mē rogāvērunt num satis pecūniae habērem.
> *They asked me whether I had enough money.*

Further examples:

a incerta eram quam longum esset flūmen.
   (Compare: 'quam longum est flūmen?')

b nēmō sciēbat num Quīntus vīveret.

c Rōmānī nesciēbant quot hostēs in castrīs manērent.

d mē rogāvit num Āfricam vīsitāvissem.

3 In Stage 26, you met the subjunctive used in *purpose clauses*:

> ad urbem iter fēcimus ut amphitheātrum vīsitārēmus.
> *We travelled to the city in order that we might visit the amphitheatre.*

Or, in more natural English:

> *We travelled to the city to visit the amphitheatre.*

Further examples:

a amīcae ad urbem festīnāvērunt ut auxilium cīvibus ferrent.

b epistulam scrīpsī ut Quīntum dē perīculō monērem.

c senātor mē arcessīvit ut rem hospitibus nārrārem.

4 In Stage 26, you also met the subjunctive used with **priusquam** (meaning *before*) and **dum** (meaning *until*):

> Vercobrix iānuam clausit priusquam mīlitēs intrārent.
> *Vercobrix shut the door before the soldiers could enter.*

> exspectābam dum amīcus advenīret.
> *I was waiting until my friend arrived.*

Further examples:

a priusquam architectus rem cōnficeret, tempestās pontem dēlēvit.

b Vilbia in tabernā exspectābat dum amitam salūtāret.

5 In Stage 27, you met the subjunctive used in *indirect commands*:

> imperātor nōbis imperāverat ut rēgnum Togidubnī occupāret.
> *The emperor had ordered us to seize Togidubnus' kingdom.*

> (Compare this with the direct command:
> 'rēgnum Togidubnī occupāte!' *'Seize Togidubnus' kingdom!'*)

Further examples:

a nūntius prīncipibus persuāsit ut dōna ad aulam ferrent.

b mātrōna deam Sūlem ōrāvit ut fūrem pūnīret.

6 In Stage 27, you also met the subjunctive used in *result clauses*:

> tanta erat calliditās philosophae ut cīvēs docēret.
> *So great was the cleverness of the philosopher that she was teaching the citizens.*

Further examples:

a tam dīligenter carcerem custōdīvī ut lēgātus ipse mē laudāret.

b mercātor tot statuās habēbat ut eās numerāre nōn posset.

7 To understand why a subjunctive is being used in a particular sentence, it is necessary to look at the whole sentence and not just the subjunctive on its own. For example, study these two sentences; one contains a *result* clause, and the other contains a *purpose* clause:

a tam anxius erat Rūfus ut dormīre nōn posset.
Rufus was so anxious that he could not sleep.

b Salvius mīlitēs ēmīsit ut Quīntum invenīrent.
Salvius sent out the soldiers to find Quintus.

Sentence **a** clearly contains the result clause: Rufus' failure to sleep was the *result* of his anxiety. The word **tam** (*so*) is a further clue; it is often followed by a result clause later in the sentence. Other similar words are **tantus** (*so great*), **tot** (*so many*) and **adeō** (*so* or *so much*).

Sentence **b** contains the purpose clause: finding Quintus was the *purpose* of sending out the soldiers.

8 Translate the following examples:

   a cīvēs templa vīsitābant ut dīs grātiās agerent.

   b lībertus, cum venēnum bibisset, mortuus prōcubuit.

   c adeō attonita erat fīlia mea ut diū immōta stāret.

   d mātrōna, priusquam pecūniam invenīret, mercātōrem īrātum cōnspexit.

   e tot hostēs castra nostra oppugnābant ut dē vītā dēspērārēmus.

   f prīncipēs mē rogāvērunt cūr pontem trānsīre vellem.

   g Rūfus mīlitibus imperāvit ut plaustra reficerent.

   h iānuās cellārum aperuimus ut amīcōs nostrōs līberārēmus.

   i Aventīna mē monuit ut latērem.

   j Britannōs ōrābāmus dum nōbīs auxilium darent.

   k Crīspus explicāre nōn poterat quō modō captīvī effūgissent.

In each sentence, give the reason why a subjunctive is being used.

Word order

The word order in the following sentences is very common:

1 In Book I, you met the following word order:

   dēspērābat vir.   *The man was in despair.*

   Further examples:

   a exiit Catia.   **b** revēnērunt artificēs.

2 From Stage 21 onwards, you have met the following word order:

   dedit signum rēgīna.   *The queen gave the signal.*

   Further examples:

   a rapuērunt pecūniam fūrēs.   **b** īnspiciēbat mīlitēs Agricola.

3 From Stage 23 onwards, you have met the following word order:

   mīsit Rūfilla epistulās.   *Rufilla sent the letters.*

   Further examples:

   a tenēbat Cephalus pōculum.   **b** sculpsērunt artificēs statuās.

4 Further examples of all three types of word order:

   a discessit puella.   **d** pulsābat nūntius iānuam.

   b fēcērunt hostēs impetum.   **e** vexābant mē puerī.

   c reficiēbat mūrum faber.   **f** plaudēbant spectātōrēs.

5 Study the word order in the following phrases containing prepositions:

   in hāc prōvinciā   ad nostrum patrem
   in this province   *to our father*

   From Stage 24 onwards, you have met a different word order:

   mediīs in undīs   hanc ad tabernam
   in the middle of the waves   *to this shop*

   Further examples:

   a hāc in urbe   **d** omnibus cum legiōnibus
   b multīs cum mīlitibus   **e** tōtam per noctem
   c parvum ad oppidum   **f** mediō in flūmine

Longer sentences

1   Study the following groups of sentences:

   a   puerī timēbant.
       The boys were afraid.

       puerī timēbant quod prope iānuam iacēbat ingēns canis.
       The boys were afraid because near the door was lying a huge dog.

       puerī timēbant quod prope iānuam iacēbat ingēns canis, vehementer lātrāns.
       The boys were afraid because near the door was lying a huge dog, barking loudly.

   b   Frontōnem cōnspexit.
       He caught sight of Fronto.

       ubi ā culīnā redībat, Frontōnem cōnspexit.
       When he was returning from the kitchen, he caught sight of Fronto.

       ubi ā culīnā in quā cēnāverat redībat, Frontōnem cōnspexit.
       When he was returning from the kitchen in which he had been dining, he caught sight of Fronto.

   c   Salvius incertus erat.
       Salvius was uncertain.

       Salvius incertus erat quō fūgisset Dumnorix.
       Salvius was uncertain where Dumnorix had fled to.

       Salvius incertus erat quō fūgisset Dumnorix, cūr abesset Quīntus.
       Salvius was uncertain where Dumnorix had fled to, and why Quintus was missing.

2   Further examples:

   a   centuriō immōtus manēbat.
       centuriō immōtus manēbat, quamquam appropinquābant hostēs.
       centuriō immōtus manēbat, quamquam appropinquābant hostēs, quī hastās vibrābant.

   b   omnēs cīvēs plausērunt.
       ubi puellae cantāre coepērunt, omnēs cīvēs plausērunt.
       ubi puellae, quae prō pompā ambulābant, cantāre coepērunt, omnēs cīvēs plausērunt.

   c   nūntius prīncipia petīvit.
       nūntius quī epistulam ferēbat prīncipia petīvit.
       nūntius quī epistulam ferēbat, simulac ad castra advēnit, prīncipia petīvit.

3   Further examples of the longer types of sentence:

   a   tantae erant flammae ut vīllam magnam dēlērent, quam architectus clārus aedificāverat.
   b   Rūfilla anxia erat quod Catia, quae in aulam manēbat, exīre nōn potuit.
   c   Salvius, Belimico diffīsus, tribūnum arcessīvit ut vērum cognōsceret.
   d   postquam ad forum vēnimus, ubi mercātōrēs negōtium agere solēbant, rem mīrābilem vīdimus.
   e   Vilbia, cum Belimicum appropinquantem cōnspexisset, post columnam sē cēlāvit.
   f   Agricola mox cognōvit ubi hostēs castra posuissent, quot mīlitēs in castrīs essent, num equōs habērent.

Part Two: Reviewing the language

Stage 21

Nouns 1

Complete and translate: Complete each Latin sentence with the correct form of the noun from the brackets. Then translate the sentence.

> Think carefully about the meaning of the sentence to work out which case of noun you need.
> **nouns**: page 184

a omnēs Britannī . . . . vīsitāre volēbant. (fōns, fontem, fontis)

b plūrimī fabrī in aulā . . . . labōrābant. (Togidubnus, Togidubnum, Togidubnī)

c 'fortasse . . . . morbum meum sānāre potest,' inquit rēx. (dea, deam, deae)

d . . . . Catiam laudāvērunt, quod līberālis et callida erat. (prīncipēs, prīncipum)

e mercātor, quī . . . . accēperat, ē forō discesserat. (dēnāriī, dēnāriōs, dēnāriōrum)

f mātrōna, quae prope iānuam stābat, multitūdinem . . . . in viā vīdit. (puellae, puellās, puellārum)

Sentences 1

Complete: Translate each English sentence into Latin by selecting correctly from the pairs of Latin words.

> Think carefully about the meaning of the sentence to work out which case of noun and which tense of verb you need.
> **nouns**: page 184
> **verbs**: page 197

For example: *The messenger heard the voice of the old man.*

| nūntius | vōcem | senem | audit |
| nūntium | vōcī | senis | audīvit |

Latin translation: nūntius vōcem senis audīvit.

a *The priests showed the statue to the architect.*

| sacerdōtēs | statuam | architectum | ostenderant |
| sacerdōtibus | statua | architectō | ostendērunt |

b *The king praised the skilful doctor.*

| rēx | medicus | perītum | laudāvit |
| rēgem | medicum | perītī | laudat |

c *A friend of the soldiers was visiting the temple.*

| amīcus | mīlitibus | templum | vīsitābat |
| amīcō | mīlitum | templī | vīsitāvit |

d *The shouts of the citizens had annoyed the soothsayer.*

| clāmōrum | cīvēs | haruspicem | vexāverant |
| clāmōrēs | cīvium | haruspicī | vexāvērunt |

e *We handed over the boy's letter to the women.*

| epistula | puerum | fēminās | trādidimus |
| epistulam | puerī | fēminīs | trādimus |

Verbs 1

Complete and translate: Complete each Latin sentence with the correct form of the verb in brackets. Then translate the sentence.

Remember to check who is doing the action in each sentence.
verbs: page 197

a tū ipse hanc rem administrāre . . . . (dēbeō, dēbēs, dēbet)

b cūr heri nōn vēnistī? per tōtum diem tē . . . . (exspectāvī, exspectāvistī, exspectāvit)

c ego, quod fontem sacrum vidēre . . . . , iter ad oppidum Aquās Sūlis fēcī. (cupiēbam, cupiēbās, cupiēbat)

d Cephalus, quī senātōrem . . . . , in tablīnum haruspicis ruit. (cōnspexeram, cōnspexerās, cōnspexerat)

e ē lectō surrēxī, quod dormīre nōn . . . . (poteram, poterās, poterat)

f in hāc vīllā . . . . Memor, haruspex nōtissimus. (habitō, habitās, habitat)

Stage 22

Nouns 2

Complete and translate: Complete each Latin sentence with the correct form of the noun from the brackets. Then translate the sentence.

Think carefully about the meaning of the sentence to work out what case of noun you need.
nouns: page 184

a   Belimicus per viās . . . . ambulābat, fībulam quaerēns. (oppidī, oppidō)

b   Vilbia, quae in tabernā labōrābat, ... cibum obtulit. (prīnceps, prīncipī)

c   clāmōrēs . . . . patrem vexāvērunt. (puerī, puerō)

d   prope vīllam . . . . , ingēns turba conveniēbat. (haruspicis, haruspicī)

e   Dumnorix, vir benignus, auxilium . . . . saepe dabat. (amīcōrum, amīcīs)

f   māter . . . . multās fābulās mīrābilēs nārrāvit. (līberōrum, līberōs)

g   prīnceps gladiōs hastāsque . . . . īnspicere coepit. (mīlitum, mīlitibus)

h   Aventīna vīnum optimum . . . . offerēbat. (hospitum, hospitibus)

Adjectives 1

Complete and translate: Complete each Latin sentence with the correct form of the adjective from the brackets. Then translate the sentence.

An adjective agrees with the noun it describes.
adjectives: page 186

a   subitō puella . . . . in ātrium cucurrit. (attonita, attonitae)

b   rēgīna, postquam hoc audīvit, fabrōs . . . . dīmīsit. (fessum, fessōs)

c   senātor, quī aderat, iuvenēs . . . . laudāvit. (callidum, callidōs)

d   omnēs cīvēs templum . . . . spectābant. (splendidum, splendida)

e   ubi in magnō perīculō eram, amīcus . . . . mē servāvit. (fidēlis, fidēlēs)

f   'in illā īnsulā,' inquit Rūfilla, 'habitant multī virī . . . .' (ferōx, ferōcēs)

g   fēmina . . . . , quae in vīllā manēbat, fūrem superāvit. (fortis, fortem, fortēs)

h   cīvēs in viīs oppidī . . . . mīlitēs vidēre solēbant. (multus, multī, multōs)

Stage 23

Verbs 2

Complete and translate: Complete each Latin sentence with the correct form of the verb from the brackets. Then translate the sentence.

Remember to check who is doing the action in each sentence.
verbs: page 197

a 'quid faciunt illī caupōnēs?' 'pōcula hospitibus . . . .' (ferimus, fertis, ferunt)

b fīlius meus vōbīs grātiās agere vult, quod mē . . . .
(servāvimus, servāvistis, servāvērunt)

c prope āram . . . . , sed sacrificium vidēre nōn poterāmus.
(stābāmus, stābātis, stābant)

d quamquam nōs puellae fessae sumus, ad templum . . . .
(currimus, curritis, currunt)

e prīncipēs fontī . . . . , ubi Cephalus stābat, pōculum tenēns.
(appropinquābāmus, appropinquābātis, appropinquābant)

f in maximō perīculō estis, quod fīlium rēgis . . . .
(vexāvimus, vexāvistis, vexāvērunt)

g nōs, quī fontem sacrum numquam . . . . , ad thermās cum rēge īre cupiēbāmus.
(vīderāmus, vīderātis, vīderant)

h amitae nostrae sunt līberālēs; nōbīs multum pecūniae . . . . (damus, datis, dant)

Participles 1

Complete and translate: Complete each Latin sentence with the most suitable perfect participle from the box below. Use each participle only once. Then translate the sentence.

A participle agrees with the noun it describes.
perfect passive participles: page 6
perfect active participles: page 28

prōgressa	locūta	ingressus	arcessīta	missum	vexātus

a Catia, haec verba . . . . , ab aulā discessit.

b dōnum, ab amīcīs meīs . . . . , erat optimum.

c fūr, vīllam . . . . , cautē circumspectāvit.

d Vilbia, ab Aventīnā . . . . , ad vīllam celeriter contendit.

e haruspex, ā Cephalō . . . . , erat īrātus.

f puella, ad fontem . . . . , tabulam in aquam iniēcit.

Stage 24

Indirect statement 1

Complete and translate: Change each sentence from a direct statement
to an indirect statement by completing the second sentence.
Then translate both sentences.

indirect statement 1:
page 46
infinitives: page 199

For example:

> pater dormit. fīlius crēdit patrem . . . .

Completed and translated, this becomes:

> pater dormit. fīlius crēdit patrem dormīre.
> *The father is sleeping.   The son believes that his father is sleeping.*

a Aventīna ex oppidō discēdit.

nūntius Rōmānus putat Aventīnam ex oppidō . . . .

b Togidubnus in carcere iacet.

Quīntus audit Togidubnum in carcere . . . .

c sacerdōtēs ad āram prōcēdunt et agnum dūcunt.

Memor dīxit sacerdōtēs ad āram . . . . et agnum . . . .

d rēx, eōs suspicātus, ultiōnem petit.

Salvius crēdidit . . . . , eōs suspicātum, ultiōnem . . . .

Adjectives 2

Complete and translate: Complete each Latin sentence with the correct form
of the adjective from the brackets. Then translate the sentence.

An adjective agrees with
the noun it describes.
adjectives: page 186

a   medicus puellae . . . . poculum dedit. (aegram, aegrae)

b   artificēs architectum . . . . laudāvērunt. (callidum, callidō)

c   faber mercātōrī . . . . dēnāriōs reddidit. (īrātum, īrātō)

d   prīncipēs rēgīnae . . . . favēre volēbant. (fortem, fortī)

e   centuriō mīlitēs . . . . vituperābat. (ignāvōs, ignāvīs)

f   Vilbia amīcīs . . . . crēdidit. (audācēs, audācibus)

g   stolās . . . . gerēbant fēminae. (novās, novīs)

h   . . . . amīcīs pecūniam obtulī. (omnēs, omnibus)

Pronouns

Replace and translate: With the help of paragraph 3 on page 193, replace the nouns in **bold** with the correct form of the pronoun **is**, **ea**, **id**. Then translate the sentence.

You may need to look up the gender of a noun in the Vocabulary.
Pronouns II: page 193

For example:

> Rūfilla in hortō ambulābat. Quīntus **Rūfillam** salūtāvit.

This becomes:

> Rūfilla in hortō ambulābat. Quīntus **eam** salūtāvit.
> *Rufilla was walking in the garden. Quintus greeted **her**.*

a   Quīntus mox ad aulam advēnit. Vitelliānus **Quīntum** in ātrium dūxit.

b   Memor in tablīnō labōrābat. Cephalus **Memorī** plūs vīnī obtulit.

c   Rūfilla laetissima erat; marītus **Rūfillae** tamen nōn erat contentus.

d   Britannī ferōciter pugnāvērunt, sed Rōmānī tandem **Britannōs** vīcērunt.

e   hostēs nōs oppugnāvērunt. **hostibus** autem restitimus.

f   multae fēminae prō templō conveniēbant. marītī **fēminārum** quoque aderant.

g   prope templum est fōns sacer; **fontem** saepe vīsitāvī.

h   in oppidō Aquīs Sūlis erant thermae maximae; multī fabrī **thermās** aedificāvērunt.

Stage 25

Subjunctive verbs 1

Complete and translate: This exercise is based on the stories **Frontō custōs I** and **II** on pages 98–99. Read the stories again. Complete each Latin sentence with the most suitable group of words from the list below. Use each group of words only once. Then translate the sentence.

Make sure that the sentence you create makes sense and is related to the plot of **Frontō custōs I** and **II**.

cum Crīspus ad culīnam abiisset

cum rem cōgitāret

cum tribūnus centuriōque discessissent

cum cēnam cōnsūmpsisset

cum Frontō ad cellam prōcēderet

cum arānea in nāsum dēcidisset

a ...., Crīspus et Frontō labōrem dēplōrāre coepērunt.

b ...., Frontō in carcere mānsit.

c ...., Vercobrix graviter dormiēbat.

d ...., Frontō fūgit perterritus.

e Crīspus, ..., ē culīnā exiit.

f Crīspus, ..., intellegere nōn potuit cūr Frontō abesset.

Participles 2

Complete and translate: Complete each Latin sentence with the most suitable participle from the box below. Use each participle only once. Then translate the sentence.

A participle agrees with the noun it describes. **participles**: page 205

missōs	līberātī	salūtāta
regressam	tenentēs	passus

a captīvī, ē cellīs subitō ...., ad portam carceris ruērunt.

b Britannī, hastās in manibus ...., castra oppugnāvērunt.

c Vilbia, ā prīncipe benignō ...., respondēre coepit.

d Togidubnus, tot iniūriās ...., Rōmānōs vehementer vituperāvit.

e māter fīliam, ā templō tandem ...., cōnspexit.

f centuriō mīlitēs, ex Ītaliā nūper ab imperātōre ...., īnspexit.

Sentences 2

Complete: Translate each English sentence into Latin by selecting correctly from the pairs of Latin words.

Think carefully about the meaning of the sentence to work out which case of noun and which tense of verb you need.
nouns: page 184
verbs: page 197

a   *The bold women had provided help.*

| fēmina | audācēs | auxilium | praebuērunt |
| fēminae | audācem | auxiliī | praebuerant |

b   *They arrested the baker in the kitchen of an inn.*

| pistōrem | per culīnam | tabernae | comprehendunt |
| pistōris | in culīnā | tabernārum | comprehendērunt |

c   *Friend! Read this letter!*

| amīce | haec | epistula | lege |
| amīcus | hanc | epistulam | legis |

d   *The words of the soothsayer frightened her.*

| verbum | haruspicis | eam | terruit |
| verba | haruspicī | eās | terruērunt |

e   *The citizens departed, praising the brave messenger.*

| cīvēs | discēdunt | fortem | nūntium | laudāns |
| cīvium | discessērunt | fortī | nūntiōs | laudantēs |

f   *How can we avoid the punishments of the gods?*

| quō modō | poenae | deōrum | ēvītantēs | possumus |
| quis | poenās | deīs | ēvītāre | poterāmus |

Stage 26

Nouns 3

Complete and translate. Complete each Latin sentence with the correct form of the noun from the brackets. Then translate the sentence.

Think carefully about the meaning of the sentence to work out which case of noun you need.
nouns: page 184

a Agricola, ubi verba . . . . audīvit, Salvium arcessīvit. (Quīntum, Quīntī, Quīntō)

b omnēs hospitēs . . . . poētae laudāvērunt. (artem, artis, artī)

c iter nostrum difficile erat, quod tot cīvēs . . . . complēbant. (viās, viārum, viīs)

d prō prīncipiīs stābat magnus numerus . . . . (mīlitēs, mīlitum, mīlitibus)

e lēgātus, postquam mandāta . . . . dedit, legiōnem ad montem proximum dūxit. (centuriōnēs, centuriōnum, centuriōnibus)

f rēgīna, quae . . . . nōn crēdēbat, īrātissima erat. (Rōmānōs, Rōmānōrum, Rōmānīs)

Subjunctive verbs 2

Complete and translate: Complete each Latin sentence with the correct form of the verb from the brackets. Then translate the sentence.

Remember to check who was doing each action in each sentence.
subjunctive verbs: page 198

a cum lēgātus legiōnem . . . . , Agricola ē prīncipiīs prōcessit. (īnstrūxisset, īnstrūxissent)

b mīlitēs quam celerrimē cucurrērunt ut hostēs . . . . (ēvītāret, ēvītārent)

c senātor scīre voluit num pater meus imperātōrī . . . . (fāvisset, fāvissent)

d cum senex . . . . , fūrēs per iānuam tacitē intrāvērunt. (dormīret, dormīrent)

e nōs, cum in Britanniā . . . . , hostēs saepe vīcimus. (essem, essēmus)

f intellegere nōn poteram cūr cīvēs istum hominem . . . . (laudāvisset, laudāvissent)

g ad vīcum vēnī ut frātrem . . . . (vīsitārem, vīsitārēmus)

h māter tua mē rogāvit quid in urbe . . . . (fēcissēs, fēcissētis)

Sentences 3

Complete and translate: Complete each Latin sentence with the most suitable word from the box below. Use each word only once. Then translate the sentence.

Think carefully about the meaning of the sentence to work out which case of noun and which tense of verb you need.
nouns: page 184
verbs: page 197

| epistulam | audīvisset | ēgressus |
| invēnērunt | equīs | salūtātae |

a Salvius, ē prīncipiīs . . . . , Belimicum quaesīvit.

b Agricola, cum haec verba . . . . , ad tribūnum sē vertit.

c feminae iuvenem in silvā iacentem . . . .

d Rūfus . . . . in manibus lacrimāns tenuit.

e Aventīna et Vilbia, ā nūntiō . . . . , eum dē ponte īnfirmō monēbant.

f aliī mīlitēs . . . . aquam dabant, aliī frūmentum in horrea īnferēbant.

Stage 27

Participles 3

Translate and identify: Translate the following sentences.

participles: page 205

a fēmina, prope iānuam tabernae stāns, multitūdinem hominum spectābat.

b Vilbia, ē casā ēgressa, Aventīnam statim quaesīvit.

c fūrēs, ad lēgātum ductī, veniam petīvērunt.

d Frontō, amphoram vīnī optimī adeptus, ad amīcōs celeriter rediit.

e subitō equōs appropinquantēs audīvimus.

f puer callidus pecūniam, in terrā cēlātam, invēnit.

Now identify the participle in each sentence and say whether it is present, perfect passive or perfect active. Then identify which noun is described by each participle.

Singulars and plurals

Change and translate: Change the words in **bold** in each Latin sentence from singular to plural. Then translate the new sentence.

You may need to look up the noun in the Vocabulary to find out what gender and declension it is. nouns: page 184

a rēgīna **īnsulam** vīsitābat.

b **nauta** pecūniam **postulābat**.

c haec verba **imperātōrem** terrēbant.

d iuvenēs **captīvum** custōdiēbant.

e puella **pōculum** īnspiciēbat.

f **fēmina** ad portum **contendēbat**.

g equī **flūmen** trānsīre nōlēbant.

h **templum** in forō **erat**.

Nouns 4

Complete and translate: Complete each Latin sentence with the correct form of the noun from the brackets. Then translate the sentence.

Think carefully about the meaning of the sentence to work out which case of noun you need. nouns: page 184

a senātor tabernam meam intrāvit. . . . . fībulam vēndidī. (senātōrem, senātōrī)

b puerī per viam currēbant. clāmōrēs . . . . mē excitāvērunt. (puerōrum, puerīs)

c Rūfilla ad aulam . . . . quam celerrimē contendit. (rēgis, rēgum)

d nūntiī prope villam stābant. . . . . duās epistulās dedimus. (nūntiōs, nūntiīs)

e Memor, ubi . . . . tuum audīvit, perterritus erat. (nōmen, nōmina)

f in hāc viā sunt duo . . . . (templī, templa)

g soror mea ad fundum meum herī vēnit. agrōs meōs . . . . ostendī. (sorōris, sorōrī)

h ingēns multitūdō . . . . nōbīs obstābat. (cīvis, cīvium)

i hostēs prōvinciam oppugnāvērunt, multāsque . . . . dēlēvērunt. (urbēs, urbibus)

j Aventīna . . . ., quem Belimicus graviter vulnerāverat, sānāvit. (Rōmānum, Rōmānōs)

Indirect statement 2

Complete and translate: Change each sentence from a direct statement to an indirect statement by completing the second sentence. Then translate both sentences.

indirect statement 2: page 50
infinitives: page 199

For example:

> pater in cubiculō dormit. fīlius dīcit . . . . in cubiculō . . . .

Completed and translated, this becomes:

> pater in cubiculō dormit. fīlius dīcit patrem in cubiculō dormīre.
> *The father is sleeping in the bedroom. The son says*
> *that the father is sleeping in the bedroom.*

a Belimicus homō magnae arrogantiae est.

Vilbia putat . . . . hominem magnae arrogantiae . . . .

b prīnceps vīnum in tabernā bibit.

Aventīna audīvit . . . . vīnum in tabernā . . . .

c architectus splendidum templum deae Sūlī Minervae aedificat.

rēx crēdit . . . . splendidum templum deae Sūlī Minervae . . . .

d imperātor Domitiānus mortem Togidubnī cupit.

Memor dīxit . . . . mortem Togidubnī . . . .

Stage 28

Subjunctive verbs 3

Complete and translate: Complete each Latin sentence with the correct form of the verb from the brackets. Then translate the sentence. For example:

Remember to check who was doing each action in each sentence.
subjunctive verbs: page 198

tam perterritī erāmus ut ex urbe . . . . (fugerēmus, fugerētis)

tam perterritī erāmus ut ex urbe **fugerēmus**.
We were so frightened that we fled from the city.

a Catia nesciēbat quō modō Togidubnus . . . . (periisset, periissent)

b cīvēs, cum tabernam . . . . , vīnum postulāvērunt. (intrāvisset, intrāvissent)

c Agricola mīlitibus imperāvit ut ad castra . . . . (redīret, redīrent)

d tantus erat clāmor ut nēmō centuriōnem . . . . (audīret, audīrent)

e nōs, cum rēgīnam . . . . , maximē gaudēbāmus. (vīdissem, vīdissēmus)

f rēxne tibi persuāsit ut sēcum templum . . . . ? (vīsitārēs, vīsitārētis)

g domum rediī ut parentēs meōs . . . . (adiuvārem, adiuvāret)

h cūr dīcere nōlēbātis ubi illō diē amīcam vestram . . . . ? (vīdissēs, vīdissētis)

Ablatives

Complete and translate: Complete each Latin sentence with the most suitable noun from the box below. Use each noun only once. Then translate the sentence.

Make sure that the sentence you create makes sense.
ablative case: page 166

| audāciā | vīnō | gladiō | fūstibus | īrā | catēnīs |

a nūntius, ... graviter vulnerātus, effugere nōn poterat.

b Salvius, ... eius attonitus, diū tacēbat.

c captīvī, ... vīnctī, in longīs ōrdinibus stābant.

d Britannī, ... armātī, pugnāre volēbant.

e Catia, ... commōta, cōnsilium capere coepit.

f hospitēs, ... solūtī, clāmāre et iocōs facere coepērunt.

Infinitives

Complete and translate: Complete each Latin sentence with the most suitable word from the box below. Use each word only once. Then translate the sentence.

Make sure that the sentence you create makes sense
infinitives: page 199

dēfendere	currere	invītāre	esse
habēre	nārrāre	retinēre	redīre

a   nōbīs decōrum est prīncipēs ad cēnam splendidam . . . .

b   līberī cupiēbant patrem fābulam novam . . . .

c   imperātor iussit mīlitēs castra cum summā fortitūdine . . . .

d   Quīntus vix crēdidit Vitelliānum in aulā rēgīnam . . . .

e   scīsne canēs per agrōs . . . . ?

f   omnēs dīcunt hominem clārissimum in forō ōrātiōnem . . . .

g   frāter meus audīvit mātrem domum . . . .

h   Vilbia iuvenī dīxit pācem . . . . meliōrem quam bellum.

Part Three: Vocabulary

1   Nouns and adjectives are listed as in the Book II Language Information section. For example:

   artifex, artificis, m.   *artist, craftsperson*

   Nouns are shown in their nominative and genitive singular forms with their gender.

   laetus, laeta, laetum   *happy*

   Adjectives are listed with the masculine, feminine and neuter forms of the nominative singular; where the nominative singular is the same for all genders, the genitive singular is added, e.g. **ingēns**, *gen.* **ingentis**.

2   Verbs are usually listed in the following way:

   parō, parāre, parāvī, parātus   *prepare*

   The first form listed (**parō**) is the 1st person singular of the present tense (*I prepare*).

   The second form (**parāre**) is the infinitive (*to prepare*).

   The third form (**parāvī**) is the 1st person singular of the perfect tense (*I prepared*).

   The fourth form (**parātus**) is the perfect passive participle in the masculine form of the nominative singular (*having been prepared*).

   The listed forms of a verb are known as the **principal parts** of the verb.

3   Study the following examples listed in the way described in paragraph 2. Notice the typical ways in which the different conjugations form their perfect tense and perfect passive participle.

   first conjugation

       amō, amāre, amāvī, amātus   *love, like*

       laudō, laudāre, laudāvi, laudātus   *praise*

   second conjugation

       moneō, monēre, monuī, monitus   *warn, advise*

       terreō, terrēre, terruī, territus   *frighten*

third conjugation

Verbs of the third conjugation form their present tense and perfect passive participle in several different ways. Here are some of them:

dūcō, dūcere, dūxī, ductus	*lead*
neglegō, neglegere, neglēxī, neglectus	*neglect, ignore*
claudō, claudere, clausī, clausus	*shut, close*
mittō, mittere, mīsī, missus	*send*
relinquō, relinquere, relīquī, relictus	*leave*
vincō, vincere, vīcī, victus	*be victorious, win*

fourth conjugation

audiō, audīre, audīvī, audītus	*hear, listen to*
custōdiō, custōdire, custōdīvī, custōdītus	*guard*

4 Use paragraph 3 to find the meaning of:

   amāvī, laudātus, monitus, terrēre, ductus, neglēxi, clausus, mīsī, vincere, vīcī, relinquō, relictus, audīvī, custōdītus.

5 Use the **Vocabulary** on pages 228–246 to find the meaning of:

   adiuvāre, comprehēnsus, nocēre, pāreō, patefēcī, audītus, suscēpī, tractus.

6 Some verbs have a perfect *active* participle, e.g. **locūtus** (*having spoken*).
   You have not yet met any other forms of these verbs and so this participle is the only form listed in the **Vocabulary**.

7 Phrases (e.g. **cōnsilium capere** *make a plan, have an idea*) are listed under both words of the phrase.

8 Many Latin words can be translated into English in a number of ways. Often the way you choose to translate a word will affect the tone of a sentence, and sometimes it will change the overall meaning. Always choose the most suitable translation for the sentence you are working on.

9 Some Latin words have meanings that are conveyed by very different words in English. Note, for example, two of the possible meanings of the verb **petō**:

> mīles iuvenem **petīvit** et facile superāvit.
> *The soldier **made for** the young man and easily overpowered him.*

> Barbillus, multōs cāsūs passus, ā tē veniam **petīvit**.
> *Barbillus, having suffered many misfortunes, **asked for** pardon from you.*

Considering the wider context of a word or sentence will help you determine which meaning is appropriate. Sometimes more than one English translation will be correct for a Latin word, and you should choose the translation that you think most suitably conveys the meaning of the Latin as you understand it.

There can also be important distinctions between the possible translations of the same word. For example, if **ancilla** is translated as *female slave* it defines a person, whereas if it is translated as *enslaved woman* it describes what has been done to that person. Consider the impact of your choice when translating for the meaning of a word or sentence.

This **Vocabulary** cannot include every possible English translation of each Latin word in this textbook. For example, **dominus** is listed as *master (of the household)*, but other translations may be more appropriate, for example, *enslaver, owner,* or *'sir'*.

Sometimes you may prefer to use a more colloquial or natural sounding translation of a word or phrase that the **Vocabulary** lists in a more literal way. For example, **placeō** is listed as *please, suit*, but when you meet this word in a sentence, you might want to translate it more naturally.

mihi placet *it pleases me*

Or, in more natural English: *I like it*

Because a single Latin word can have a range of English meanings, you should feel free to use alternative translations where it is appropriate to do so.

10 Where a word appears in a **Vocabulary checklist** in Stages 1–28, it is marked with the relevant Stage number. For example:

5	audiō, audīre, audīvī, audītus	*hear, listen to*

This means that **audiō** appears as a **Vocabulary checklist** word in Stage 5.

a

18, 21	ā, ab	*from; by*
10	abeō, abīre, abiī	*go away*
	absēns, *gen.* absentis	*absent*
6	absum, abesse, āfuī	*be out, be absent, be away*
	absurdus, absurda, absurdum	*absurd*
28	ac	*and*
20	accidō, accidere, accidī	*happen*
10	accipiō, accipere, accēpī, acceptus	*accept, take in, receive*
	accurrō, accurrere, accucurrī, accursus	*run up*
	accūsō, accūsāre, accūsāvī, accūsātus	*accuse*
3	ad	*to, towards, at*
	addō, addere, addidī, additus	*add*
	addūcō, addūcere, addūxī, adductus	*lead (on), urge (on)*
27	adeō	*so much, so greatly*
20	adeō, adīre, adiī	*go up to, pay a visit to*
	adeptus, adepta, adeptum	*having received, having obtained*
	adest *see* adsum	
	adhūc	*until now, so far*
23	adiuvō, adiuvāre, adiūvī	*help*
	administrō, administrāre, administrāvī, administrātus	*manage*
	adōrō, adōrāre, adōrāvī, adōrātus	*worship*
	adstō, adstāre, adstitī	*stand in attendance*
5	adsum, adesse, adfuī	*be here, be present*
14	adveniō, advenīre, advēnī	*arrive*
	adventus, adventūs, m.	*arrival*
	aedificium, aedificiī, n.	*building*
16	aedificō, aedificāre, aedificāvī, aedificātus	*build*
13	aeger, aegra, aegrum	*sick, ill*
	Aegyptius, Aegyptia, Aegyptium	*Egyptian*
	Aegyptus, Aegyptī, f.	*Egypt*
	afferō, afferre, attulī, adlātus	*bring*
	afflīgō, afflīgere, afflīxī, afflīctus	*afflict, hurt*
	ager, agrī, m.	*field*

8	agitō, agitāre, agitāvī, agitātus	*chase, hunt*
	agmen, agminis, n.	*column (of soldiers)*
9	agnōscō, agnōscere, agnōvī, agnitus	*recognise*
	agnus, agnī, m.	*lamb*
4	agō, agere, ēgī, āctus	*do, act*
	age!	*come on!*
	grātiās agere	*thank, give thanks, be grateful*
	persōnam agere	*play the part (of)*
	vītam agere	*lead a life*
	quid agit?	*how is he?*
5	agricola, agricolae, m.	*farmer*
	ālea, āleae, f.	*dice*
	āleam lūdere	*play dice*
	Alexandrīa, Alexandrīae, f.	*Alexandria*
	aliquandō	*sometimes*
25, 17	aliquis, aliquid	*someone, something*
	aliquid novī	*something new*
15	alius, alia, aliud	*other, another*
21	aliī . . . aliī	*some . . . others*
15	alter, altera, alterum	*the other, the second*
	alter . . . alter	*one . . . the other*
	altitūdō, altitūdinis, f.	*depth*
	altus, alta, altum	*deep*
	amātor, amātōris, m.	*(male) lover*
	ambō, ambae, ambō	*both*
5	ambulō, ambulāre, ambulāvī	*walk*
	amīca, amīcae, f.	*(female) friend, girlfriend*
	amīcitia, amīcitiae, f.	*friendship*
2	amīcus, amīcī, m.	*(male) friend*
	amīcus, amīca, amīcum	*friendly*
	amita, amitae, f.	*aunt*
12	āmittō, āmittere, āmīsī, āmissus	*lose*
17	amō, amāre, amāvī, amātus	*love, like*
26	amor, amōris, m.	*love*
	amphitheātrum, amphitheātrī, n.	*amphitheatre*
	amphora, amphorae, f.	*wine jar, storage jar*
	amplexus, amplexa, amplexum	*having hugged*
2	ancilla	*(female) slave, enslaved woman*
	angulus, angulī, m.	*corner*
	anīlis, anīle	*of an old woman*
	animal, animālis, n.	*animal*

27	animus, animī, m.	*soul, spirit, mind*
	in animō volvere	*wonder, turn over in the mind*
21	annus, annī, m.	*year*
18	anteā	*before*
	antenna, antennae, f.	*yardarm*
	antīquus, antīqua, antīquum	*old, ancient*
4	ānulus, ānulī, m.	*ring*
	anxius, anxia, anxium	*worried*
25	aperiō, aperīre, aperuī, apertus	*open*
	apertē	*openly*
	apodytērium, apodytēriī, n.	*changing room*
16	appāreō, appārēre, appāruī	*appear*
17	appropinquō, appropinquāre, appropinquāvī	*approach, come near to*
	aptus, apta, aptum	*suitable*
14	apud	*among, at the house of*
15	aqua, aquae, f.	*water*
	Aquae Sūlis, Aquārum Sūlis, f.pl.	*Bath*
23	āra, ārae, f.	*altar*
	arānea, arāneae, f.	*spider, spider's web*
	arbor, arboris, f.	*tree*
	arca, arcae, f.	*strongbox, chest*
24	arcessō, arcessere, arcessīvī, arcessītus	*summon, send for*
	architectus, architectī, m.	*builder, architect*
	ardeō, ardēre, arsī	*burn, be on fire*
	ārea, āreae, f.	*courtyard*
	argenteus, argentea, argenteum	*(made of) silver*
27	arma, armōrum, n.pl.	*weapons, arms*
	armārium, armāriī, n.	*chest, cupboard*
	armō, armāre, armāvī, armātus	*arm*
	arrogāns, gen. arrogantis	*arrogant, conceited*
	arrogantia, arrogantiae, f.	*arrogance, conceit*
20	ars, artis, f.	*art*
	artifex, artificis, m.	*artist, craftsperson*
17	ascendō, ascendere, ascendī	*climb, rise*
	asinus, asinī, m.	*donkey*
	aspiciō, aspicere, aspexī	*look towards*
	assiduē	*continually*
	Athēnae, Athēnārum, f.pl.	*Athens*
28	atque	*and*
	ātrium, ātriī, n.	*atrium (reception room)*

14	attonitus, attonita, attonitum	*astonished*
24	auctōritās, auctōritātis, f.	*authority*
	auctus *see* augeō	
	audācia, audāciae, f.	*boldness, audacity*
	audācter	*boldly*
13	audāx, *gen* audācis	*bold, courageous*
18	audeō, audēre	*dare*
5	audiō, audīre, audīvī, audītus	*hear, listen to*
26	auferō, auferre, abstulī, ablātus	*take away, carry off, steal*
	augeō, augēre, auxī, auctus	*increase*
15	aula, aulae, f.	*palace*
	aureus, aurea, aureum	*golden, (made of) gold*
	aureus, aureī, m.	*gold coin*
	auris, auris, f.	*ear*
	aut	*or*
23	autem	*but*
16	auxilium, auxiliī, n.	*help*
	avāritia, avaritiae, f.	*greed*
	avārus, avāra, avārum	*greedy, miserly*
	avē	*hello*
	avidē	*eagerly*
	avidus, avida, avidum	*eager*

b

	balneum, balneī, n.	*bath*
	barbarus, barbarī, m.	*foreigner, barbarian*
	bellicōsus, bellicōsa, bellicōsum	*warlike*
26	bellum, bellī, n.	*war*
15	bellum gerere	*wage war*
	bellus, bella, bellum	*pretty*
17	bene	*well, good*
	beneficium, beneficiī, n.	*act of kindness, favour*
	benignē	*kindly*
	benignitās, benignitātis, f.	*kindness*
17	benignus, benigna, benignum	*kind, generous*
	bēstia, bēstiae, f.	*wild animal, beast*
3	bibō, bibere, bibī	*drink*
	blanditiae, blanditiārum, f.pl.	*flattery*
	blandus, blanda, blandum	*flattering*
12	bonus, bona, bonum	*good, worthy*
16	melior, melius	*better*
	melius est	*it would be better*

5	optimus, optima, optimum	*very good, excellent, best*
	bracchium, bracchiī, n.	*arm*
	brevī	*in a short time*
25	brevis, breve	*short, brief*
	breviter	*briefly, shortly*
	Britannī, Britannōrum, m.pl.	*Britons*
	Britannia, Britanniae, f.	*Britain*
	Britannicus, Britannica, Britannicum	*British*
	Britunculus, Brittunculī, m.	*poor little Briton*

C

	C. = Gāius	
	cachinnō, cachinnāre, cachinnāvī	*roar with laughter*
13	cadō, cadere, cecidī	*fall*
	caecus, caeca, caecum	*blind*
	caedō, caedere, cecīdī	*kill, slaughter*
22	caelum, caelī, n.	*sky*
	calceus, calcei, m.	*shoe*
	Calēdonia, Calēdoniae, f.	*Scotland*
	calidus, calida, calidum	*hot, warm*
	calliditās, calliditātis, f.	*shrewdness, cleverness*
10	callidus, callida, callidum	*clever*
1	canis, canis, m.	*dog*
15	cantō, cantāre, cantāvī	*sing, chant*
10	capiō, capere, cēpī, captus	*catch, capture, take*
	cōnsilium capere	*make a plan, have an idea*
25	captīvus, captīvī, m.	*prisoner, captive*
18	caput, capitis, n.	*head*
24	carcer, carceris, m.	*prison*
19	cārus, cāra, cārum	*dear*
	casa, casae, f.	*small house, cottage*
25	castra, castrōrum, n.pl.	*camp*
	casus, cāsūs, m.	*misfortune*
	catēna, catēnae, f.	*chain*
	caudex, caudicis, m.	*idiot*
	caupō, caupōnis, m.	*innkeeper*
	caupōna, cauponae, f.	*innkeeper*
	cautē	*cautiously*
	cautus, cauta, cautum	*cautious*
	caveō, cavēre, cāvī	*beware*
	cecidī *see* cadō	
	cecīdī *see* caedō	
23	cēdō, cēdere, cessī	*give in, give way*

14	celer, celeris, celere	*quick, fast*
	celerrimus, celerrima, celerrimum	*very fast*
	celeritās, celeritātis, f.	*speed*
9	celeriter	*quickly, fast*
	celerrimē	*very quickly, very fast*
	celerius	*faster*
	quam celerrimē	*as quickly as possible*
	cella, cellae, f.	*cell, sanctuary*
22	cēlō, cēlāre, cēlāvī, cēlātus	*hide*
2	cēna, cēnae, f.	*dinner*
	cēnō, cēnāre, cēnāvī	*eat dinner, dine*
28	centum	*a hundred*
	centuriō, centuriōnis, m.	*centurion*
	cēpī *see* capiō	
	certāmen, certāminis, n.	*struggle, contest*
	certō, certāre, certāvī	*compete*
	certus, certa, certum	*certain*
	prō certō habēre	*know for certain*
	cerva, cervae, f.	*deer*
	cessī *see* cēdō	
13	cēterī, cēterae, cētera, pl.	*the others, the rest*
2	cibus, cibī, m.	*food*
21	circum	*around*
3	circumspectō, circumspectāre, circumspectāvī	*look round*
	circumveniō, circumvenīre, circumvēnī, circumventus	*surround*
11	cīvis, cīvis, m.f.	*citizen*
	clādēs, clādis, f.	*disaster*
	clam	*in secret, privately*
3	clāmō, clāmāre, clāmāvī	*shout*
5	clāmor, clāmōris, m.	*noise, shouting, shout*
21	clārus, clāra, clārum	*famous*
	claudicō, claudicāre, claudicāvī	*walk with a limp*
	claudō, claudere, clausī, clausus	*shut, close*
	clēmēns, *gen.* clēmentis	*merciful*
	Cn. = Gnaeus	
18	coepī	*I began*
20	cōgitō, cōgitāre, cōgitāvī	*think, consider*
	sēcum cōgitāre	*consider to himself*
18	cognōscō, cognōscere, cognōvī, cognitus	*find out, get to know*
25	cōgō, cōgere, coēgī, coāctus	*force, compel*
	cohors, cohortis, f.	*cohort*

	colligō, colligere, collēgī, collēctus	*gather, collect, assemble*
	collocō, collocāre, collocāvī	*place, put, apply*
	colō, colere, coluī, cultus	*cultivate, make friends with*
	columna, columnae, f.	*column*
24	comes, comitis, m.f.	*comrade, companion*
	cōmiter	*politely, courteously*
	commemorō, commemorāre, commemorāvī	*talk about*
	committō, committere, commīsī, commissus	*commit*
26	commōtus, commōta, commōtum	*moved, alarmed, excited, distressed, upset*
19	comparō, comparāre, comparāvī, comparātus	*obtain*
12	compleō, complēre, complēvī, complētus	*fill*
24	comprehendō, comprehendere, comprehendī, comprehēnsus	*arrest, seize*
20	cōnficiō, cōnficere, cōnfēcī, cōnfectus	*finish*
	rem cōnficere	*finish the job*
21	cōnfīdō, cōnfīdere	*trust*
	coniūrātiō, coniūrātiōnis, f.	*plot, conspiracy*
	cōnscendō, cōnscendere, cōnscendī	*embark, go on board*
	cōnsecrō, cōnsecrāre, cōnsecrāvī	*dedicate*
16	cōnsentiō, cōnsentīre, cōnsēnsī	*agree*
	cōnsīdō, cōnsīdere, cōnsēdī	*sit down*
16	cōnsilium, cōnsiliī, n.	*plan, idea, advice*
	cōnsilium capere	*make a plan, have an idea*
	cōnsistō, cōnsistere, cōnstitī	*stand one's ground, stand firm*
	cōnspectus, cōnspectūs, m.	*sight, view*
23	cōnspicātus, cōnspicāta, cōnspicātum	*having caught sight of*
7	cōnspiciō, cōnspicere, cōnspexī, cōnspectus	*catch sight of, notice*
28	cōnstituō, cōnstituere, cōnstituī, cōnstitūtus	*decide*
	cōnsulō, cōnsulere, cōnsuluī, cōnsultus	*consult*
8	cōnsūmō, cōnsūmere, cōnsūmpsī, cōnsūmptus	*eat*
5	contendō, contendere, contendī	*hurry*
	contentiō, contentiōnis, f.	*argument*

10	contentus, contenta, contentum	*satisfied*
	contineō, continēre, continuī, contentus	*contain*
	continuus, continua, continuum	*continuous, on end*
25	contrā	*against*
	contrārius, contrāria, contrārium	*opposite*
	rēs contrāria	*the opposite*
	convalēscō, convalēscere, convaluī, convalitus	*get better, recover*
11	conveniō, convenīre, convēnī	*gather, meet*
	conversus, conversa, conversum	*having turned*
	convertō, convertere, convertī	*turn*
	sē convertere	*turn*
27	cōpiae, cōpiārum, f.	*forces, troops*
4	coquō, coquere, coxī	*cook*
1	coquus, coquī, m.	*cook*
28	corpus, corporis, n.	*body*
	corrumpō, corrumpere, corrūpī, corruptus	*corrupt*
16	cotīdiē	*every day*
11	crēdō, crēdere, crēdidī	*believe in, trust, have faith in*
	creō, creāre, creāvī, creātus	*make, create*
20	crūdēlis, crūdēle	*cruel*
	crūdēlitās, crūdēlitātis, f.	*cruelty*
	cubiculum, cubiculī, n.	*bedroom*
	cucurrī *see* currō	
	cui (*dative of* quī)	*to whom, to which*
	cuius (*genitive of* quī)	*whose, of which*
	culīna, culīnae, f.	*kitchen*
	culpa, culpae, f.	*blame, fault*
24	cum	*(1) when; since*
7	cum	*(2) with*
	cupīdō, cupīdinis, f.	*desire*
	Cupīdō, Cupīdinis, m.	*Cupid, the god of desire*
9	cupiō, cupere, cupīvī	*want, desire*
4	cūr?	*why?*
23	cūra, cūrae, f.	*care*
19	cūrō, cūrāre, cūrāvī, cūrātus	*care for, supervise*
5	currō, currere, cucurrī	*run*
12	custōdiō, custōdīre, custōdīvī, custōdītus	*guard*
13	custōs, custōdis, m.f.	*guard*

d

dare *see* dō

damnō, damnāre, damnāvī,   *condemn*
damnātus

11 dē   *down from; about*

19 dea, deae, f.   *goddess*

15 dēbeō, dēbēre, dēbuī,   *owe; should, must, ought*
dēbitus

20, 28 decem   *ten*

dēcidō, dēcidere, dēcidī   *fall down*

decimus, decima, decimum   *tenth*

dēcipiō, dēcipere, dēcēpī,   *deceive, fool*
dēceptus

14 decōrus, decōra, decōrum   *right, proper*

dedī *see* dō

dēfendō, dēfendere,   *defend*
dēfendī

dēfēnsor, dēfēnsōris, m.   *defender*

dēfīxiō, dēfīxiōnis, f.   *curse*

dēiciō, dēicere, dēiēcī,   *throw down*
dēiēctus

16 deinde   *then*

dēlectō, dēlectāre,   *delight, please*
dēlectāvī, dēlectātus

14 dēleō, dēlēre, dēlēvī,   *destroy*
dēlētus

dēligō, dēligāre, dēligāvī,   *bind, tie, tie up, moor*
dēligātus

dēmittō, dēmittere, dēmīsī   *lower, let down*

dēmoveō, dēmovēre,   *dismiss, remove*
dēmōvī, dēmōtus

dēnārius, dēnāriī, m.   *denarius (small coin)*

20 dēnique   *at last, finally*

dēnsus, dēnsa, dēnsum   *thick*

dēnūntiō, dēnūntiāre,   *denounce, reveal*
dēnūntiāvī, dēnūntiātus

dēplōrō, dēplōrāre,   *complain about*
dēplōrāvī, dēplōrātus

dēpōnō, dēpōnere, dēposuī,   *put down, take off*
dēpositus

dērīdeō, dērīdēre, dērīsī   *laugh at, make fun of*

24 dēscendō, dēscendere,   *come down, go down*
dēscendī

dēserō, dēserere, dēseruī,   *desert*
dēsertus

dēsertus, dēserta, dēsertum   *deserted*

dēsiliō, dēsilīre, dēsiluī   *jump down*

dēsistō, dēsistere, dēstitī   *stop*

20 dēspērō, dēspērāre,   *despair*
dēspērāvī

dēstinō, dēstināre,   *intend*
dēstināvī, dēstinātus

dēstringō, dēstringere,   *draw out*
dēstrīnxī, dēstrictus

dētestātus, dētestāta,   *having cursed*
dētestātum

15 deus, deī, m.   *god*

    dī immortālēs!   *heavens above!*

Dēva, Dēvae, f.   *Chester*

    Dēvae   *at Chester*

dēvorō, dēvorāre, dēvorāvī,   *devour, eat up*
dēvorātus

Diāna, Diānae, f.   *Diana (goddess of hunting)*

13 dīcō, dīcere, dīxī, dictus   *say*

dictō, dictāre, dictāvī,   *dictate*
dictātus

9 diēs, diēī, m.   *day*

difficilē   *with difficulty*

14 difficilis, difficile   *difficult*

    difficillimus, difficillima,   *very difficult*
difficillimum

difficultās, difficultātis, f.   *difficulty*

diffīsus, diffīsa, diffīsum   *having distrusted*

25 dignitās, dignitātis, f.   *importance, prestige, dignity*

dignus, digna, dignum   *worthy, appropriate*

21 dīligēns *gen.* dīligentis   *hardworking, careful*

15 dīligenter   *carefully*

dīligentia, dīligentiae, f.   *carefulness, attentiveness*

dīligō, dīligere, dīlēxī,   *be fond of*
dīlēctus

dīmittō, dīmittere, dīmīsī,   *send away, dismiss*
dīmissus

dīripiō, dīripere, dīripuī,   *pull apart, ransack*
dīreptus

dīrus, dīra, dīrum   *dreadful*

dīs *see* deus

19 discēdō, discēdere, discessī   *depart, leave*

dissentiō, dissentīre,   *disagree*
dissēnsī, dissēnsus

dissimilis, dissimile   *different*

dissuādeō, dissuādēre,   *dissuade*
dissuāsī, dissuāsus

17 diū   *for a long time*

    diūtius   *any longer*

19 dīves, *gen.* dīvitis   *rich*

dīxī *see* dīcō

9	dō, dare, dedī, datus	*give*
	poenas dare	*pay the penalty, be punished*
26	doceō, docēre, docuī, doctus	*teach*
	doleō, dolēre, doluī	*hurt, be in pain, grieve*
	dolor, dolōris, m.	*pain, grief*
	dolus, dolī, m.	*trickery*
13	domina, dominae, f.	*lady (of the household), mistress*
2	dominus, dominī, m.	*master (of the household)*
	Domitiānus, Domitiānī, m.	*Domitian*
	domum	*(towards) home*
20	domus, domūs, f.	*house, home*
20	domī	*at home*
14	dōnum, dōnī, n.	*present, gift*
2	dormiō, dormīre, dormīvī	*sleep*
	Druidae, Druidārum, m.pl.	*Druids*
	dubium, dubiī, n.	*doubt*
8	dūcō, dūcere, dūxī, ductus	*lead, take*
	dulcis, dulce	*sweet*
26	dum	*while; until*
12, 20, 28	duo, duae, duo	*two*
21	dūrus, dūra, dūrum	*harsh, hard*
	dux, ducis, m.	*leader*

e

4	ē, ex	*out of, from*
	ea	*those things*
	eādem	*the same*
	eam	*her, it*
	eās	*them*
	Eborācum, Eborācī, n.	*York*
4	ecce!	*look!*
23	efficiō, efficere, effēcī, effectus	*carry out, accomplish*
	effluō, effluere, efflūxī	*pour out, flow out*
16	effugiō, effugere, effūgī	*escape*
	effundō, effundere, effūdī, effūsus	*pour out*
	ēgī *see* agō	
4	ego, meī	*I, me*
	mēcum	*with me*
22	ēgressus, ēgressa, ēgressum	*having gone out*
	ehem!	*well, well!*
4	ēheu!	*oh dear! oh no!*

	eī	*to him, to her, to it, to them (singular)*
	eīs	*to them, for them (plural)*
	eius	*his, her*
	ēlāpsus, ēlāpsa, ēlāpsum	*having escaped*
	ēlegāns, *gen.* ēlegantis	*tasteful, elegant*
25	ēligō, ēligere, ēlēgī, ēlēctus	*choose*
9	ēmittō, ēmittere, ēmīsī, ēmissus	*throw, send out*
6	emō, emere, ēmī, ēmptus	*buy*
	ēmptor, ēmptōris, m.	*buyer*
	ēmoveō, ēmovēre, ēmōvī	*move, clear away*
	ēn!	*look!*
	ēn iūstitia!	*so this is justice!*
20	enim	*for*
11	eō, īre, iī	*go*
	obviam īre	*(go to) meet*
	eō	*it*
	eōrum	*their*
	eōs	*them*
12	epistula, epistulae, f.	*letter*
	eques, equitis, m.	*horseman*
	equitō, equitāre, equitāvī	*ride*
15	equus, equī, m.	*horse*
	eram *see* sum	
	ergō	*therefore*
	errō, errāre, errāvī	*make a mistake: wander*
	longē errāre	*make a big mistake*
	est *see* sum	
	estō	*be!*
3	et	*and*
	et . . . et	*both . . . and*
17	etiam	*even, also*
	nōn sōlum . . . sed etiam	*not only . . . but also*
	euge!	*hurray!*
8	eum	*him, it*
4	ex, ē	*out of, from*
	exanimātus, exanimāta, exanimātum	*unconscious*
	excipiō, excipere, excēpī, exceptus	*take in, receive*
	excitō, excitāre, excitāvī, excitātus	*wake up, rouse*
10	exclāmō, exclāmāre, exclāmāvī	*exclaim, shout out*
	excruciō, excruciāre, excruciāvī, excruciātus	*torture, torment*
3	exeō, exīre, exiī	*go out*

	exerceō, exercēre, exercuī, exercitus	*exercise, practise*
27	exercitus, exercitūs, m.	*army*
	expellō, expellere, expulī, expulsus	*throw out*
	explicō, explicāre, explicāvī, explicātus	*explain; unroll*
	exquīsītus, exquīsīta, exquīsītum	*special*
	exspectātus, exspectāta, exspectātum	*welcome*
3	exspectō, exspectāre, exspectāvī, exspectātus	*wait for*
	exstinguō, extinguere, exstīnxī, exstīnctus	*extinguish, destroy*
	exsultō, exsultāre, exsultāvī	*exult, be triumphant*
	extorqueō, extorquēre, extorsī, extortus	*extort*
	extrā	*outside*
	extrahō, extrahere, extrāxī, extractus	*pull out, take out*
	extulī *see* efferō	
	extrēmus, extrēma, extrēmum	*edge, last*
	extrēma pars	*edge*

f

23	faber, fabrī, m.	*craftsman, craftsperson*
5	fābula, fābulae, f.	*play, story*
8	facile	*easily*
16	facilis, facile	*easy*
	facinus, facinoris, n.	*crime*
7	faciō, facere, fēcī, factus	*make, do*
	impetum facere	*charge, make an attack*
	fallō, fallere, fefellī, falsus	*deceive*
	falsum, falsī, n.	*lie, untruth*
	falsus, falsa, falsum	*untrue, false, dishonest*
	familiāris, familiāris, m.	*relation, relative*
11	faveō, favēre, fāvī	*favour, support*
	favor, favōris, m.	*favour, support*
	fēcī *see* faciō	
	fefellī *see* fallō	
	fēlīcitās, fēlīcitātis, f.	*luck, fortune*
18	fēlīx, *gen.* fēlīcis	*lucky, fortunate*
5	fēmina, fēminae, f.	*woman*
	fenestra, fenestrae, f.	*window*
9	ferō, ferre, tulī, lātus	*bring, carry*
	graviter ferre	*take badly*

6	ferōciter	*fiercely*
8	ferōx, *gen.* ferōcis	*fierce, ferocious*
	ferrārius, ferrāriī, m.	*blacksmith*
11	fessus, fessa, fessum	*tired*
6	festīnō, festīnāre, festīnāvī	*hurry*
	fībula, fībulae, f.	*brooch, decorative pin*
28	fidēs, fideī, f.	*loyalty, trustworthiness*
15	fidēlis, fidēle	*faithful, loyal*
	fidēliter	*faithfully, loyally*
1	fīlia, fīliae, f.	*daughter*
1	fīlius, fīliī, m.	*son*
	fīnis, fīnis, m.f.	*end*
	ad fīnem	*to the end*
	firmē	*firmly*
	fistulam	*pipe*
12	flamma, flammae, f.	*flame*
	flōs, flōris, m.	*flower*
19	flūmen, flūminis, n.	*river*
	foedus, foeda, foedum	*foul, disgusting*
21	fōns, fontis, m.	*fountain, spring*
	fōrma, fōrmae, f.	*(outward) appearance*
17	fortasse	*perhaps*
28	forte	*by chance*
6	fortis, forte	*brave, strong*
12	fortiter	*bravely*
	fortitūdō, fortitūdinis, f.	*courage*
	fortūna, fortūnae, f.	*destiny, fate*
4	forum, forī, n.	*forum (market place)*
	fossa, fossae, f.	*ditch*
	frāctus, frācta, frāctum	*broken*
10	frāter, frātris, m.	*brother*
	fraus, fraudis, f.	*trick*
	frūmentum, frūmentī, n.	*grain*
12	frūstrā	*in vain*
	fuga, fugae, f.	*escape*
12	fugiō, fugere, fūgī	*run away, flee*
	fugitīvus, fugitīvī, m.	*fugitive*
	fuī *see* sum	
12	fundus, fundī, m.	*farm*
	fūnus, fūneris, n.	*funeral*
6	fūr, fūris, m.	*thief*
	furcifer, furciferī, m.	*scoundrel, rascal*
	furēns, *gen.* furentis	*furious, in a rage*
	furō, furere, furuī	*raging*
	furor, furōris, m.	*rage*
	fūstis, fūstis, m.	*club, stick*

g

	garriō, garrīre, garrīvī	*chatter, gossip*
	garum, garī, n.	*fish sauce*
27	gaudeō, gaudēre	*be pleased, rejoice*
	gemitus, gemitūs, m.	*groan*
	gemma, gemmae, f.	*jewel, gem*
27	gēns, gentis, f.	*family, tribe, race, people*
	ubi gentium?	*where in the world?*
	genū, genūs, n.	*knee*
15	gerō, gerere, gessī, gestus	*wear; wage*
15	bellum gerere	*wage war*
8	gladius, gladiī, m.	*sword*
	Graecus, Graeca, Graecum	*Greek*
	grātiae, grātiārum, f.pl.	*thanks*
	grātiās agere	*thank, give thanks, be grateful*
	grātīs	*free*
21	gravis, grave	*heavy, serious*
	gravitās, gravitātis, f.	*heaviness, seriousness*
17	graviter	*seriously, heavily*
	graviter dolēre	*be in extreme pain*
	graviter ferre	*take badly*
	gustō, gustāre, gustāvī	*taste*
	guttur, gutturis, n.	*throat*

h

4	habeō, habēre, habuī, habitus	*have*
	in memoriā habēre	*keep in mind, remember*
	ōrātiōnem habēre	*make a speech*
	prō certō habēre	*know for certain*
	sermōnem habēre	*have a conversation, talk*
10	habitō, habitāre, habitāvī	*live*
	hāc, hae, haec *see* hic	
	haereō, haerēre, haesī	*cling*
	haesitō, haesitāre, haesitāvī	*hesitate*
	hanc *see* hic	
	haruspex, haruspicis, m.	*soothsayer*
	hās *see* hic	
19	hasta, hastae, f.	*spear*
	haud	*not*
	haudquāquam	*not at all*
	hauriō, haurīre, hausī, haustus	*drain*

	hercle!	*by Heavens! good heavens!*
	hērēs, hērēdis, m.f.	*heir*
7	herī	*yesterday*
	heus!	*hey!*
8	hic, haec, hoc	*this*
25	hīc	*here*
	hiems, hiemis, f.	*winter*
	hilarē	*in high spirits*
	hinc	*from here*
	Hispānia, Hispāniae, f.	*Spain*
	hoc, hōc *see* hic	
5	hodiē	*today*
9	homō, hominis, m.	*person, human being, man*
	homunculus, homunculī, m.	*poor little man*
	honor, honōris, m.	*honour, public office*
	honōrō, honōrāre, honōrāvī, honōrātus	*honour*
21	hōra, hōrae, f.	*hour*
	horreum, horreī, n.	*barn, granary*
1	hortus, hortī, m.	*garden*
9	hospes, hospitis, m.	*guest*
27	hostis, hostis, m.f.	*enemy*
17	hūc	*here, to this place*
	huic	*to this (dative of **hic**)*
	huius	*of this (genitive of **hic**)*
	humilis	*lowly, of humble birth*
	humus, humī, f.	*ground*
24	humī	*on the ground*
	hunc *see* hic	

i

12	iaceō, iacēre, iacuī	*lie, rest*
22	iaciō, iacere, iēcī, iactus	*throw, hurl*
12	iam	*now, already*
	iamprīdem	*a long time ago*
3	iānua, iānuae, f.	*door*
	ībam *see* eō	
18	ibi	*there*
	id	*it*
	identidem	*repeatedly*
	iecur, iecoris, n.	*liver*
	iēcī *see* iaciō	
11	igitur	*therefore, and so*
28	ignārus, ignāra, ignārum	*not knowing, unaware*
8	ignāvus, ignāva, ignāvum	*cowardly, lazy*

	ignis, ignis, m.	*fire*
	ignōtus, ignōta, ignōtum	*unknown*
9	ille, illa, illud	*he, she, it, they, that*
	illūc	*there, to that place*
	illūcēscō, illūcēscere, illūxī	*grow bright, dawn*
	immineō, imminēre, imminuī	*hang over, threaten*
	immortālis, immortāle	*immortal*
	dī immortālēs!	*heavens above!*
	immortālitās, immortālitātis, f.	*immortality*
	immōtus, immōta, immōtum	*still, motionless*
	impatiēns, *gen.* impatientis	*impatient*
	impellō, impellere, impulī, impulsus	*drive, force*
15	imperātor, imperātōris, m.	*emperor*
10	imperium, imperiī, n.	*empire, power*
27	imperō, imperāre, imperāvī, imperātus	*order, command*
	impetus, impetūs, m.	*attack*
	impetum facere	*charge, make an attack*
	impiger, impigra, impigrum	*lively, energetic*
	impōnō, impōnere, imposuī, impositus	*impose*
	importō, importāre, importāvī, importātus	*import*
	imprecātiō, imprecātiōnis, f.	*curse*
	imprōvīsus, imprōvīsa, imprōvīsum	*unexpected, unforeseen*
	impulī *see* impellō	
	impūne	*safely*
1	in	*in, on; into, onto*
	inānis, ināne	*empty, meaningless*
27	incendō, incendere, incendī, incēnsus	*burn, set on fire*
	incēnsus, incēnsa, incēnsum	*incensed, angered*
	incertus, incerta, incertum	*uncertain*
	incidō, incidere, incidī	*fall into*
22	incipiō, incipere, incēpī, inceptus	*begin, start*
	incitō, incitāre, incitāvī, incitātus	*urge on, encourage*
	inclūsus, inclūsa, inclūsum	*shut up, imprisoned*
	indicium, indiciī, n.	*sign, evidence*
	induō, induere, induī, indūtus	*put on*
	inest *see* īnsum	
22	īnfēlīx, *gen.* īnfēlīcis	*unlucky*

	īnferō, īnferre, intulī, inlātus	*bring in, bring on*
	īnfestus, īnfesta, īnfestum	*hostile, dangerous*
	īnfirmus, īnfirma, īnfirmum	*weak*
23	ingenium, ingeniī, n.	*character*
7	ingēns, *gen.* ingentis	*huge*
22	ingressus, ingressa, ingressum	*having entered*
	iniciō, inicere, iniēcī, iniectus	*throw in*
	inimīcitia, inimīcitiae, f.	*feud, quarrel*
14	inimīcus, inimīcī, m.	*enemy*
	iniūria, iniūriae, f.	*injustice, injury*
	innocēns, *gen.* innocentis	*innocent*
4	inquit	*says, said*
	īnsānia, īnsāniae, f.	*madness, insanity*
	īnsāniō, īnsānīre, īnsānīvī	*be mad, be insane*
	īnsānus, īnsāna, īnsānum	*mad, crazy*
	īnsidiae, īnsidiārum, f.pl.	*trap, ambush*
	īnsolēns, *gen.* īnsolentis	*rude, insolent*
	īnsolenter	*rudely, insolently*
9	īnspiciō, īnspicere, īnspexī, īnspectus	*examine, inspect*
	īnstruō, īnstruere, īnstrūxī, īnstrūctus	*draw up*
17	īnsula, īnsulae, f.	*island; block of flats*
7	intellegō, intellegere, intellēxī, intellēctus	*understand*
	rem intellegere	*understand the truth*
6	intentē	*closely, carefully*
16	inter	*among*
	inter sē	*among themselves, with each other*
24	intereā	*meanwhile*
13	interficiō, interficere, interfēcī, interfectus	*kill*
	interrogō, interrogāre, interrogāvī, interrogātus	*question*
	intrā	*inside, within*
2	intrō, intrāre, intrāvī	*enter*
	intulī *see* īnferō	
	inūtilis, inūtile	*useless*
10	inveniō, invenīre, invēnī, inventus	*find*
	invīsus, invīsa, invīsum	*unseen*
11	invītō, invītāre, invītāvī, invītātus	*invite*
17	invītus, invīta, invītum	*unwilling, reluctant*
	iō!	*hurray!*
14	ipse, ipsa, ipsum	*himself, herself, itself*

28	īra, īrae, f.	*anger*
3	īrātus, īrāta, īrātum	*angry*
	īre *see* eō	
	is, ea, id	*he, she, it*
14	iste, ista, istud	*that*
16	ita	*in this way*
13	ita vērō	*yes*
	Ītalia, Ītaliae, f.	*Italy*
18	itaque	*and so*
17	iter, itineris, n.	*journey, progress*
9	iterum	*again*
21	iubeō, iubēre, iussī, iussus	*order*
	iugulum, iugulī, n.	*throat*
	iussum, iussī, n.	*order, instruction*
	iūstitia, iūstitiae, f.	*justice*
5	iuvenis, iuvenis, m.f.	*young person*

l

	L. = Lūcius	
25	labor, labōris, m.	*work*
1	labōrō, labōrāre, labōrāvī	*work*
7	lacrimō, lacrimāre, lacrimāvī	*cry, weep*
	laedō, laedere, laesī, laesus	*harm*
	laetē	*happily*
2	laetus, laeta, laetum	*happy*
	lāpsus, lāpsa, lāpsum	*having fallen*
	lateō, latēre, latuī	*lie hidden*
	lātitūdō, lātitūdinis, f.	*width*
	latrō, latrōnis, m.	*(hired) criminal, ruffian*
27	lātus, lāta, lātum	*wide*
2	laudō, laudāre, laudāvī, laudātus	*praise*
	lavō, lavāre, lāvī, lautus	*wash*
	lēctor, lēctōris, m.	*reader*
15	lectus, lectī, m.	*couch, bed*
26	lēgātus, lēgātī, m.	*commander, governor*
26	legiō, legiōnis, f.	*legion*
	lēgō, lēgāre, lēgāvī, lēgātus	*bequeath*
11	legō, legere, lēgī, lēctus	*read*
23	lentē	*slowly*
19	lentus, lenta, lentum	*slow*
8	leō, leōnis, m.	*lion*
	lēx, lēgis, f.	*law*
18	libenter	*gladly, willingly*
10	liber, librī, m.	*book*
	līber, lībera, līberum	*free*
11	līberālis, līberāle	*generous*

	līberālitās, līberālitātis, f.	*generosity*
	līberāliter	*generously*
	līberātor, līberātōris, m.	*liberator*
	līberātrīx, līberātrīcis, f.	*liberator*
14	līberī, līberōrum, m.pl.	*children*
25	līberō, līberāre, līberāvī, līberātus	*free, set free*
	lībertās, lībertātis, f.	*freedom*
6	lībertus, lībertī, m.	*freedman (male), ex-slave*
	ligāmenta	*bandage*
	lingua, linguae, f.	*language, tongue*
	lītus, lītoris, n.	*shore (of the sea)*
	līvidus, līvida, līvidum	*dull, greyish blue*
19	locus, locī, m.	*place*
22	locūtus, locūta, locūtum	*having spoken*
	Londinium, Londiniī, n.	*London*
	longē	*far, a long way*
	longē errāre	*make a big mistake*
	longitūdō, longitūdinis, f.	*length*
13	longus, longa, longum	*long*
	lūceō, lūcēre, lūxī	*shine*
	lūcus, lūcī, m.	*grove, small wood*
	lūdō, lūdere, lūsī	*play*
	āleam lūdere	*play dice*
	lūx	*light*
	mea lūx!	*light of my life!*

m

	madidus, madida, madidum	*soaking wet*
	magis	*more*
	multō magis	*much more*
	magister, magistrī, m.	*captain (of a ship)*
	magnificus, magnifica, magnificum	*impressive, magnificent*
26	magnopere	*greatly, very much*
21	maximē	*very greatly, very much, most of all*
3	magnus, magna, magnum	*big, large, great*
23	maior, *gen.* maiōris	*bigger, larger, greater*
	maximus, maxima, maximum	*very big, very large, very great*
	magnitūdō, magnitūdinis, f.	*greatness, magnitude, size*
	maledictus	*insult, slander*
25	mālō, mālle, māluī	*prefer*
	mālim	*I would prefer*
28	malus, mala, malum	*evil, bad*

	peior, *gen.* peiōris	*worse*
	pessimus, pessima, pessimum	*worst, very bad*
23	mandātum, mandātī n.	*instruction, order*
	mandō, mandāre, mandāvī, mandātus	*entrust*
19	māne	*in the morning*
9	maneō, manēre, mānsī	*remain, stay*
	mānsuētus, mānsuēta, mānsuētum	*tame*
	mānsuētūdō, mānsuētūdinis, f.	*tameness*
19	manus, manūs, f.	*hand; band, group (of people)*
15	mare, maris, n.	*sea*
14	marītus, marītī, m.	*husband*
	Mārs, Mārtis, m.	*Mars (god of war)*
1	māter, mātris, f.	*mother*
	mātrimōnium, mātrimōniī, n.	*marriage*
	mātrōna, mātrōnae, f.	*lady*
21	maximē	*very greatly, very much*
17	maximus, maxima, maximum	*very big, very large, very great*
	mē *see* ego	
	medica, medicae, f.	*doctor*
	medicus, medicī, m.	*doctor*
9	medius, media, medium	*middle*
	mel, mellis, n.	*honey*
16	melior, meliōris	*better*
	melius est	*it would be better*
	memoria, memoriae, f.	*memory*
	in memoriā habēre	*keep in mind, remember*
	mendāx, mendācis, m.	*liar*
	mendāx, *gen.* mendācis	*lying, deceitful*
2	mercātor, mercātōris, m.	*merchant*
28	metus, metūs, m.	*fear*
5	meus, mea, meum	*my, mine*
	mihi *see* ego	
13	mīles, mīlitis, m.	*soldier*
28	mīlle	*a thousand*
28	mīlia	*thousands*
	Minerva, Minervae, f.	*Minerva (goddess of wisdom)*
11	minimē!	*definitely not! no!*
25	minimus, minima, minimum	*very little, least*
24	minor, *gen.* minōris	*smaller, less*
	minus	*less*

12	mīrābilis, mīrābile	*extraordinary, strange*
	misceō, miscēre, miscuī, mixtus	*mix*
16	miser, misera, miserum	*wretched, miserable*
	o mē miserum!	*oh wretched me! oh dear!*
12	mittō, mittere, mīsī, missus	*send*
	modo	*just now, recently*
23	modus, modī, m.	*manner, way, kind*
	quō modō?	*how?*
	rēs huius modī	*a thing of this kind*
	molestus, molesta, molestum	*troublesome, disruptive*
	mollis, molle	*soft*
	mōmentum, mōmentī, n.	*importance*
	Mona, Monae, f.	*Ynys Môn, Anglesey*
22	moneō, monēre, monuī, monitus	*warn, advise*
12	mōns, montis, m.	*mountain*
	monumentum, monumentī, n.	*monument*
	mora, morae, f.	*delay*
21	morbus, morbī, m.	*illness*
	moribundus, moribunda, moribundum	*almost dead*
20	mors, mortis, f.	*death*
	mortālis, mortāle	*mortal*
7	mortuus, mortua, mortuum	*dead*
	mōs, mōris, m.	*custom*
24	moveō, movēre, mōvī, mōtus	*move*
9	mox	*soon*
	multitūdō, multitūdinis, f.	*crowd, throng*
28	multō, multum	*much*
	multō magis	*much more*
5	multus, multa, multum	*much*
5	multī, multae, multa	*many*
	plūs, *gen.* plūris	*more*
	plūrimī, plūrimae, plūrima	*very many*
	plūrimus, plūrima, plūrimum	*most*
11	mūrus, mūrī, m.	*(outside) wall*
	mūs, mūris, m.f.	*mouse*
	mūtō, mūtāre, mūtāvī, mūtātus	*change*

n

| 18 | nam | *for* |

7	nārrō, nārrāre, nārrāvī, nārrātus	*tell, narrate, relate*
	rem nārrāre	*tell the story*
	nāsus, nāsī, m.	*nose*
	natō, natāre, natāvī	*swim*
	naufragium, naufragiī, n.	*shipwreck*
15	nauta, nautae, m.	*sailor*
16	nāvigō, nāvigāre, nāvigāvī	*sail*
3	nāvis, nāvis, f.	*ship*
22	-ne	*(turns a statement into a question)*
14	necesse	*necessary*
7	necō, necāre, necāvī, necātus	*kill*
	neglegēns, *gen.* neglegentis	*careless*
	neglegenter	*carelessly*
	neglegō, neglegere, neglēxī, neglēctum	*ignore, disregard*
17	negōtium, negōtiī, n.	*business*
18	nēmō	*no one, nobody*
	neque	*and not*
24	neque . . . neque	*neither . . . nor*
25	nescio, nescīre, nescīvī	*not know*
7	nihil	*nothing*
	nihil perīculī	*no danger*
	nimis	*too*
	nimium	*too much*
25	nisi	*except, unless*
	nōbīs *see* nōs	
	nocēns, *gen.* nocentis	*guilty*
	noctū	*at night*
13	nōlō, nōlle, nōluī	*not want*
	nōlī, nōlīte	*do not, don't*
18	nōmen, nōminis, n.	*name*
	nōmine	*named*
3	nōn	*not*
28	nōnāgintā	*ninety*
16	nōnne	*surely?*
19	nōnnūllī, nōnnūllae, nōnnūlla	*some, several*
	nōnus, nōna, nōnum	*ninth*
10	nōs	*we, us*
	nōbīscum	*with us*
11	noster, nostra, nostrum	*our*
26	nōtus, nōta, nōtum	*known, famous, well known*
20, 28	novem	*nine*
	nōvī	*I know*

13	novus, nova, novum	*new*
20	nox, noctis, f.	*night*
	noctū	*at night*
14	nūllus, nūlla, nūllum	*not any, no*
14	num	*(1) surely . . . not?*
26	num	*(2) whether*
	numerō, numerāre, numerāvī	*count*
	numerus, numerī, m.	*number*
17	numquam	*never*
11	nunc	*now*
10	nūntiō, nūntiāre, nūntiāvī, nūntiātus	*announce*
8, 23	nūntius, nūntiī, m.	*messenger; message, news*
21	nūper	*recently*
	nusquam	*nowhere*

O

	ō!	*oh!*
	obstinātē	*stubbornly*
	obstinātus, obstināta, obstinātum	*obstinate, stubborn*
18	obstō, obstāre, obstitī	*stand in the way, obstruct*
	obtulī *see* offerō	
	obviam eō, obviam īre, obviam iī	*(go to) meet*
28	occīdō, occīdere, occīdī, occīsus	*kill*
	occupātus, occupāta, occupātum	*busy*
	occupō, occupāre, occupāvī, occupātus	*seize, take over*
20, 28	octō	*eight*
28	octōginta	*eighty*
25	oculus, oculī, m.	*eye*
	ōdī	*I hate*
9	offerō, offerre, obtulī, oblātus	*offer*
6	ōlim	*once, some time ago*
	ōmen, ōminis, n.	*omen, sign (from the gods)*
	omnīnō	*completely*
7	omnis, omne, omnia	*all*
	omnia	*all, everything*
28	opēs, opum, f.pl.	*money, wealth*
21	oppidum, oppidī, n.	*town*
27	opprimō, opprimere, oppressī, oppressus	*crush, overwhelm*

27	oppugnō, oppugnāre, oppugnāvī, oppugnātus	attack
12	optimē	very well
5	optimus, optima, optimum	very good, excellent, best
	optiō, optiōnis, m.	optio (officer ranked below a centurion)
	ōrātiō, ōrātiōnis, f.	speech
	ōrātiōnem habēre	make a speech
	orbis, orbis, m.	world
	ōrdō, ōrdinis, m.	row
	ōrnāmentum, ōrnāmentī, n.	ornament
	ōrnātus, ōrnāta, ōrnātum	elaborate, showy
27	ōrō, ōrāre, ōrāvī	beg, beg for
	ōs, ōris, n.	face
	ōsculum, ōsculī, n.	kiss
9	ostendō, ostendere, ostendī, ostentus	show
	ōtium, ōtiī, n.	leisure

p

12	paene	nearly, almost
	pallēscō, pallēscere, palluī	grow pale
	pallidus, pallida, pallidum	pale
	pallium, palliī, n.	cloak
	parcō, parcere, pepercī	spare
	parēns, parentis, m.f.	parent
23	pāreō, pārēre, pāruī	obey
7	parō, parāre, parāvī, parātus	prepare
18	pars, partis, f.	part
6	parvus, parva, parvum	small, little
24	minor, gen. minōris	smaller, less
	minimus, minima, minimum	very little, least
24	passus, passa, passum	having suffered
	pāstor, pāstōris, m.	shepherd
26	patefaciō, patefacere, patefēcī, patefactus	reveal
1	pater, patris, m.	father
	patera, paterae, f.	bowl, dish
	patiēns, gen. patientis	patient
16	paucī, paucae, pauca	a few, few
	paulātim	gradually
	paulīsper	for a short time
	paulum, paulī, n.	little, a little
	paulō	a little
	pauper, gen. pauperis	poor
	paupertās, paupertātis, f.	poverty

10	pāx, pācis, f.	peace
	pecus, pecoris, n.	farm animal
4	pecūnia, pecūniae, f.	money
	peior, gen. peiōris	worse
	pellō, pellere, pepulī, pulsus	drive
6	per	through, along
	perdomitus, perdomita, perdomitum	conquered
16	pereō, perīre, periī	die, perish
	perfidia, perfidiae, f.	treachery
	perfidus, perfida, perfidum	treacherous, untrustworthy
	perīculōsus, perīculōsa, perīculōsum	dangerous
19	perīculum, perīculī, n.	danger
	periī see pereō	
	perītē	skilfully
	perītia, perītiae, f.	skill
	perītus, perīta, perītum	skilful
	permōtus, permōta, permōtum	alarmed, disturbed
	persecūtus, persecūta, persecūtum	having pursued
	persōna, persōnae, f.	character
	persōnam agere	play the part (of)
	perstō, perstāre, perstitī	persist, stand firm
20	persuādeō, persuādēre, persuāsī	persuade
4	perterritus, perterrita, perterritum	terrified
17	perveniō, pervenīre, pervēnī	reach, arrive at
8	pēs, pedis, m.	paw, foot
20	pessimus, pessima, pessimum	very bad, worst
	pestis, pestis, f.	pest, nuisance
5, 19	petō, petere, petīvī, petītus	make for, head for, attack, beg for, ask for
	philosopha, philosophae, f.	(female) philosopher
	philosophus, philosophī, m.	(male) philosopher
	pictūra, pictūrae, f.	painting, picture
	pingō, pingere, pīnxī	paint
	pistor, pistōris, m.	baker
11	placeō, placēre, placuī	please, suit
	placidē	calmly
	placidus, placida, placidum	calm, peaceful
	plānē	clearly
5	plaudō, plaudere, plausī	applaud, clap
	plaustrum, plaustrī, n.	wagon, cart
21	plēnus, plēna, plēnum	full

	plumbeus, plumbea, plumbeum	*(made of) lead*
	plūrimus, plūrima, plūrimum	*most*
19	plūrimī, plūrimae, plūrima	*very many*
22	plūs, *gen.* plūris	*more*
	plūs vīnī	*more wine*
	pōculum, pōculī, n.	*cup*
25	poena, poenae, f.	*punishment*
25	poenās dare	*pay the penalty, be punished*
	poēta, poētae, m.	*poet*
	poliō, polīre, polīvī, polītus	*polish*
	pompa, pompae, f.	*procession*
	Pompēiānus, Pompēiāna, Pompēiānum	*Pompeian*
16	pōnō, pōnere, posuī, positus	*place, put up*
	pōns, pontis, m.	*bridge*
	populus, populī, m.	*people*
	porrō	*what's more, furthermore*
8	porta, portae, f.	*gate*
3	portō, portāre, portāvī, portātus	*carry*
10	portus, portūs, m.	*harbour*
	possideō, possidēre, possēdī	*possess*
13	possum, posse, potuī	*can, be able*
9	post	*after, behind*
18	posteā	*afterwards*
6	postquam	*after, when*
	postrēmō	*finally, lastly*
13	postrīdiē	*(on) the next day*
8	postulō, postulāre, postulāvī, postulātus	*demand*
	posuī *see* pōnō	
	potēns, *gen.* potentis	*powerful*
	potestās, potestātis, f.	*power*
	potius	*rather*
	potuī *see* possum	
22	praebeō, praebēre, praebuī, praebitus	*offer, present, provide*
	praeceps, *gen.* praecipitis	*headlong*
21	praemium, praemiī, n.	*reward, prize, profit*
	praesidium, praesidiī, n.	*protection*
	praestō, praestāre, praestitī	*be superior to, surpass*
	praetereā	*besides*
	prāvus, prāva, prāvum	*evil*

22	precātus, precāta, precātum	*having prayed (to)*
	precēs, precum, f.pl.	*prayers*
	prēnsō, prēnsāre, prēnsāvī, prēnsātus	*clutch, take hold of*
	pretiōsus, pretiōsa, pretiōsum	*precious, expensive*
	prīdiē	*the day before*
27	prīmō	*at first, first*
11	prīmus, prīma, prīmum	*first*
	in prīmīs	*in particular*
15	prīnceps, prīncipis, m.	*chief, chieftain*
	prīncipia, prīncipiōrum, n.pl.	*headquarters*
	prius	*earlier*
	priusquam	*before*
18	prō	*in front of, for, in return for*
	prō certō habēre	*know for certain*
	probē	*honestly*
	probitās, probitātis, f.	*honesty*
	probus, proba, probum	*honest*
9	prōcēdō, prōcēdere, prōcessī	*advance, proceed*
	procul	*some distance away, far off*
	prōcumbō, prōcumbere, prōcubuī	*bow down, fall, fall down*
	prōcūrātor, prōcūrātōris, m.	*manager*
	prōdō, prōdere, prōdidī, prōditus	*betray*
	prōditōr, prōditōris, m.	*traitor, betrayer*
28	profectus, profecta, profectum	*having set out*
22	prōgressus, prōgressa, prōgressum	*having advanced*
	prohibeō, prohibēre, prohibuī, prohibitus	*prevent*
11	prōmittō, prōmittere, prōmīsī, promissus	*promise*
7	prope	*near*
	prōpōnō, prōpōnere, prōposuī, prōpositus	*propose, put forward*
27	propter	*on account of, because of*
	prōsiliō, prōsilīre, prōsiluī	*leap forward*
	prōvincia, prōvinciae, f.	*province*
27	proximus, proxima, proximum	*nearest*
	prūdens, *gen.* prūdentis	*intelligent, sensible*
	prūdenter	*sensibly*
	prūdentia, prūdentiae, f.	*good sense, intelligence*
5	puella, puellae, f.	*girl*
8	puer, puerī, m.	*boy*

	pugiō, pugiōnis, m.	*dagger*
11	pugna, pugnae, f.	*fight*
8	pugnō, pugnāre, pugnāvī	*fight*
9	pulcher, pulchra, pulchrum	*beautiful, handsome*
	pulchritūdō, pulchritūdinis, f.	*beauty*
6	pulsō, pulsāre, pulsāvī	*knock at, hit, punch*
18	pūniō, pūnīre, pūnīvī, pūnītus	*punish*
	pūrgō, pūrgāre, pūrgāvī, pūrgātus	*clean*
	puteus, puteī, m.	*well (for water)*
23	putō, putāre, putāvī	*think*
	pȳramis, pȳramidis, f.	*pyramid*

q

	quā *see* quī	
20, 28	quadrāgintā	*forty*
	quae *see* quī	
4	quaerō, quaerere, quaesīvī, quaesītus	*look for, search for*
27	quālis, quāle	*what sort of*
10	quam	*(1) how*
	quam celerrimē	*as quickly as possible*
10	quam	*(2) than*
	quam	*(3) see* **quī**
14	quamquam	*although*
26	quantus, quanta, quantum	*how big, how great*
	quārtus, quārta, quārtum	*fourth*
20, 28	quattuor	*four*
14	-que	*and*
15	quī, quae, quod	*who, which*
28	quicquam (*also spelt* quidquam)	*anything*
	quid?	*what?*
	quid agis?	*how are you?*
	quid vīs?	*what do you want?*
22	quīdam, quaedam, quoddam	*one, a certain*
	quidem	*indeed*
	quiēscō, quiēscere, quiēvī	*rest*
	quiētus, quiēta, quiētum	*quiet*
	quīngentī, quīngentae, quingenta	*five hundred*
20, 28	quīnquāgintā	*fifty*
20, 28	quīnque	*five*
4	quis? quid?	*who? what?*
19	quō?	*(1) where (to)?*

	quō	*(2) see* **quī**
22	quō modō?	*how? in what way?*
6	quod	*(1) because*
	quod	*(2) see* **quī**
17	quondam	*one day, once*
2	quoque	*also, too*
	quōs *see* quī	
26	quot?	*how many?*
	quotiēns	*whenever*

r

	raeda, raedae, f.	*carriage*
23	rapiō, rapere, rapuī, raptus	*seize, grab*
	raptim	*hastily, quickly*
	recitō, recitāre, recitāvī	*recite*
	rēctā	*directly, straight*
	recumbō, recumbere, recubuī	*lie down, recline*
18	recūsō, recūsāre, recūsāvī, recūsātus	*refuse*
4	reddō, reddere, reddidī, redditus	*give back*
14	redeō, redīre, rediī	*go back, return*
	reditus, reditūs, m.	*return*
26	referō, referre, rettulī, relātus	*carry, bring back, deliver; tell, relate, report*
	reficiō, reficere, refēcī, refectus	*repair, restore*
15	rēgīna, rēgīnae, f.	*queen*
28	rēgnum, rēgnī, n.	*kingdom*
22	regressus, regressa, regressum	*having returned*
20	relinquō, relinquere, relīquī, relictus	*leave behind*
	remedium, remediī, n.	*cure*
	remittō, remittere, remīsī	*let go, drop*
	repetō, repetere, repetīvī, repetītus	*claim*
6	rēs, reī, f.	*thing, matter*
	rem cōgitāre	*consider the problem*
	rem cōnficere	*finish the job*
	rem intellegere	*understand the truth*
	rem suscipere	*undertake the task*
	rēs contrāria	*the opposite*
18	resistō, resistere, restitī	*resist*
3	respondeō, respondēre, respondī	*reply*
	respōnsum, respōnsī, n.	*answer*

24	retineō, retinēre, retinuī, retentus	*hold back, keep (back)*
	rettulī *see* referō	
9	reveniō, revenīre, revēnī	*come back, return*
15	rēx, rēgis, m.	*king*
3	rīdeō, rīdēre, rīsī	*laugh, smile*
	rīdiculus, rīdicula, rīdiculum	*ridiculous, laughable*
	rīpa, rīpae, f.	*bank (of a river)*
7	rogō, rogāre, rogāvī, rogātus	*ask*
	Rōma, Romae, f.	*Rome*
	Rōmae	*at Rome, in Rome*
	Rōmānī, Rōmānōrum, m.pl.	*Romans*
	Rōmānus, Rōmāna, Rōmānum	*Roman*
13	ruō, ruere, ruī	*rush*
	rūrsus	*again*

S

	saccus, saccī, m.	*bag, sack*
18	sacer, sacra, sacrum	*holy, sacred*
15	sacerdōs, sacerdōtis, m.f.	*priest*
	sacrificium, sacrificiī, n.	*sacrifice, offering*
	sacrificō, sacrificāre, sacrificāvī, sacrificātus	*sacrifice*
8	saepe	*often*
	saevē	*furiously*
	saeviō, saevīre, saeviī	*be in a rage*
24	saevus, saeva, saevum	*savage, cruel*
	salūs, salūtis, f.	*safety*
2	salūtō, salūtāre, salūtāvī, salūtātus	*greet*
3	salvē!	*hello!*
	sānē	*obviously*
8	sanguis, sanguinis, m.	*blood*
	sānō, sānāre, sānāvī, sānātus	*heal, cure*
	sānus, sāna, sānum	*well, healthy*
21	sapiēns, *gen.* sapientis	*wise*
	sapienter	*wisely*
4	satis	*enough*
	scaena, scaenae, f.	*stage*
23	scelestus, scelesta, scelestum	*wicked*
28	scelus, sceleris, n.	*crime*
	scēptrum, scēptrī, n.	*sceptre*
	scindō, scindere, scidī, scissus	*tear up*
23	scio, scīre, scīvī	*know*

6	scrībō, scrībere, scrīpsī, scrīptus	*write*
	scrīptor, scrīptōris, m.	*writer*
	sculpō, sculpere, sculpsī	*carve*
13	sē	*himself, herself, themselves*
	inter sē	*among themselves, with each other*
	sēcum	*with him, with her, with them; to himself*
	sēcum cōgitāre	*consider to themselves*
	sēcrētus, sēcrēta, sēcrētum	*secret*
	secundus, secunda, secundum	*second*
24	secūtus, secūta, secūtum	*having followed*
4	sed	*but*
3	sedeō, sedēre, sēdī	*sit*
	sēditiō, sēditiōnis, f.	*rebellion*
	sella, sellae, f.	*chair*
	sēmirutus, sēmiruta, sēmirutum	*rickety, half-collapsed*
10	semper	*always*
11	senātor, senātōris, m.	*senator*
5	senex, senis, m.	*old man*
	sententia, sententiae, f.	*opinion*
12	sentiō, sentīre, sēnsī, sensus	*feel, notice*
	sepeliō, sepelīre, sepelīvī, sepultus	*bury*
20, 28	septem	*seven*
	septimus	*seventh*
28	septuāgintā	*seventy*
	serēnus, serēna, serēnum	*calm, reassuring*
	sermō, sermōnis, m.	*conversation*
	sermōnem habēre	*have a conversation, talk*
10	servō, servāre, servāvī, servātus	*save, keep (safe), look after*
1	servus, servī, m.	*(male) slave, enslaved man*
	sevērus, sevēra, sevērum	*severe, stern*
20, 28	sex	*six*
28	sexāgintā	*sixty*
26	sī	*if*
	sibi *see* sē	
28	sīc	*thus, in this way*
20	sīcut	*like, just as*
	significō, significāre, signifiāvī, significātus	*mean, indicate*

	signō, signāre, signāvī, signātus	*sign, seal*
8	signum, signī, n.	*seal, signal, sign*
	silentium, silentiī, n.	*silence*
8	silva, silvae, f.	*wood, forest*
	similis, simile	*like, similar*
22	simul	*at the same time*
14	simulac, simulatque	*as soon as*
19	sine	*without*
	situs, sita, situm	*located, situated*
	sōl, sōlis, m.	*sun*
18	soleō, solēre	*be accustomed*
	sōlitūdō, sōlitūdinis, f.	*solitude, loneliness*
	sollicitūdō, sollicitūdinis, f.	*worry, anxiety*
11	sollicitus, sollicita, sollicitum	*troubled, anxious*
	sōlum	*only*
	nōn sōlum . . . sed etiam	*not only . . . but also*
10	sōlus, sōla, sōlum	*alone, lonely, only, on one's own*
	solūtus, solūta, solūtum	*relaxed*
	solvō, solvere, solvī, solūtus	*undo, loosen*
	sonitus, sonitūs, m.	*sound*
	sonō, sonāre, sonuī, sonitus	*sound*
	sonus, sonī, m.	*sound*
	sordidus, sordida, sordidum	*dirty, filthy*
17	soror, sorōris, f.	*sister*
	spectāculum, spectāculī, n.	*spectacle, show*
	spectātor, spectātōris, m.	*spectator*
5	spectō, spectāre, spectāvī, spectātus	*look at, watch*
	spernō, spernere, sprēvī, sprētus	*despise, reject*
	spērō, spērāre, spērāvī	*hope, expect*
28	spēs, speī, f.	*hope*
	splendidē	*splendidly*
	splendidus, splendida, splendidum	*splendid*
8	statim	*at once, immediately*
	statiō, statiōnis, f.	*post*
	statua, statuae, f.	*statue*
5	stō, stāre, stetī	*stand*
	stola, stolae, f.	*(long) dress*
	stultitia, stultitiae, f.	*foolishness*
11	stultus, stulta, stultum	*foolish*
	suāvis, suāve	*sweet*
	suāviter	*sweetly*
24	sub	*under, beneath*

	subdūcō, subdūcere, subdūxī, subductus	*draw up, raise*
6	subitō	*suddenly*
	Sūlis, Sūlis, f.	*Sulis*
1	sum, esse, fuī	*be*
16	summus, summa, summum	*highest, greatest, top*
	sūmptuōsē	*lavishly*
	sūmptuōsus, sūmptuōsa, sūmptuōsum	*expensive, lavish*
	superbē	*proudly*
	superbus, superba, superbum	*arrogant, proud*
6	superō, superāre, superāvī, superātus	*overcome, overpower*
7	surgō, surgere, surrēxī	*get up, rise*
	suscipiō, suscipere, suscēpī, susceptus	*undertake, take on*
	suspicātus, suspicāta, suspicātum	*having suspected*
	suspīrō, suspīrāre, suspīrāvī, suspīrātus	*sigh, draw breath*
	sustulī *see* tollō	
	susurrō, susurrāre, susurrāvī	*whisper, mutter*
10	suus, sua, suum	*his, her, their, their own*

t

	T. = Titus	
3	taberna, tabernae, f.	*shop, inn*
	tabernārius, tabernāriī, m.	*shopkeeper*
	tablīnum, tablīnī, n.	*study*
	tabula, tabulae, f.	*(writing) tablet*
10	taceō, tacēre, tacuī	*be silent, be quiet*
	tacē! tacēte!	*shut up! be quiet!*
7	tacitē	*quietly, silently*
22	tālis, tāle	*such*
20	tam	*so*
7	tamen	*however*
12	tandem	*at last, finally*
	tangō, tangere, tetigī, tāctus	*touch*
	tantum	*only*
27	tantus, tanta, tantum	*so great, such a great*
	tē *see* tū	
	tēctum, tēctī, n.	*roof, ceiling*
	tēla, tēlae, f.	*cloth, tapestry*
20	tempestās, tempestātis, f.	*storm*
12	templum, templī, n.	*temple*

19	temptō, temptāre, temptāvī, temptātus	*try, attempt*
	tenebrae, tenebrārum, f.pl.	*darkness*
15	teneō, tenēre, tenuī, tentus	*hold*
	tergum, tergī, n.	*back*
12	terra, terrae, f.	*ground, land*
7	terreō, terrēre, terruī, territus	*frighten*
	terribilis, terribile	*terrible*
	terror, terrōris, m.	*terror*
	tertius, tertia, tertium	*third*
	testāmentum, testāmentī, n.	*will*
26	testis, testis, m.f.	*witness*
	texō, texere, texui, textus	*weave*
	thermae, thermārum, f.pl.	*baths*
	tibi *see* tū	
12	timeō, timēre, timuī	*be afraid (of), fear*
	timor, timōris, m.	*fear*
	tintinō, tintināre, tintināvī	*ring*
	toga, togae, f.	*toga*
16	tollō, tollere, sustulī, sublātus	*raise, lift up*
27	tot	*so many*
8	tōtus, tōta, tōtum	*whole*
9	trādō, trādere, trādidī, trāditus	*hand over*
13	trahō, trahere, trāxī, tractus	*drag*
	tranquillus, tranquilla, tranquillum	*calm, peaceful*
	trāns	*across*
	trānseō, trānsīre, trānsiī	*cross*
	tranquillitās, tranquillitātis, f.	*calmness*
	tremō, tremere, tremuī	*tremble, shake*
	tremēns, *gen.* trementis	*trembling, shaking*
	tremor, tremōris, m.	*shaking*
12, 20, 28	trēs, tria	*three*
	tribūnal, tribūnālis, n.	*platform*
	tribūnus, tribūnī, m.	*tribune (high-ranking officer)*
	trīclīnium, trīclīniī, n.	*dining room*
20, 28	trīgintā	*thirty*
	tripodes, tripodum, m.pl.	*tripods*
16	trīstis, trīste	*sad*
	trīste	*sadly*
4	tū, tuī	*you (singular)*
	tēcum	*with you*
	tuba, tubae, f.	*trumpet*
	tulī *see* ferō	

6	tum	*then*
5	turba, turbae, f.	*crowd*
17	tūtus, tūta, tūtum	*safe*
	tūtius est	*it would be safer*
6	tuus, tua, tuum	*your, yours (singular)*

u

5, 14	ubi	*where; when*
	ubīque	*everywhere*
	Ulixēs, Ulyxis, m.	*Ulysses (Roman name for Odysseus)*
	ūllus, ūlla, ūllum	*any*
24	ultimus, ultima, ultimum	*final, last, furthest*
	ultiō, ultiōnis, f.	*revenge*
25	umquam	*ever*
21	unde	*from where*
12, 20, 28	ūnus, ūna, ūnum	*one*
	ūnum	*one thing*
5	urbs, urbis, f.	*city*
	ursa, ursae, f.	*bear*
	usquam	*anywhere*
28	ut	*(1) as*
26	ut	*(2) that, so that, in order that*
	ūtilis, ūtile	*useful*
10	uxor, uxōris, f.	*wife*

v

	vah!	*ugh!*
7	valdē	*very much, very*
11	valē! valēte!	*goodbye! farewell!*
	valedīcō, valedīcere, valedīxī, valedictus	*say goodbye*
	valeō, valēre, valuī, valitus	*be well*
	valēscō, valēscere, valuī	*grow strong, begin to get well*
	valētūdinārium valētūdināriī, n.	*hospital*
	valētūdō, valētūdinis, f.	*health*
	validus, valida, validum	*strong*
	vallis, vallis, f.	*valley*
	varius, varia, varium	*different*
10	vehementer	*loudly, energetically*
	vehō, vehere, vēxī	*carry*
	vēla, vēlōrum, n.pl.	*sail*
	velim, vellem *see* volō	

	vēnātiō, vēnātiōnis, f.	hunt
	vēnātor, vēnātōris, m.	hunter
	vēnditor, vēnditōris, m.	seller, vendor
6	vēndō, vēndere, vēndidī, vēnditus	sell
	venēnātus, venēnāta, venēnātum	poisoned
	venēnum, venēnī, n.	poison
	venia, veniae, f.	mercy, pardon
5	veniō, venīre, vēnī	come
	venter, ventris, m.	stomach
	ventus, ventī, m.	wind
	Venus, Veneris, f.	Venus (highest dice roll)
	vēr, vēris, n.	spring
11	verberō, verberāre, verberāvī, verberātus	strike, beat
22	verbum, verbī, n.	word
	versus, versa, versum	having turned
16	vertō, vertere, vertī, versus	turn
	sē vertere	turn around
24	vērum, vērī, n.	the truth, truth
13	ita vērō	yes
	vērus, vēra, vērum	true, real
	vesperāscō, vesperāscere, vesperāvī	grow dark
26	vester, vestra, vestrum	your (plural)
	vestīgium, vestīgiī, n.	footprint, track
23	vestīmenta, vestīmentōrum, n.pl.	clothes
19	vexō, vexāre, vexāvī, vexātus	annoy
1	via, viae, f.	street, road
	vibrō, vibrāre, vibrāvī, vibrātus	wave, brandish
	vīcī see vincō	
	victī, victōrum, m.pl	the conquered
	vīcīnus, vīcīna, vīcīnum	neighbouring, nearby
	victima, victimae, f.	victim
	victor, victōris, m.	victor, winner
28	victōria, victōriae, f.	victory
	victrīx, victrīcis, f.	victor, winner
	vīcus, vīcī, m.	village

3	videō, vidēre, vīdī, vīsus	see
20, 28	vīgintī	twenty
13	vīlla, vīllae, f.	villa, house, country house
15	vincō, vincere, vīcī, victus	be victorious, win
	victī, victōrum, m.pl.	the conquered
3	vīnum, vīnī, n.	wine
11	vir, virī, m.	man
26	virtūs, virtūtis, f.	courage, virtue
	vīs see volō	
	vīsitō, vīsitāre, vīsitāvī, vīsitātus	visit
13	vīta, vītae, f.	life
6	vituperō, vituperāre, vituperāvī, vituperātus	rebuke, tell off
19	vīvō, vīvere, vīxī	be alive, live
25	vīvus, vīva, vīvum	alive, living
19	vix	hardly, scarcely, with difficulty
	vōbīs see vōs	
4	vocō, vocāre, vocāvī, vocātus	call
13	volō, velle, voluī	want
	quid vīs?	what do you want?
	velim	I would like
	volvō, volvere, volvī, volūtus	turn
	in animō volvere	wonder, turn over in the mind
	vōmer, vōmeris, m.	ploughshare (the blade of a plough)
10	vōs	you (plural)
	vōbīscum	with you
	vōtum, vōtī, n.	votive offering
17	vōx, vōcis, f.	voice
	vulnerātus, vulnerāta, vulnerātum	wounded
13	vulnerō, vulnerāre, vulnerāvī, vulnerātus	wound, injure
20	vulnus, vulneris, n.	wound
	vult see volō	
24	vultus, vultūs, m.	expression, face

Index of grammatical topics

Index of cultural topics

Acknowledgements

This edition of the Cambridge Latin Course is the result of over fifty years of research, classroom testing, feedback, revision and development. During that period millions of students, tens of thousands of teachers, hundreds of experts in the fields of Classics, History and Education and dozens of authors have contributed to make the CLC the success that it is today. To list everyone who has played a part would be impossible, but particular thanks are due to the following individuals for their work on this 5th edition of Book III.

All team members – past and present – at the Cambridge School Classics Project, without whom this course simply would not exist. A special mention is due to Lisa Hay for her outstanding dedication and work on this edition.

All the teachers and collaborators who took the time to review our materials and offer helpful feedback and suggestions.

Ben Harris for his crucial authorial input and generous sharing of expertise.

James Watson and Benjamin Joffe for their authorial contributions and never wavering support.

Lottie Mortimer, Rob Hancock-Jones, Jane Ainsworth and Caroline Musgrove for their work on the cultural background sections.

The following individuals who undertook academic reviews of material: Eleri Cousins, Ingo Gildenhard, Stuart Mckie.

Chris Tuckley and the team at Yorkshire Archaeological Trust who shared their expertise and resources with such enthusiasm.

The team behind Roman Inscriptions of Britain whose expertise and incredible website have been truly essential to the creation of this book.

Jasmine Elmer, Pria Jackson and Annis Wiltshire for their important and insightful reviews.

And finally, the CSCP team would like to thank their Director, Caroline Bristow, for her ever enthusiastic and collaborative leadership. Her energy has carried this project from strength to strength and produced a new, vibrant and inclusive CLC edition for the waiting Classics community.

The authors and publishers acknowledge the following sources of copyright material and are grateful for the permissions granted. While every effort has been made, it has not always been possible to identify the sources of all the material used, or to trace all copyright holders. If any omissions are brought to our notice, we will be happy to include the appropriate acknowledgements on reprinting.

Thanks to the following for permission to reproduce images:

Cover main image and inside pp 7, 8, 9t, 12, 13, 17tr,b, 18l,r, 19tr,bl,br, 21, 22, 23, 45, 58bc,br © The Roman Baths, Bath and North East Somerset Council; cover background and inside pp 1, 11, 27, 28r, 60r, 72, 81, 83, 100, 107l, 109l, 110br, 116, 117, 124r, 151, 157t, 181 © The Trustees of the British Museum; pp viii, ix, 60c, 88t, 94, 165 West Cheshire Museums; pp9, 38 drawings by R.S.O. Tomlin, pp9, 61, 133, 155 drawings by R.G. Collingwood, p61 drawings by R.P. Wright, p61 drawing reproduced from Cotton Julius MS, all reproduced by kind permission of the Haverfield Trust (Roman Inscriptions of Britain); p5 DEA/G. Nimatallah/GI; pp9b, 38 Mike Peel (www.mikepeel.net) CC-BY-SA-4.0; p15 wjarek/GI; p17l David Coleman/Alamy Stock Photo; p20l,r Brian Jannsen/Alamy Stock